ENGENDERING RESISTANCE:
AGENCY AND POWER IN WOMEN'S PRISONS

KV-638-213

In recognition of the friendship and generosity that I experienced from all the women who took part in my research in HMP/YOI Drake Hall, HM Remand Centre Pucklechurch and in the Women's Annex of HMP Winchester, I dedicate this book to them, in the hope that they may continue to resist the pains of imprisonment.

Advances in Criminology
Series Editor: David Nelken

Titles in the Series

Engendering Resistance: Agency and Power in Women's Prisons
Mary Bosworth

Integrating a Victim Perspective with Criminal Justice
International debates
Adam Crawford and Jo Goodey

Contrasts in Criminal Justice
David Nelken

Critique and Radical Discourses on Crime
George Pavlich

Blood in the Bank
Social and legal aspects of death at work
Gary Slapper

Governable Places
Readings on governmentality and crime control
Russell Smandych

Engendering Resistance: Agency and Power in Women's Prisons

MARY BOSWORTH
Department of Sociology and Anthropology
Fordham University, New York

Ashgate

DARTMOUTH

Aldershot • Brookfield USA • Singapore • Sydney

© Mary Bosworth 1999

All rights reserved. No part of this publication may be reproduced, stored in a retrieval system, or transmitted in any form or by any means electronic, mechanical, photocopying, recording or otherwise without the prior permission of the publisher.

Published by
Dartmouth Publishing Company Limited
Ashgate Publishing Limited
Gower House
Croft Road
Aldershot
Hants GU11 3HR
England

Ashgate Publishing Company
Old Post Road
Brookfield
Vermont 05036
USA

British Library Cataloguing in Publication Data
Bosworth, Mary
Engendering Resistance : agency and power in women's prisons.
   – (Advances in criminology)
   1.Women prisoners – England   2.Women prisoners – Wales
   3.Women – Identity   4.Women – Psychology   5.Women – Legal
   status, laws, etc. – England   6.Women – Legal status, laws,
   etc. – Wales
   I.Title
   365.6'082'0942

Library of Congress Cataloging-in-Publication Data
Bosworth, Mary.
     Engendering Resistance : agency and power in women's prisons / Mary
     Bosworth
        p.   cm.
     Includes bibliographical references.
     ISBN (invalid) 1-84014-739-3 (hardback)
     1. Women prisoners—England—Research.   2. Women prisoners—
England—Psychology.   3. Women prisoners—Civil rights—England.
4. Prison administration—England.   5. Sex discrimination in
criminal justice administration—England.   6. Prisons—Government
policy—England.   I. Title
     HV9649.E5B67   1999
     365'.6'0820942—dc21   98-52034
                                                                                  CIP

ISBN 1 84014 739 3

Typeset by Manton Typesetters, 5–7 Eastfield Road, Louth, Lincs, LN11 7AJ, UK.
Printed and bound by Athenaeum Press Ltd., Gateshead, Tyne & Wear.

Contents

Contents   vii

Acknowledgements

Many people have given me support throughout the completion of this research and its transition from a doctoral thesis to a book. First I would like to thank the Wakefield Committee at the Institute of Criminology, Cambridge, for awarding me a generous three-year scholarship which enabled me to survive during my Ph.D. I would also like to thank Trinity Hall which funded much of the research, and the staff and Governors of each of the establishments I visited who made me welcome throughout the research. Likewise, I am grateful to the School of Criminal Justice at Rutgers University, Newark, for awarding me a visiting library fellowship so that I could complete my thesis in New York, and to the Prison Inspectorate who allowed me to reproduce their map of women's prisons.

Many thanks are due to Alison Liebling, Tony Bottoms, Eamonn Carrabine, Alison Young, Richard Sparks, Adrian Howe and Dragan Milovanovic for their constructive comments on earlier drafts. Kathy Daly helped me to conceptualize the thesis as a book, as did Professor David Nelken, who also gave me the opportunity to be part of this exciting new series at Ashgate. All of these individuals provided indispensible intellectual and personal guidance, without which this study would not have been possible.

On a more personal level, I would like to thank my family and friends for offering advice, encouragement and enthusiasm. My parents in particular were a constant source of love and support. They read many drafts, most recently in the sweltering heat of a New York summer. Mari, Eleanor, Sarah and Kirsty gave me ideas and affection, offering rich female companionship and laughter when I needed it most. Finally, a special acknowledgement is due to Anthony, with whom I have started a new life in New York. He has been steadfast in his emotional and intellectual encouragement, acting as editor, companion and best friend – Thank you.

New York City

Series Preface

The new series *Advances in Criminology* builds on the success of the *International Library of Criminology, Criminal Justice and Penology.* But rather than being dedicated to anthologising the best of existing work this venture seeks to publish original cutting-edge contributions to these fields. Volumes so far in press include discussions of Foucault and *governmentality*; critical criminology; victims and criminal justice; corporate crime; postmodern policing; and women's prisons.

The monograph by Mary Bosworth, *Engendering Resistance: Agency and Power in Women's Prisons* is a valuable and sophisticated contribution to recently revived sociological studies of the prison. The author offers an original and often surprising account of the way female prisoners use femininity in their attempt to cope with the 'pains of imprisonment'. Her open espousal of a standpoint methodology geared to understanding and sharing the point of view of her informants should also stimulate interest and debate.

DAVID NELKEN
Series Editor

1. Low Newton (North East)
2. Durham (North East)
3. Askham Grange (Yorkshire)
4. New Hall (Yorkshire)
5. Risley (Mersey and Manchester)
6. Styal (Mersey and Manchester)
7. Foston Hall (Mersey and Manchester)
8. Drake Hall (Mercia)
9. Brockhill (Mercia)
10. Highpoint (London North and East Anglia)
11. Bullwood Hall (London North and East Anglia)
12. Holloway (London North and East Anglia)
13. Eastwood Park (Wales and the West)
14. Cookham Wood (Kent)
15. East Sutton Park (Kent)
16. Winchester (South Coast)

Map of the Women's Penal Establishments in England and Wales

Introduction
Agency and Power in Women's Prisons: An Overview

In [research] typically we start off with a question, which we know to be badly formed at the outset. We hope that in struggling with it, we shall find that its terms are transformed, so that in the end we will answer a question which we could not properly conceive at the beginning. We are striving for conceptual innovation which will allow us to illuminate some matter, say an area of human experience, which would otherwise remain dark and confused (Taylor 1985a: 41).

[Feminists] locate individual experience in society and history, embedded within a set of social relations which produce both the possibilities and limitations of that experience (Acker, Barry and Esseveld 1991: 135).

Make sure you get it right then, and tell them how it really is in here (Allison:[1] HM Remand Centre Pucklechurch, November, 1995).

There have never been as many men, women and children incarcerated in England and Wales as there are today. The most dramatic increases in the prison population have occurred only in the last few years, soaring from 40,606 at the end of 1992 to just over 65,000 by May 1998 (Braggins 1998: 10). This unforeseen rise has been accompanied by a variety of policy changes including: the conversion of the prison service into a semi-autonomous agency, the building of many new prisons, the commitment to privatizing 10 per cent of the penal estate by the year 2000, and the shift in managerial rhetoric from a concern with 'justice' to a concern with 'custody' (Lygo 1991; HM Prison Service 1993c; Kemp 1996; Home Affairs Committee 1993, 1997: v–x; Woolf 1991; Learmont 1995).

Within the overall increase of the penal population, the number of women has been growing at a rate far greater than it has for men, doubling over the

1

last six years, and increasing by 21 per cent in the last twelve months alone (HM Prison Service 1998: 1). At the time of writing, there are approximately 3100 women dispersed throughout some 16 female penal establishments of England and Wales, with a current plan to 're-role' a number of establishments for men to hold women, in order to avoid using police cells to house them (HM Prison Service, 1998: 1).[2] Most of the women in prison are poor. Almost a third of them are on remand. Usually, they are repeat offenders, imprisoned for petty, non-violent crimes, and, increasingly, for drug-related offences. Most have at least one child. Often they are single mothers. A quarter of them belong to minority ethnic groups, and Afro-Caribbean women are particularly over-represented (FitzGerald and Marshall 1996). Half of the women of colour are overseas nationals (PAC 1996: 2). Studies estimate that up to 60 per cent of all the women have suffered sexual and/or physical violence from a member of their family or from a stranger, with the figure rising to 80 per cent once all physical violence is included (Home Office 1992a: §4). Finally, female prisoners generally have a low level of formal education, and, at best, sporadic employment histories (Home Office 1992a; HM Prison Service 1996; Player 1994; Morris, et al. 1995; Morris and Wilkinson 1995; NACRO 1996; HMCIP 1997: §2.04–2.15).

Such is the constitution of the female prison estate. Each of these elements has been documented in prison service surveys and annual reports, in a way which forms an image of a 'typical' female inmate.[3] Together these facts are usually understood to constitute the identity of the average woman in prison, an abstract figure to whom criminologists, practitioners and prison officers alike refer, and from whom it is suggested policy should flow (HMCIP 1997: §2.22). Yet, without further refinement, such abstractions are little more than descriptive categories with scant intrinsic meaning. They form the image of a normative 'type', removed from any context. Only in a general sense can this information about female prisoners communicate 'who' the women are. It cannot explain why the women came to prison nor how they feel about it. It does not give an account of the women's own understanding of incarceration, nor of the role and function of prison in their own lives.

Yet it is precisely the women's subjectivity – their motivations and sense of self – that can serve to elaborate how they evaluate and negotiate power relations in prison. Formed through their life experiences and their socio-economic status, prisoners connect their sense of self within the prison to broader social constructions of race, gender and class. Their subjectivity, in other words, provides a context in which to understand their actions in penal institutions and with each other for it goes beyond the empirical characteristics of the 'women's estate', to embrace the individual woman's own sense of identity.

Identity Politics: A New Approach for Criminology?

Identity and subjectivity are currently fashionable terms in much feminist and critical theory (Calhoun 1994; Taylor 1989; Braidotti 1994; Griffiths 1995; see Chapter 4 below). Emerging in part from the ashes of Marxism, this work provides some basis for a replacement ideology for the Left and has been particularly influential in feminist circles. By destabilizing the restrictive immutability previously attached both to the notion of 'Woman' and to gender, contemporary feminists have indicated the possibility of transforming unequal power relations (Butler 1990, 1993; Schor and Weed 1994; Weir 1996). Building on feminist thought, much of which problematizes the categories of sex, sexuality and gender, in this book I examine the effects of femininity upon women in prison. Questions I ask include: To what extent are practices of imprisonment based on rigid stereotypes of women? Do the prisoners accept or reject traditional feminine identities? Is femininity a source of oppression, or can it also enable resistance? In short, are the women able to transform or challenge power relations from their 'embodied' positions, as feminist theorists suggest?

By raising such questions, I am attempting to explain how the identities of women in prison are constituted by a variety of changing social relations. As prisoners they must negotiate discourses of punishment and responsibility, while as women they are subject to notions of femininity. However, the effects of imprisonment are not uniform. Rather, both the collective and individual identities of the women are active and changing, constantly under formation and never complete.

An investigation of identity introduces the related concepts of agency and resistance to prison studies, since it requires an appreciation of inmates as independent actors whose actions help to determine the meanings and effects of punishment. To be an 'agent', or to have 'agency' denotes the ability to negotiate power. It requires a certain self-image as active and participatory, entailing the subject's 'capacity to make meanings in her interaction with others' (Mahoney and Yngvesson 1992: 45). Power, in prison, is constantly negotiated on the level of identity. The prisoners are clearly at a disadvantage in this negotiation, because they are restricted not only in their movements and opportunities, but also in most of the characteristics typically deemed necessary for active, adult agency, namely choice, autonomy and responsibility. However, these restrictions do not entirely disempower them. Rather, the prisoners are able, to some extent, to 'get what they want done' and so to assert themselves as agents.

Such stubborn assertion of agency raises profound questions about how women in prison manage power relations despite their limited choices and opportunities. In investigating this matter, I draw upon contemporary feminist and social theory in order to illuminate the paradoxical ways in which women in three English penal establishments – HMP/YOI Drake Hall, HM Remand Centre Pucklechurch and the Women's Annex of HMP Winchester – strive to resist the restrictions placed upon them by imprisonment.[4] Without wishing to overstate the case for their resistance, I demonstrate many subtle ways in which they rebel against the authority of the institution. In particular, I argue that women rely on notions of an idealized femininity to survive imprisonment which are often similar to those used to punish them. Thus there are paradoxical continuities and contradictions between women's agency and their confinement. Rather than searching for a singular definition of 'women in prison', I suggest that it may be in the variety of possible subject positions occupied by individual prisoners that the ability to resist emerges.

In sum, this study has a liberationist-critical goal. It aims to challenge criminological and popular understanding of imprisonment and punishment through a consideration of gender, race and class. The prison is used in this text to denote both a specific site or institution, and a representation of the state's power to punish. The prison is considered both as a material structure and as a symbolic institution. By grounding my analysis in the women's own words and experiences, as well as in contemporary feminist theories of agency and identity, I offer a reading of the relationship between gender and punishment.

Considering imprisonment through an analysis of identity suggests that institutional order and control may not be fixed. In this way my work builds on recent criminological accounts of legitimacy and power in prison (Sparks, Bottoms and Hay 1996). Ultimately it enables criminologists to go beyond traditional prison studies by making connections between the embodied characteristics of the penal population and power arrangements outside. Thus it broadens the study from one conducted within the prison walls to locate the institution and its inhabitants in the social world.

An Outline of the Chapters

Chapter 1 summarizes criminological literature on the prison. Beginning with the work of Michel Foucault (1979) and David Garland (1990), it examines how prisoners are able to wield power. To this end, it builds upon elements already present in prison literature, thereby revealing that issues of identity, subjectivity and agency have long been implicit in studies of imprisonment. Here it is demonstrated for example, how early sociological analyses of female prisoners identified continuities between social expectations of female identity and behaviour, and the corresponding organization of women in prison (Ward and Kassebaum 1965; Giallombardo 1966a; Heffernan 1974). Likewise, this chapter indicates how more recent feminist studies argue that women in prison are controlled and punished through the enforcement of ideals of feminine behaviour (Carlen 1983; Eaton 1993), while autobiographical accounts and the literature on self-harm are shown to provide expressions of agency by female prisoners (Padel and Stevenson 1988; Liebling 1992: Chapter 7, 1994).

The first chapter ends by outlining the key characteristics of the emerging literature on legitimacy (Sparks 1994; Sparks and Bottoms 1995; Sparks, Bottoms and Hay 1996). I argue that these contemporary studies of legitimacy have focused on how order and compliance among male prisoners are maintained, without considering the implications of the prisoners' identities. Because the nature of women's imprisonment rests, in part, upon gender inequalities, the concept of legitimacy must be broadened to explore how agency, choice and resistance are influenced by identity. While this new literature encourages an appreciation of prisoners as agents, I suggest that these studies do not adequately define inmates as subjects.

In Chapter 2, three recent official inquiries into the general penal system of England and Wales are compared with the two contemporaneously produced government publications about women's prisons (Woolf 1991; Woodcock 1994; Learmont 1995; Home Office 1992a; HMCIP 1997). Through this comparison, I argue that women fit uneasily into the rhetoric of justice and security which characterizes the contemporary management of the prison service as a whole. Despite the ethos of equal treatment that supposedly underlies the prison system, women are understood to exhibit alternative needs and qualities. While men are seen as active, dangerous and in need of justice, women are described as resigned, as suffering from low self-esteem, and as being in need of care. The practices and legitimacy of imprisonment thus differ for women and men along a gender binary.

Once imprisonment is viewed as gendered, it becomes apparent that many of the stereotypes upon which women's punishment is based are contradictory. For example, femininity requires women to be both dependent daughters and wives, and responsible mothers; women are represented as the mainstay of the home, as well as its source of greatest weakness. Chapter 2 examines the extent to which these paradoxes of femininity underlie the treatment of women inmates. I conclude in this section that, if these contradictions are to be overcome, a more acute appreciation will be needed of how the prisoners themselves evaluate their experiences of imprisonment.

Chapter 3 outlines the range of practical and theoretical strategies and techniques which I adopted in my fieldwork. Here I argue that prison research has been shaped by a particular vision of rationality and objectivity marginalizing women's experiences of crime and punishment. I investigate the rationale for qualitative research methods, concluding that any empirical findings are conceptually limited unless they are located within a precise, theoretical context. Recent feminist epistemology and methodology are reviewed with attention given to many feminist advocates' failure to acknowledge the pressures and emotional demands of fieldwork.

This chapter functions as a hinge between the two halves of the book. While it has become more usual to locate a discussion of methodological issues in a separate appendix (see, for example, Maher 1997), I have chosen to place mine at the centre of the text in order to reflect on the process of research. By disclosing the development of my ideas, I suggest that the women's testimonies which appear in the second half of the text should be carefully interpreted rather than taken to be self-explanatory.

Chapter 4 explores both how prison challenges and confronts women's identity and agency, as well as how power relations are constantly under negotiation. The subjectivity of women in prison is a contested intellectual terrain in criminological literature. Frequently characterized as 'poor copers' (Fox in Toch 1992; Maden 1996; Sim 1990: Chapter 6) or as having 'chaotic' lives or lifestyles, women paradoxically are also often portrayed as more deviant and culpable than their male counterparts (Eaton 1993; Shaw 1995). Through examples from my empirical research, I show how women, despite the inevitable erosion of their self-image in response to the institutional restrictions, expend a considerable amount of energy inside attempting to maintain a self-identity as active, reasoning agents.

The women's positive images of themselves are undermined by institutional constraints which encourage them to exhibit traditional, passive, feminine behaviour at the same time as their identities and responsibilities as mothers, wives, girlfriends and sisters are denied. Women in prison – and in the community – are expected to conform to a particular ideal of feminine behaviour, which is predicated upon a silencing of their desire for autonomy and agency. In order to survive the pains of imprisonment, women must redefine the meaning of femininity and so break through its limitations.

Chapter 5 builds directly on the discussion of identity in order to demonstrate how women in prison manage to resist the 'pains of imprisonment'. It outlines a number of ways in which women constitute an alternative self-identity to the *passive* femininity fostered by the institution. For example, the prison encourages a particular vision of femininity, through the provision of such traditional work and education options as the beauty classes in which prisoners are taught how to craft a neat, feminine appearance. However, rather than being limited by such classes, many of the prisoners are able to use them either to survive, or to resist imprisonment. In the apparently simple process of taking care of their appearance, for example, female prisoners manage to maintain self-respect, and so defy their image as weak and defeated. In other words, while the prisoners do not appear to be challenging many of the key notions of femininity favoured by the prison regime, the women none the less reshape ideas of femininity in terms of their race, class and sexuality in such a way that enables some practical, verbal, resistance to the restricted regimes. Despite their seeming passivity, and the notorious absence of large-scale disturbances in female prisons, women constantly engage in strategies to reduce the pains of imprisonment. Femininity plays a crucial, albeit paradoxical, role in their resistance: while it represents the goal and form of their imprisonment, it is also the means by which they achieve their own ends.

Identity and Agency: Encouraging Expressions of Resistance

Familiarity and Difference, Insider and Outsider, Self and Other – these elements of identity, subjectivity and knowledge are destabilized within criminology, feminism and, of course, within the prison. They are, however, issues which govern how we react to each other, both consciously and unconsciously (Goffman 1969). Therefore, they are useful themes for a theoretical analysis of the prison. Although the prison is deeply hidden within our society, going inside is not simply a matter of greeting the unfamiliar, it is also about recognizing the well-known. Writing about imprisonment therefore requires being attuned to subjectivity and identity in the most profound and subtle sense.

The current discussion of subjectivity and identity occurs across disciplines and across ideological persuasions. However, the contemporary debate has often been restricted to the abstract areas of social theory and philosophy. Surprisingly little has been written on the practical and 'lived experience' of the modern (or postmodern) 'fragmentation' of our identities. There is, therefore, a real need for a grounding of theory. Yet, in order to understand women in prison, the criminologist must be able to speak to them in ways which are mutually comprehensible. This requires a subtle use of language and a clarity of ideas. Given that sociologists of imprisonment have revealed how prisoners import ideas, values and morals from currents within society at large, the criminologist must have an understanding of the implications of the relationship of the 'inside' to the 'outside'. Indeed, criminologists can (and should) theorize beyond what 'goes on' in prison, to what 'goes on' in society. An analysis of the prison must therefore be reflexive and multifaceted. The criminologist must be honest about her own structuring 'prejudices', both as an individual and as a criminologist.

In conclusion, I argue that examining prison through the notions of agency and identity illuminates elements of the complex relationship between gender and power both inside and outside the prison. It helps to uncover the finer details of the effects of imprisonment, and to appreciate the ways in which everyday pressures undermine the women's sense of identity. With this approach we enrich our understanding of the complexities and contradictions of the experience of punishment. Studying identity extends the boundaries of contemporary prison studies by utilizing an alternative, smaller-scale analysis of the distribution of power. Introducing the issues of agency and identity into an analysis of imprisonment also requires that criminologists transgress the boundaries of their discipline and engage with contemporary debates occurring elsewhere. In this way, a consideration of subjectivity not only deepens analysis of imprisonment, it also broadens the scope of criminological research.

Through interrogating how women sustain their sense of self in prison, I hope to deepen the understanding of the meaning and role of imprisonment today. I propose that women resist by relying on similar notions of femininity that are used to restrain them. Such a paradox reveals the contingency of the gender binaries that reinforce the prison and its study. If the women are able to use elements of femininity to challenge the prison regime, there is no reason to think those binaries fixed. It is in these very contradictions and paradoxes that I find the possibility of transformation and change. Thus, I conclude that criminologists may well be able to destabilize the seemingly constant 'reality' of imprisonment, and propose alternatives to current practice, which is generally ineffective and frequently inhumane.

Notes

1   Not her real name.
2   This proportion of women to men in prison corresponds with most other industrialized nations, superseded only by the US which currently boasts an incarcerated female population of around six per cent of its total penal estate (HM Prison Service, 1996; Immarigeon and Chesney-Lind, 1992).
3   Although I am conscious that the word 'inmate' carries paternalist overtones, it is the term which most women in prison used to describe themselves, and so I use it advisedly throughout this text.
4   Although my research is exclusively about women, much of the argument is applicable to prisons in general. The gynocentric approach is a strategic and ideological choice, but it is not meant to exclude a gendered analysis of masculinity and men's imprisonment.

1   Reading the Prison: A Review of the Literature

Today's penal complex does not prevent or stop crime in the main – the normal forms of socialisation and integration do that. Nor does it generally reform criminals. Rather, it administers criminals and criminality, managing 'social failures' and not repairing them. Its effect is to propel these individuals into a deterred conformity or, more usually, into closely supervised spirals of failure and continued failure ... It places them in a position of being known and predictable, properly connected with either social or penal institutions – 'within control'. (Garland 1985: 260)

Women's imprisonment ... has traditionally been characterised by its invisibility, its domesticity and its infantilisation (Carlen 1983: 18).

Going to prison is like going through the looking glass. It is entering an unreal world (Hélène: HMP/YOI Drake Hall, June 1995).

The prison has long been a popular site of analysis. Jeremy Bentham portrayed it as central to the utilitarian vision of an ordered society (Bentham 1995). Lombroso and Ferrero found, calibrated and quantified their sample of criminogenic types there (Lombroso and Ferrero 1895). Interwar and postwar sociologists conducted detailed analyses of social organization and subcultures inside maximum secure establishments (Clemmer 1940; Sykes 1958; Giallombardo 1966a). Historians have mapped the prison's relationship to the development of capitalism (Ignatieff 1978; Melossi and Pavarini 1981). Foucault traced the roots and representations of the contemporary disciplinary society in its genealogy (Foucault 1979), and feminists uncovered continuities between women's domesticization throughout society and their treatment within penal institutions (Carlen 1983, 1985; Faith 1993). Most recently, prisons have become the locus of battles for and against the free market and privatization (Sparks 1994), and sites of analysis of the politics of managerialism (DiIulio 1987; Feeley and Simon 1992; Bottoms

9

1995; Adler and Longhurst 1994; Genders and Player 1995). Even the boundaries of the field of 'prison studies' are unclear, since accounts of imprisonment are frequently written by scholars from disciplines other than criminology. Analyses of the prison can spring from the history and sociology of punishment (Ignatieff 1978; Melossi and Pavarini 1981; Garland 1990), the sociology of imprisonment (Clemmer 1940; Sykes 1958), penology (DiIulio 1987, 1991), government inquiries and reviews (Woolf 1991; Home Office 1992a; Woodcock 1994; Learmont 1995), and, more recently, penality (Foucault 1979; Howe 1994).[1]

Yet, despite the range and breadth of scholarship about punishment and imprisonment, most studies have been characterized by an implicit instrumentalism which has obscured the complex material and symbolic power relations embodied by the prison. Although there has been analysis of the 'power to punish' (Foucault 1979; Garland and Young 1983), there has been little application of this work to contemporary, empirical, prison research. Aside from historical reviews of the prison, there has been limited reciprocity between theoretical studies of punishment and practical analyses of imprisonment. When 'power' has been discussed, it has generally been considered in terms of 'coercion' or 'order' by criminologists who have focused on relations inside.[2]

The overall absence of an inclusive, theoretical articulation of power relations in prison studies has had broad empirical and epistemological effects upon the understanding of incarceration: 'Studies of imprisonment, in common with other areas of social inquiry, tend to stand on one or other side of certain dualisms' (Sparks, Bottoms and Hay 1996: 63). These oppositions range from early debates about freedom/determinism (Howard, 1777; Lombroso and Ferrero, 1895), through importation/deprivation (Irwin and Cressey 1962; Sykes 1958) to the more recent concerns with rehabilitation/ just deserts (May 1979) and justice/custody (Woolf 1991; Learmont 1995). These rigid parameters have drawn attention away from the small-scale negotiations which characterize daily prison life, and have tended to disguise the manner in which prisoners themselves contribute to the configuration of power inside. As a result, power has been equated with such measurable phenomena as 'order' and 'control', and its symbolic qualities have all but been ignored.[3]

In order to illuminate the ways in which power is under constant negotiation in prison, it is helpful to reflect on how prisoners 'get things done' as well as addressing how they evaluate what they want done. If it is accepted that prisoners are always in some manner engaged in the negotiation of power inside – however limited their role may be – then it is necessary to consider how prisoners manage to retain a sense of themselves as agents, despite the restrictions they face. Consequently, as the following chapter will demonstrate in more detail, issues of identity inevitably arise once prisoners are recognized to be agents.

Prisoners, like other individuals, formulate judgements and act with reference to the community from which they come, where their sense of self is based. However, prison studies have rarely been concerned with questions of subjectivity. Criminologists have tended to focus upon white men's experiences of the 'pains of imprisonment' (Sykes 1958) to the exclusion of other groups of prisoners (although see Jacobs 1977; Irwin 1970; Carroll 1974). For many years, women, if they were considered in studies of prisons at all, were simply added on, with no new categories or frameworks of analysis (Ward and Kassebaum 1965; Giallombardo 1966a). Similarly, until recently there was little attempt to incorporate notions of gender or ethnicity into mainstream analyses of the prison (although see Carlen 1983; Carroll 1974; Genders and Player 1989; Díaz-Cotto 1996; FitzGerald and Marshall 1996). While it is no longer possible to claim that there have been *no* studies of female offenders, nor that race has been completely ignored, it is still apparent that much research continues to avoid these topics altogether. In particular, despite the emerging field of masculinity studies in criminology (Messerschmidt 1986, 1993; Newburn and Stanko 1994; Jefferson and Carlen 1996), there has been limited application of it to men in prison (although, see Newton 1994; Sim 1994a; Carrabine and Longhurst 1998).

Perhaps most disappointingly, those scholars who have endeavoured to develop a complex, philosophical understanding of power relations through empirical research in prison have often reached conclusions which have been ignored or censured by policy makers (Cohen and Taylor 1972, 1976). Without a relational and dynamic understanding of power, prison studies have been unable to break free from the instrumental question typically associated with imprisonment: at its simplest, 'what works'? Prisons are, therefore, usually measured – by the government, by the public, and by many criminologists – according to practical achievements.[4] Yet, clearly, the prison means much more than the sum of its instrumental failures or successes. A sentence of imprisonment has profound moral, economic and psychological implications, while the treatment of prisoners depends on wider societal concerns with rehabilitation, labour and security. Most importantly, the prisoners themselves constantly interpret their experience of imprisonment. They act as, and consider themselves to be, independent agents – to some degree – despite their confinement.

In this chapter and the next, I outline and challenge many of the empirical and epistemological traditions of prison studies and reports. In this section I develop work which has touched upon issues of agency and identity. Such studies, as, for example, Mandaraka-Sheppard's depiction of changes to women's self-identity in British prisons (Mandaraka-Sheppard 1986), are often influenced by Goffman's paradigmatic analysis of 'impression management' and 'presentation of self' in total institutions (Goffman 1961). There are also phenomenological accounts of 'survival' (Cohen and Taylor 1972), psychological descriptions of 'coping' (Toch et al. 1989), identification of 'suicide-risks' (Liebling 1992) and feminist studies which list the strategies women undertake in order to prevent reoffending (Eaton 1993). Complementing prison studies, but slightly separate from them are analyses of the images of femininity invoked in the treatment of juvenile female offenders (Cain 1989; Gelsthorpe 1989) and feminist discourse analysis of female law breakers (Allen 1987a; Worrall 1990). Much useful and theoretically informed work has thus already been done. Yet a rigorous use of the conceptual fields which surround the terms 'agency', 'identity' and 'subjectivity' can take matters further and potentially bridge the gap between studies of punishment and research into imprisonment.

The Origins of the Prison: Freedom vs. Responsibility

Dualities in prison studies date to the formation of the first penitentiaries during the eighteenth and nineteenth centuries, when social reformers competed with social scientists to define the purpose and the form of imprisonment. According to David Garland, understanding of the prison was transformed in this period from a 'moral philosophy' to a 'penological science' (Garland 1990: 185). The changing modes and comprehension of punishment reflected contemporary ideological and economic concerns which typically legitimated competing discourses about free will, responsibility and determinism (Pasquino 1991). In eighteenth and early nineteenth-century Britain, religious reformers – who most commonly were members of the ascending capitalist classes of industrialists, bankers and merchants like Elizabeth Fry and John Howard – were central to the development of minimum standards of penal regimes (Howard, 1777; Fry, 1827).[5] Underlying their actions was a belief that offenders were ultimately responsible for their actions and could be transformed into 'good' members of society through a combination of religious instruction, meaningful labour and time for solitary reflection.

However, the influence of these philanthropists on prison reform was soon undermined by a growing belief in biological determinism and a deepening fear of the 'dangerous classes' (Lombroso and Ferrero, 1895). Penal policy was transformed by Victorian ideas of 'less eligibility' and the 'deserving poor', and consequently, by the mid-nineteenth century, the impact of philanthropic, religious reformers had markedly declined (Platt 1969; Simon 1993; Sparks 1996). Prisons became governed by the 'separate system', and ideals of order and rationality prevailed over religious morality (Ignatieff 1978; Garland 1990: 185; Zedner 1991: 122–4; McConville 1995: 15–16). *Homo Penalis*, capable of exercising free will, had been replaced by *Homo Criminalis*, 'whose acts are not results of a false calculation ... but manifestations of an evil nature' (Pasquino 1991: 238). As a result, instead of striving to reform by good example, prison officials now sought to gather as much information about the criminal underclass to ensure the most effective techniques of confinement. In short, philanthropy was succeeded by science.

Indicating the continuing influence of nineteenth-century ideas of criminological 'science', prison studies are still frequently marked by a pernicious instrumentalism. Yet, critical studies of a broader scope also possess a considerable history. In particular, many contemporary explanations of the historical development of techniques of punishment have their roots in Georg Rusche and Otto Kirchheimer's *Punishment and Social Structure* (1939) which explained changes in the dominant mode of punishment in terms of shifts in the economic structure. Focusing upon the relationship between 'penal methods' and 'basic social relations', the authors traced the evolution of the prison in Europe from the sixteenth century, relating practices of punishment to economic transformations. By destabilizing the seemingly self-evident and irreducible relationship between crime and punishment, Rusche and Kirchheimer enabled later research into the symbolic role of the prison. For, as they wrote:

> It is necessary to strip from the social institution of punishment its ideological veils and juristic appearance and to describe it in its real relationships ... Punishment is neither a simple consequence of crime, nor the reverse side of crime, nor a mere means which is determined by the end to be achieved. Punishment must be understood as a social phenomenon. (Rusche and Kirchheimer 1968: 5)

Notwithstanding widespread criticism of their overly mechanistic approach (Garland 1990: Chapter Four; Zimring and Hawkins 1991: Chapter 3; Sparks 1996), Rusche and Kirchheimer have had an enduring influence upon analyses of the relationship between the economy, unemployment and imprisonment. Their work has also shaped recent discussions of 'less eligibility' and punishment (see *inter alia*, Platt and Takagi 1980; Melossi and Pavarini 1981; Box and Hale 1985; Melossi 1989; Simon 1993). Yet, despite the later popularity of *Punishment and Social Structure*, particularly among Marxist historians and criminologists, Rusche and Kirchheimer had little effect on the studies immediately following theirs, which instead took a more empirical, sociological approach to an analysis of the prison (Clemmer 1940;

Sykes 1958). Only with the rediscovery of their text, and its reprinting in 1968, could their views contribute to new criminological analyses of the implications of the symbolic and structural nature of imprisonment (Howe 1994: 5–7, 14–15; Foucault 1979; Melossi and Pavarini 1981; Melossi 1989).

In particular, the publication and the later translation into English of Foucault's 'genealogical' text, *Discipline and Punish* (Foucault 1979), which is clearly beholden to *Punishment and Social Structure*, permanently altered the mode of theoretical investigation of punishment and the prison. Described as 'the most influential late twentieth-century text on the question of punishment', Foucault's study is perceived by many to have 'transformed our understanding of the field which he redefined as "penality"' (Howe 1994: 14). Even so, Foucault's work has received scant recent academic attention in British criminological circles, since scholars have favoured either an ethnographic or a psychological approach in investigating the prison.[6] In the late twentieth century, therefore, prison studies have, in many ways become polarized in a manner reminiscent of the first reformers. Now, as then, criminologists have either sided with (empirical, objective) science, or they have tried to find new moral and intellectual means to challenge the legitimacy of imprisonment, often without actually entering a prison themselves.

Punishment, Discipline and Modern Society

Discipline and Punish represents the most celebrated contemporary attack on the 'science' of imprisonment.[7] In it, Foucault depicts the prison as a metaphor for modern life, and uses it to describe the distribution of power within society. Desirous of 'demonstrating the [historical] precariousness' of the prison, he aims to show how the practice of imprisonment 'was capable of being accepted at a certain moment as a principal component of the penal system, thus coming to seem an altogether natural, self-evident and indispensable part of it' (Foucault 1991a: 75). In his opinion there was a transformation of penal practices between 1760 and 1840 from punishment directed at the body to punishment directed at the mind (Foucault 1979: 9–16). Like Rusche and Kirchheimer, Foucault relates the development of punitive techniques to the rise of modernity, contrasting the relatively homogenous contemporary practice of confinement to the variety of capital and corporal punishments applied in the *ancien régime*. Yet, rather than portraying the transformation of penal practice as instrumentally tied to changes in the economic structure, Foucault connects techniques of punishment to developments in knowledge, particularly in the areas of science, medicine and technology. For Foucault, the prison is central to a modern web of disciplinary power in which all citizens, regardless of their guilt or innocence, are monitored, ordered and controlled by competing discourses and social structures (Foucault 1979: 195–228). Foucault questions whether there has been real improvement in the humanity of penal treatment by characterizing the goal of the early 'reformers' as being 'not to punish less, but to punish better; to punish with an attenuated severity perhaps, but in order to punish with more universality and necessity; to insert the power to punish more deeply into the social body' (Foucault 1979: 82). Finally, he claims that, despite the manifest failure of the prison to reform or deter criminals, it remains central to the criminal justice system because its real role is to control the working class through the constant reproduction of a fringe population who are excluded from unions and other blue-collar organizations (see Foucault's interview by Simon 1974).

Having provided an account of the historical development of methods of punishment from the seventeenth century, Foucault employs the idea of 'discipline' to articulate and explore the relationship between power and knowledge. According to him, 'discipline produces subjected and practised bodies, "docile bodies", through a combination of routine, punishment and knowledge' (Foucault 1979: 138). While disciplinary methods had long been used in monasteries, armies and workshops, such 'formulas of domination' became more diffused and institutionalized throughout the seventeenth and eighteenth centuries (Foucault 1979: 137). Following Foucault's analysis:

> The historical moment of the disciplines [in the eighteenth century] was the moment when an art of the human body was born, which was directed not only at the growth of its skills, nor at the intensification of its subjection, but at the formation of a relation that in the mechanism itself makes it more obedient as it becomes more useful. (Foucault 1979: 137–8)

The exercise of these new disciplines, which appeared in such 'modern' institutions as factories, schools and hospitals, led to practices of enclosure, partitioning, classification, examination, and to the temporal control of all activity (Foucault 1979: 141–51). In turn, the disciplines of modernity required new strategies of information collection about all aspects of life. In particular, they presupposed

> ... a mechanism that coerces by means of observation; an apparatus in which the techniques that make it possible to see induce effects of power, and in which, conversely, the means of coercion make those on whom they are applied clearly visible. (Foucault 1979: 170–1)

Foucault's usage of the term 'discipline' thus refers both to particular areas of intellectual expertise – notably medicine and the human and social sciences – and to techniques of order and punishment (see also Foucault 1967, 1970). In his analysis, the prison is at the very heart of this 'disciplinized' modern social order.

Already by the mid-nineteenth century, the penitentiary stood at the centre of the exercise of a disciplinary power that was based on surveillance, classification and segmented space. Where a variety of punishments had previously been put to use in sanctioning criminal behaviour, confinement was now the norm. Time had become the measure of power, and it was applied in conjunction with 'a whole set of techniques and institutions for measuring, supervising and correcting' (Foucault 1979: 199), in such a way that irrevocably linked discipline, surveillance and punishment.

According to Foucault, Bentham's Panopticon is the architectural figure which best exemplifies this relationship between power, knowledge and punishment since it induces in the inmates 'a state of conscious and permanent visibility that assures the automatic functioning of power ... in short ... the inmates should be caught up in a power situation of which they themselves are the bearers' (Foucault 1979: 201). In the panopticon, inmates are segregated in solitary cells which are arranged so that the prisoners are constantly visible to an overseer who is conversely invisible to the captives (Semple 1993; Bentham 1995; Foucault 1979: Chapter 3). As a result, the panopticon 'automatizes and disindividualizes power ... [and] whatever use one may wish to put it to, produces homogenous effects of power' (Foucault 1979: 202).[8]

The panopticon, which stands for society's power to punish, radically disempowers prisoners, Foucault's analysis continues. Its domination is based on the authorities' knowledge of the inmates, and springs from its very architectural design. Most importantly, the panopticon is able to control without employing physical retribution, and in this sense represents the new, 'modern', expression of power, which is more hidden at the same time as it is stronger and more pervasive.

As in many of his other texts, Foucault in *Discipline and Punish* challenges the Marxist class analysis and historical materialism which had hitherto influenced many academic fields, and also rejects assumptions about the inevitability of progress. In Foucault's eyes, power is not a hierarchical relationship, controlled by the dominant class, rather it is capillary and multidirectional. Although in his later work on the history of sexuality, Foucault claimed that power inevitably invoked resistance, there is little sense of opposition in his depiction of the prison (Foucault 1980b: 53).

As a result, according to one feminist theorist, much of Foucault's work has marginalized an appreciation of agency and identity because he mistakenly depicts power in *Discipline and Punish* as

> ... a centralized, monolithic force with an inexorable grip on it subjects [because his] examination of power is one-sided; *power relations are only examined from the perspective of how they are installed in institutions and they are not considered from the point of view of those subject to power.* (McNay 1993: 38–39; emphasis added)

When Foucault's ideas are accepted at their simplest, prisoners in the modern world are classified, ordered and surveyed. They are subject to a regime in which they can only be objects. They are deprived of any special subjectivity in their gender, race or class; they are made neither subjects nor agents.

In a recent examination of Foucault, David Garland suggests an alternative interpretation of the development of modern forms of punishment which, in part, is built upon his rejection of Foucault's articulation of power and subjectivity (Garland 1990). Starting with the foundationalist work of Emile Durkheim (1964), Garland outlines and critiques the major theoretical schools of the sociology of punishment, including work by Foucault (1979) and Pieter Spierenburg (1984). Owing some debt to Rusche and Kirchheimer, whose book he also discusses, Garland is concerned with showing that

> ... juridical punishment is not the transparent and rather self-evident institution of crime control that it is commonly taken to be ... Punishment today is a deeply problematic and barely understood aspect of social life, the rationale for which is by no means clear. (Garland 1990: 3)

However, rather than adopting either the historical materialism of Rusche and Kirchheimer, or the post-structuralism of Foucault, Garland uses the work of Norbert Elias (1978) to examine the relationship between punishment, 'culture' and 'sensibilities' in order to 'focus on the ways in which particular values and commitments enter into the penal process and become embodied there, and, more broadly, how cultural mentalities and sensibilities influence penal institutions' (Garland 1990: 193). Garland's exploration of culture is intended to provide an alternative explanation for the enduring popularity of penal institutions. To that end he suggests 'languages, discourses, and sign systems ... must be interpreted and understood if the social meaning and motivations of punishment are to become intelligible' (Garland 1990: 198). Most importantly, he challenges the reification of notions of punishment and imprisonment by arguing that punishment

... is not reducible to a single meaning or a single purpose. It is not susceptible
to a logical or formulaic definition ... because it is a social institution embody-
ing and 'condensing' a range of purposes and a stored-up depth of historical
meaning. (Garland 1990: 17)

Both Garland and Foucault allege that the logic, or the legitimacy, of imprisonment is reinforced by historically determined social values. Thus, punishment, while subject to change, often successfully rebuts it. Ultimately, Garland
disrupts the apparent immutability of prisons much more persuasively than
Foucault had done, by linking punishment to sensibilities rather than to the
abstract notions of power/knowledge. These notions of culture change and
their shifts can be documented over time; by contrast, Foucault's power/
knowledge nexus remains an inaccessible and rather forbidding construct.
Moreover, as Garland points out:

Power is not a thing in itself, despite Foucault's tendency to use the term as if it
were a proper noun. Power is a relational concept. It is the name we give to the
capacity to realize a desired goal in a particular situation, and in human cultures,
the goals which may be valued and sought after are many and varied. (Garland
1990: 169)

In his analysis, power cannot be understood unless it is contextualized.

Perhaps most strikingly, Garland is critical of Foucault's tendency to
depict a seamless web of control, suggesting instead a more nuanced appreciation of forms of agency and resistance. Accordingly, Garland argues:

By studying more closely the nature of resistance, Foucault would have done
something to balance his account of power ... In particular, he might have been
led to describe the operation of power upon individuals as being less of an
'automatic' process and more of a matter of micro-political conflict in which the
individual subject may draw upon alternative sources of power and subjectivity
to resist that imposed by the institution. (Garland 1990: 173)

In short, he criticizes Foucault for neglecting the power of the inmates.
However, like Foucault, Garland does not discuss in any detail the resistance
or subjectivity of individual prisoners. As a result, he too ignores their role
in the creation of the meaning of punishment. Although Garland is critical
of Foucault's reductionist portrayal of control, he also depicts a realm
devoid of subjects. The elements of race, gender and class are particularly
absent from both texts[9] with the result that both authors detach their critique
of punishment from a critique of society.

Few, apart from feminists, have challenged the androcentrism of Garland
and Foucault (on Foucault see Nicholson 1990; McNay 1993; on Foucault

and Garland see Howe 1994). In England, there are only two texts about the history of women's imprisonment which have engaged with aspects of Foucault's work (Zedner 1991; Dobash et al. 1986). Likewise, in the United States, work is confined to that of two women, both of whom have produced studies of life inside eighteenth and nineteenth-century women's penitentiaries which owe more to the revisionism of David Rothman (1971) than to European debates about punishment (Hahn Rafter 1990; Freedman 1981). Despite their small numbers, however, these texts about the history of women's imprisonment pose a considerable challenge to Foucault and Garland simply by introducing gender into the history of imprisonment.

In particular, work by Lucia Zedner disputes earlier writers' accounts both of periodization and of the success of the penological shift towards rationality. Criticizing the revisionist historians *en masse*, Zedner claims that '[b]y ignoring the existence of conflict or even dissension they deny the possibility of change' (Zedner 1991: 97). Similarly, she argues that scholars need to take greater interest in individual agency and identity in order to differentiate between penal populations. In contrast to other historical accounts, her study of the treatment of alcoholic women in nineteenth-century Britain suggests that punishment and imprisonment cannot be fully understood without a consideration of gender. According to her, women posed a severe problem for the penal authorities long after the mid-nineteenth century, delaying the full implementation of modern practices of punishment (Zedner 1991: 3–8; Chapter 6). Her text indicates, in sum,

> ... how notions of appropriate male and female roles figured in the development of penal theory; how far penal policy was directed towards one sex; and how, in practice, the very presence of women in prison generated major anomalies. (Zedner 1991: 97)

Historians of punishment and its philosophers have thus greatly contributed both to our empirical knowledge about the subject and to our conceptual approach to it. They have indicated how practices and ideas change over time, and in response to diverse influences. None the less, sociologists and criminologists dominate the study of actual prisons. What then, have these approaches contributed to an understanding of imprisonment? Specifically, what have they written about women?

The Founding Fathers: Importation/Deprivation

Empirical accounts of the prison began during the first half of this century in the United States, when new ethnographic methods were employed in the emerging field of the sociology of imprisonment (Clemmer 1940; Sykes 1958; Goffman 1961). In these early studies, sociologists conducted detailed analyses of the social organization of relationships in prison. They examined role playing, offender groups and inmate argot with a view to explaining the maintenance of order in prison. Reflecting the more empirical and 'hands-on' approach within sociology and anthropology which had been established by the Chicago school of sociology (Park and Burgess 1927), most of the sociologists of imprisonment actively engaged in fieldwork, and utilized information which they personally gathered from the prisoners. In such work, the prison was perceived to be both a micro society, in which all elements had a function, and a microcosm of the world outside the prison walls 'in which the conditions and processes in the broader society are observable' (Cressey, in Clemmer 1940: vii). Although the majority of texts included in the canon of early prison sociology were concerned solely with men's prisons, a handful of writers considered female establishments (Ward and Kassebaum 1964, 1965; Giallombardo 1966a, 1966b; Heffernan 1974). Their studies diverged from analyses of men's prisons through an emphasis upon the private, the domestic and the sexual. Specifically, they used sex role theory to illuminate women's experiences of imprisonment.

The sociology of imprisonment was originally configured by a binary relationship between 'deprivation' and 'importation'. This dichotomy is typically illustrated by contrasting the work of Gresham Sykes and Erving Goffman with that of John Irwin and Donald Cressey. The former depict relations in prison as a consequence of the 'pains of imprisonment' and the 'deprivations' suffered in the 'total institution' (Sykes 1958; Goffman 1961), while the latter argue that walls are 'permeable' and that prison life is a result of values imported from outside (Irwin and Cressey 1962; Irwin 1970). However, this early polarity of importation and deprivation was rapidly disrupted by scholars who demonstrated that prison culture (both of the inmates and of the staff) was constituted by a combination of factors (Carroll 1974; Thomas and Petersen 1977).

More recently, there has been an attempt to explain the inner organization of prison with reference to the negotiation of power, and without using the concepts of importation and deprivation (Sparks et al. 1996: Chapter 2; see below). In so doing, these new studies of prison order have reinterpreted the early sociologies of imprisonment to illustrate the centrality of prisoners' agency in creating prison life. Yet, as I shall argue below, such work does not move from an account of agency to one of identity. Identity, therefore, has rarely been of interest to sociologists of male imprisonment, contemporary or otherwise. Hence it is necessary to reconsider the early studies of women's imprisonment, where research raised questions of identity because female offenders were perceived as anomalous prisoners and deviant women.

The 'Community' of Women: Importation, Deprivation or Inadequacy?

Three studies characterize the approach of the early, non-feminist and largely descriptive literature on women's imprisonment: David Ward and Gene Kassebaum's account of 'sex roles' in Frontera, Rose Giallombardo's work in Alderson, and Ester Heffernan's systems analysis of life in Occoquan.[10] Although these criminologists differed in their specific focus, they all concluded that women coped with the 'pains of imprisonment' in ways that were different from the male inmates. Despite limitations in their analyses – particularly in the emphasis they each placed on sexual relations in women's establishments – these early texts warrant a closer re-reading than it has become the fashion to give them.

Ward and Kassebaum produced the first book-length sociological study of women's imprisonment in 1965. Describing their intentions in their preface, they claimed that '[t]his study began with our interest in gathering data on women in prison to see whether there were female prisoner types consistent with the reported characteristics of male prisoners' (Ward and Kassebaum 1965: v). Drawing on contemporary sociological and phenomenological research, particularly that of Goffman (1961) and Sykes (1958), the authors found many differences between the imprisoned female and male communities which they explained in terms of the 'latent social identities' that inmates bring to prison (Ward and Kassebaum 1965: 57). Such identities, which pre-date prison life, meant they argued that prisoners react to the pains of imprisonment though such factors as race, class, sex and sex roles. Hence, Ward and Kassebaum wrote:

> The inmates at Frontera respond to the experience of imprisonment not only because they are reacting to deprivations and restrictions, but also because they have internalized, to varying degrees, the values of delinquent subcultures, of prisoner codes, and of the conventional community; and finally *they react as women. These norms and this identity are significant in that they provide frames of reference which influence behavior in the prison setting.* (Ward and Kassebaum 1965: 58; emphasis added)

The differences between women and men's 'latent social identities' – which, in turn, constitute their different reactions to imprisonment – were, they averred, a direct result of the 'sex roles' present in the wider community. Accordingly,

Women bring to prison with them identities and self-conceptions which are based principally on familial roles as wives, mothers, and daughters, and their related roles (fiancées and girlfriends). These differences reflect the division of labor in kinship systems which place on women the principal responsibilities of house keeping and care of the children. (Ward and Kassebaum 1965: 70)

Despite their initial recognition of the influence of identity, the central conclusion drawn by Ward and Kassebaum was that the most important way in which women reacted to the pains of imprisonment was by forming homosexual relationships. Defining 'homosexuality' rather specifically (and in italics) as '*kissing and fondling of the breasts, manual or oral stimulation of the genitalia and simulation of intercourse between two women*' (Ward and Kassebaum 1965: 80), they then spent the majority of the book recounting lesbian activity in Frontera.[11] As a result, their study seems dated, sensationalist and obsessed with sex and sexuality, fitting only with difficulty into contemporary analysis of women's imprisonment.

While many of the details of *Women's Prisons: Sex and Social Structure* can certainly be dismissed as obsolete, and frequently inaccurate, the text continues to carry some significance for contemporary accounts of female imprisonment because it draws attention to the existence of a relationship between agency and identity. Even though their description of women as 'inclined to be more passive and gentle' appears only to reflect the limitations of the paternalist ideology of femininity in which they operated, their belief that '[i]n prison, the inmate is stripped of identifying and distinctive qualities, capabilities, and symbols until she comes to resemble all others around her' resonates with more critical commentaries on the alienating effects of total institutions (Ward and Kassebaum 1965: 74–75). At the same time, their distinction between 'sex' and 'sex roles' prefigures more recent analyses of the confining role of femininity in women's prisons (Carlen 1983).

Not dissimilarly, Giallombardo explored relationships of conflict and cohesion in a women's prison in her book *Society of Women*, emulating the research conducted almost a decade earlier by Sykes (Giallombardo 1966a). Claiming that the 'female prison community has been overlooked' (Giallombardo 1966a: 1), she challenged the conclusions of Sykes and Clemmer that 'the most important features of the inmate culture emerge as a response to the conditions of imprisonment' (Giallombardo 1966b: 269). Rather, Giallombardo argued that female prison culture was determined by a combination of the internal system of roles and status with values and attitudes brought into the prison from outside (Giallombardo 1966b: 288). Like Ward and Kassebaum, she made explicit the thesis that 'differences in the informal social structure in male and female prison communities can be

understood in terms of the differential cultural definitions ascribed to male
and female roles in American society' (Giallombardo 1966b: 270).

Despite her implicit criticism of the absence of information about women
in prison, however, Giallombardo was not a proto-feminist. Her analysis
was confined by negative stereotypes of female behaviour and she did not
perceive women to be fully responsible adults. Although she described
some disputes between the prisoners, Giallombardo implied that the 'generally passive orientation of the female' resulted in a more stable prison
environment (Giallombardo 1966a: 102). Similarly, she typecast women as
untrustworthy and fickle, concluding that 'the female's self-orientation and
the tendency to see one another as rivals both function to decrease expectations of rigid alliance from one another' (Giallombardo 1966b: 275). Finally, echoing the earlier findings of Ward and Kassebaum (1964, 1965),
she allegedly discovered the so-called 'homosexual dyadic relationship' in
American women's prisons to be the most significant structuring factor for
daily life and inmate relationships (Giallombardo 1966a: 133–57). Ultimately, then, Giallombardo approvingly implied that order and harmony
were maintained in women's prisons in much the same way as they were in
the home. Not only did the prison enforce ideals of domesticity and femininity, but the women arranged themselves accordingly. In short,
Giallombardo gave little sense of the women as responsible or autonomous
agents who were capable of resistance.

Of these early sociological inquiries, Heffernan's was the most analytical
and critical. Many of the issues that she raised remain central to an understanding of imprisonment today, particularly her sensitive analysis of 'time
management', trust, and staff-inmate relations (Heffernan 1974: 66–86; 134–
43; 164–87). However, her penchant for describing various *sub rosa* activities, again with a primary emphasis upon lesbian relations, weakened an
otherwise sophisticated analysis of women's experience of imprisonment
(Heffernan 1974: 87–106). Initially designed as a 'replication of Wheeler's
testing of Clemmer's concept of prisonization' (Heffernan 1974: 10),
Heffernan's preliminary research suggested that different questions had to
be asked of the women in prison because the 'female social system' did not
correspond with that previously identified in the masculine literature.
Heffernan argued that women rejected the roles typically associated with
inmate systems. They did not function in complete exclusion from one
another but rather exhibited sufficient levels of solidarity to ensure that the
prison did not collapse into rioting (Heffernan 1974: 10–14).

Heffernan, in contrast to the claims of Sykes and Clemmer, proposed that
there was not a single, unified inmate system functioning in response to
standardized experiences of deprivation. Rather, she identified three different ways of 'doing time' which formed the subtitle of her text: 'the cool, the

square and the life' (Heffernan 1974: 16–17). She concluded that '[t]he prisoners' "community of fate" did not produce normative uniformity so much as functional interdependence' (Heffernan 1974: 184). The 'inmate system' was thus both an 'adaptive system' as proposed by Sykes, and one in which, as Irwin and Cressey claimed (1962), 'there is constant interplay between normative orientation to prison and the situational framework of each institution' (Heffernan 1974: 184). In order to understand imprisonment, therefore, Heffernan concluded that we must transgress the binary opposition of visions of deprivation/importation to appreciate that these qualities are reflexive. As a result, it becomes possible to appreciate prisoners as individuals who act and possess some autonomy, yet who are acted upon by the institution.

Despite the differences among these texts, and despite the challenge which the authors posed to the male traditions of the sociology of imprisonment, their reliance upon sex-role theory limited the critical possibilities of their work. Most importantly, even though the studies destabilized the division between 'importation' and 'deprivation', they maintained a traditionalist Cartesian dichotomy between women/men, domestic (or private)/public and passive/active. Such rigid dualism had the effect ultimately of disqualifying women's actions from attempting to subvert the dominant paradigm and prevented an analysis of women's agency. It was not until the 1980s that sociologists of female imprisonment began to propose a more political interpretation of identity and agency, through analysis of ideals of femininity. As the following section will demonstrate, this new literature enabled criminologists to move beyond the walls of the prison in their work and to contemplate more seriously the full social role and meaning of female incarceration.

Disciplining Women: Sociology and Autobiography

In Britain, sociological studies of female imprisonment are comparatively recent. There has been little research into role playing and inmate groups (Mandaraka-Sheppard 1986: 19). As late as 1983, Pat Carlen set the tone for most of the scholarship thereafter, in her book *Women's Imprisonment*. Prior to its publication, British discussion of women's prisons had been limited to a smattering of first-hand accounts of imprisonment from staff (Field 1963; Kelley 1967) and prisoners (Henry 1952), along with biographies of inmates (Parker 1965), government reports on female offenders (Home Office 1967; 1972; 1976), and historical monographs (Fry, 1827; Carpenter 1872). Carlen's analysis of the Scottish female establishment, Cornton Vale, in which she explores the influence of notions of femininity and domesticity upon the treatment of incarcerated women, was thus a decisive break from traditional research.

Based on a series of brief interviews with 20 short-term offenders, sheriffs, prison officers and other members of staff (Carlen 1983: 5–9), *Women's Imprisonment* is unashamedly partisan. In it, Carlen is critical of both the Scottish Prison Service and the wider, cultural gender order (Carlen 1983: 17). She contends that the women in prison are characterized as 'failures' of the ideals of the family and motherhood (Carlen 1983: 16–18), claiming that '[t]he Scottish female offenders most likely to be imprisoned are those who have stepped outwith domestic discipline' (Carlen 1983: 16). Similarly, she finds that women at Cornton Vale are not taught 'general survival skills which would enable them to live without a man', but rather are instructed in specific skills to help them 'to fill their ideal place in the ideal family' (Carlen 1983: 73).

Carlen avoids the dichotomies of earlier sex-role sociology by exploring the effect of ideological notions of femininity upon the form of women's imprisonment. She describes her task as being 'to theorize about the relationships between the biographies of women prisoners, the discourses which constitute them and the politics which render them the "female" subject (albeit denied) of penology' (Carlen 1983: 3). However, despite using the women's testimonies as evidence, when Carlen characterizes their experiences of imprisonment she gives little sense of the possibility of resistance. Rather, the regimes of femininity within and 'without' prison appear to prevent an active subjectivity.

Many criminologists built on Carlen's foundationalist study. In particular, research by Alexandra Mandaraka-Sheppard (1986) and Mary Eaton (1993) complement and develop many of her findings.[12] Although very different from one another, the findings of these two women suggest that understanding subjectivity entails an appreciation of agency.

In *The Dynamics of Aggression in Women's Prisons in England*, Mandaraka-Sheppard explores the relationship between women's self-image and their behaviour in prison through an empirical application of work by Goffman (1961) and Mead (1934).[13] Drawing on fieldwork conducted in three open and three closed prisons in England, she examines 'the "law breaking" by the women prisoners within the prisons and the controls exercised by the institutional authorities to curb such behaviours' (Mandaraka-Sheppard 1986: 13). Agency and identity are implicit in much of her text, especially where she investigates women's coping mechanisms.

Briefly, Mandaraka-Sheppard claims that 'upon entering the institution, the prisoner's self is constantly invaded either by the institutional procedures or by the close proximity of other inmates' (Mandaraka-Sheppard 1986: 113). Furthermore, she argues that the destabilization of the women's sense of self has an effect on their compliance. Differentiating between forms of obedience, from 'ritualistic' to 'committed' compliance and 'defiance or individualistic rebellion', Mandaraka-Sheppard suggests that the majority of women 'do not conform to the rules because they recognize and respect their "legitimacy" but because there is no other path to follow which would lead them to the outside with the least harm' (Mandaraka-Sheppard 1986: 121). The women's ability to act is, therefore, largely circumscribed by practical concerns which are controlled by the institution and which determine the prisoners' behaviour.

In a key section of her book, Mandaraka-Sheppard develops her consideration of agency and identity by probing the extent to which the 'women's self-esteem is affected by the prison experiences and ... whether inmates' self-concepts are related to (i) inmates' biographical data, and (ii) inmates' modes of adapting in prison, or overt behaviour' (Mandaraka-Sheppard 1986: 145). She detects no significant difference between the prisons. The women's 'self-esteem' is not dependent on the level of coercion or control in establishments, but rather is determined by their life experiences and their modes of adapting to prison. The most important influence on their behaviour is the number of times that they have been incarcerated before, with recidivists undergoing fewer changes to their sense of self than first offenders.

Many of the issues raised by Mandaraka-Sheppard continue to be relevant for women's experiences of imprisonment today. However, perhaps because of her reliance upon Goffman and Mead, she excludes the impact of socio-economic influences upon women's agency or subjectivity. There is no discussion of the women's ethnic or cultural identities, even though so many women in prison belong to minority groups. Similarly, the psychological explanations which she favours curtails the otherwise liberationist implications of her thesis, since they prevent a comprehensive theoretical critique of imprisonment. None the less, her study is rich, and when combined with work by Mary Eaton, provides important insights into the relationship between agency and identity in women's prisons.

In *Women After Prison* (1993) Eaton describes research with 34 women, all of whom had been in prison. Overall, she identifies three strategies of survival: 're-direction', 'recognition' and 'reciprocal relationships', each of which is imperative to establishing a successful life on the outside (Eaton 1993: 19–20). Although specifically concerned with women's life after prison, she none the less acknowledges that '[p]rison affords little space for the development of a sense of self' (Eaton 1993: 18). As a result, '[w]omen coming out of prison bring with them the sense of self that was cultivated in response to the prison. This may well continue to exclude the woman from the world about her' (Eaton 1993: 18). Describing her book as being 'about the enabling conditions conducive to women taking charge of their lives and changing' (Eaton 1993: 99), Eaton is refreshingly optimistic. She argues that personal change is possible, given appropriate networks of support, and sufficient self-knowledge. As a result, she turns her attention to the structural blocks that prevent 'changes in subjectivity', suggesting reform in 'housing; the labour market and educational provision; social services and health' (Eaton 1993: 19, and Chapter Six). According to Eaton, the women who successfully renegotiate their lives on the outside, only do so when they are able to find meaningful employment, supportive relationships and secure housing. Their ability to succeed and to become responsible agents is thus dependent on their sense of self.

A final area of scholarship which deserves to be mentioned is that of autobiographical accounts of women's imprisonment. These books have long played an important role in raising awareness of issues specific to female prisoners and have often been used to build a profile of the 'typical' woman in prison in order to supplement official accounts (see for example, Henry 1952; Carlen 1985; Padel and Stevenson 1988; Ward 1993; Maguire 1994). Life stories, like those recounted in Pat Carlen's interviews with five prisoners (Carlen 1985), or in Una Padel and Prue Stevenson's edited collection, document women's experiences of abuse and self-harm, highlighting the hardships of their lives (Padel and Stevenson 1988).

Such descriptive accounts are designed to provide a 'view from below', thereby allowing the women a voice, despite their confinement. However, the unquestioned primacy given to 'experience' which often accompanies these collections renders them problematic for an appreciation and analysis of power. Moreover, despite their liberationist intent, they frequently construct their subjects as victims. Accounts of women's suicide and self-harm in prison and in the community are characterized by a similar paradoxical representation of women as both victims and agents (Fox, in Toch 1992; Liebling 1994; Jack 1992). Many of these studies describe practices of self-mutilation – which women engage in far more frequently than men wherever their location – as responses to experiences of childhood abuse or 'stress', yet they also define such actions as 'coping mechanisms' (Liebling 1994). These contradictions in the definition and description of women in prison underline the importance of considering the women's own accounts and life stories. Rather than relying simply on autobiographical accounts, it is necessary to develop a more detailed, theoretical understanding of the relationship between agency and identity and their role in the negotiation of power in the prison.

Feminism and Critique: Social Theory

In a recent criticism of the traditions of women's prisons studies, Carlen chides criminologists (particularly feminist criminologists) for having provided 'more insight into the ways in which penal practices are related to other institutional forms than about the specifically penal power, penal functions, and penal dimensions of such relationships' (Carlen 1994: 134). In particular, she admonishes scholars for failing to conceptualize the prison's punitive capacity. Because of Carlen's crucial role in defining the field of prison studies for women, her revisionist article signifies a decisive rupture in criminological thought. Although she herself has yet to provide solutions to some of her criticisms, many of her challenges have been met by Australian criminologist Adrian Howe who, in 1994, published the first full-length, self-consciously feminist and post-structuralist theoretical critique of punishment and penality.

In her book, *Punish and Critique*, Howe traces the development of thinking about punishment in Western criminology from the historical materialism of Rusche and Kirchheimer, to the revisionist histories by Foucault, Garland and others (Howe 1994). Overall, she is harshly critical of the eurocentrism, masculinism and conservatism of penology and penality. She claims: 'It is as if the prison – quintessentially masculine because its populations are predominantly male – demands a masculine, more penile-than-penal discourse in which women prisoners are peripheral and feminism beyond consideration' (Howe 1994: 40).

According to Howe, the male domination of prison studies has in part resulted from problems within feminist criminology because 'feminist research initiatives have remained ... disparate empirical studies which are still today missing the benefit of a sustained critical dialogue, let alone an active theoretical engagement with issues raised by critical but non-feminist analysts' (Howe 1994: 123). In response, Howe endeavours to construct a new analysis of punishment. Dividing her text into three sections, she first outlines research findings by male revisionist historians (Howe 1994: 5–122), before turning her attention to feminist empirical criminology (1994: 123–64). She concludes her comprehensive review of the literature by advocating a 'postmodern feminist penality' (1994: 165–217), arguing that 'feminist studies of the disciplined female body', conducted outside criminology, 'have an as yet untapped potential to transform our understanding of punishment in the Western world' (1994: 206; see for example, Bartky 1988; Bordo 1993). Her attempt to incorporate insights drawn from postmodern feminist theory rejects the isolationist stance taken by many criminologists towards other more theoretical disciplines, and broadens the discussion from the problematic of 'punishment' to those of 'penality'.

Of central importance to her conceptualization of a 'feminist penality' is a consideration of the myriad of ways in which women are always already subject to mechanisms of discipline. By drawing on contemporary feminist theory, she is able to construct an image of the 'punishment continuum' in contrast to the 'crime-punishment equation' (Howe 1994: 163). That is to say, Howe argues that women's experience of institutionalized punishment is influenced by the manner in which women are always under some form of discipline in the 'free society'. As a result, issues of identity and subjectivity are finally placed at the centre of an analysis of the prison. Although Howe does not include an account of personal research with incarcerated women in this study, she sets out a powerful alternative to the sociological traditions which had hitherto defined analysis of women's punishment and imprisonment.

The Current 'Crisis' in Prison Studies: Questions of Legitimacy

The final area of literature which needs to be analysed is that concerned with legitimacy. Since this approach has yet to be extended to women in prison, it is necessary to consider accounts of men's imprisonment.

Studies of men's prisons have long been concerned with the twin issues of order and compliance (Home Office 1984; Bottoms and Light 1987; Ditchfield 1990). Recently, it has been suggested that the so-called 'problem of order', on which these texts have centred, may be more usefully conceptualized as representing a 'legitimacy deficit' wherein the distribution of power in prison is under constant negotiation by the staff and by the prisoners (Cavadino and Dignan 1992; Adler and Longhurst 1994; Vagg 1994; Sparks 1994; Sparks and Bottoms 1995; Sparks et al. 1996). The identification of legitimate relations is proffered both as a type of penal reform – since all kinds of everyday events are said to contribute to the maintenance of order – and as a new approach to understanding the distribution of power in prison. Most importantly, legitimacy is said by criminologists Richard Sparks, Tony Bottoms and Will Hay to illuminate how prisoners themselves contribute to the maintenance of order, suggesting that, despite their confinement, prisoners are able to be agents (see in particular, Sparks et al. 1996: 62–90).

Legitimacy is a term which is central to political philosophy (Hobbes 1960; Locke 1967; Rousseau 1993; Hegel 1953; Rawls 1971), sociology (Weber 1968; Giddens 1984; Beetham 1991), critical theory (Habermas 1976) and moral philosophy (Taylor 1985b). Yet, despite the current popularity of the notion of legitimacy in prison studies, the implications of the history of the idea remain largely unexamined by criminologists. The version which appears in Sparks, Bottoms and Hay's work builds on a recent re-working of Max Weber's theory by political scientist David Beetham. According to Weber, 'without exception every sphere of social action is profoundly influenced by structures of domination' (Weber 1968: 941), and every system of control 'attempts to establish and cultivate the belief in its legitimacy' (Weber 1968: 213). Domination is not a simple relationship of asymmetry, but rather is dependent on compliance from those who are subordinate in the power relationship and who need to believe in the legitimacy of their domination.[14]

In contrast to Weber, Beetham claims that a 'given power relationship is not legitimate because people believe in its legitimacy, but because it can be *justified in terms of* their beliefs' (Beetham 1991: 11). Power is, therefore, rarely a simple matter of oppression. Power is, instead, under constant negotiation. Legitimate power is

> ... power that is valid according to rules, and where the rules themselves are justifiable by and in conformity with underlying norms and beliefs, then the main way in which the powerful will maintain their legitimacy is by respecting the intrinsic limits set to their power by the rules and the underlying principles on which they are grounded. *Legitimate power, that is to say, is limited power.* (Beetham 1991: 35; emphasis added)

Such a notion of limited power seems particularly appropriate for analysis of the prison, not least because, according to Sparks, constituting 'legitimacy' is 'a deeply vexed, but generally unarticulated problem that haunts most discussions of prisons, prison disorders, and other aspects of penal politics' (Sparks 1994: 14).

Based on a piece of research commissioned by the Research Advisory Group (Home Office 1987), elements of which were later submitted to Lord Justice Woolf's Inquiry into Prison Disturbances (Sparks et al. 1996: 11–14), *Prisons and the Problem of Order* by Sparks, Bottoms and Hay (1996) delineates the current state of the art in British penological thinking.[15] The most detailed articulation of their work on prisons to date, it builds on a series of their earlier studies (see for example, Bottoms et al. 1990; Hay et al. 1990; Hay and Sparks 1991; Sparks 1994; Sparks and Bottoms 1995). In their new work, the authors combine fieldwork data gathered at Albany and Long Lartin (Dispersal) prisons during 1987 and 1988 with sociological literature on social order in and out of prison, point to new directions for thinking about order and control, and the management of inmates. Drawing on a variety of social theory, most notably that of sociologist Anthony Giddens (1984), they conclude

... a general way forward for future thinking about control in long-term prisons would include ... a 'social' crime prevention, aimed at enhanced legitimacy ... whilst ... considering creatively how 'situational' dimensions of the prison environment could be adapted to reduce opportunities for control problems, without destroying the legitimacy of social relations and trust necessary for effective *social* control. (Sparks et al. 1996: 322–3; see also 91–3)

They employ Giddens' notion of the 'dialectic of control', in which there is an ongoing relationship between agents and structures, in conjunction with conventional criminological accounts of social control and situational crime prevention, to provide the basis for a new penology (Giddens 1984: 16, 32, Chapter 2).

The notion of legitimacy provides a way to investigate the complexities of prison order and prison life, through an appreciation of the points of view of all parties in a given power relationship. The conceptual usefulness of legitimacy

... lies in the connections it illuminates between the interior life of penal systems and the social relations that characterize them, and the centrally important 'external' issue of the conditions under which it is judged appropriate to impose prison sentences in the first place. (Sparks 1994: 16)

By recognizing that there must be some connections between the views formed on the outside and action taken on the inside, Sparks, Bottoms and Hay open the empirical field to a theoretical analysis. They also challenge the position of both radical and conservative criminologists whose work 'assumes the *non-legitimate* nature of power in penal social relations' (Sparks et al. 1996: 302), by illustrating that order is assured only through an ongoing negotiation of power between staff and inmates:

Imprisonment (in common with but in a more extreme form than other contemporary forms of punishment) is the practical embodiment of the state's claim to moral authority in the delivery of justice ... the state's authority claims [cannot] be sustained if the practice of imprisonment routinely belies them (whether in the material conditions of confinement – such as overcrowding, and sanitary arrangements; *or* in its formal and procedural aspects; or its 'cultural', relational, and discretionary features) ... At least within a democratic society, no abstract justification of penological rationales can indefinitely survive a practical failure to deliver regimes or standards that conform to its claims. (Sparks et al. 1996: 308).

Their work allows scope for an investigation of the socio-economic experiences which influence prisoners' viewpoints. Moreover, it suggests that there is a relationship between the 'condition of modernity', in which prisons are central to our system of punishment, and how prisoners and staff experience the sentence of imprisonment.

It is important to add, however, that a focus on 'legitimacy' can also depoliticize otherwise critical criminology. For, although 'legitimacy' is directly related to 'power', Sparks, Bottoms and Hay often avoid using the language of power and inequality, thereby diluting their critique. Portraying their work as an alternative to both radical (Sim 1990; Scraton et al. 1991) and reactionary (DiIulio 1987, 1991) criminology, they strive for the middle-ground. Moreover, as already noted, the gendered element of legitimacy has yet to be explored, since recent studies have not distinguished between inmates in terms of race, age, or gender. Therefore, it is necessary to question whether legitimacy illuminates women's experiences of imprisonment: is it useful for a critical understanding of women's imprisonment? Does the concept illuminate and challenge the normative justifications for prison regimes and punishment for women? Can it acknowledge their experiences of incarceration? Is 'legitimacy' in fact a gendered concept which must be altered significantly before it can facilitate a useful appraisal of the experience of imprisonment? Can legitimacy illuminate how power relations are negotiated by individuals who are gendered, who belong to an ethnic group, and who can be identified in terms of their sexuality and/or their religion? Although it allows for an appreciation of agency, legitimacy as it is currently configured excludes issues of identity and subjectivity. In other words, while this literature portrays individual prisoners as agents, it does not view them as subjects.

Implications of Re-viewing the Literature: New Directions?

All in all, then, despite the amount of empirical research which is conducted into prison life, it can be argued that theoretical studies of the prison have remained underdeveloped – if by theoretical is meant a conceptual apparatus with which to interrogate, appreciate, and critique apparently practical and 'real' aspects of our social world. In particular, issues of gender and race have been markedly absent from mainstream analysis. The prison emerged at the same time as the foundationalist liberal notion of the individual, who is bound by rights and responsibilities. The prison is, therefore, at the centre of the paradox of free will and determinism, since it both upholds and challenges faith in the responsibility of rational individuals. As the next chapter will demonstrate, this paradox is most apparent in the treatment of female prisoners because the ideal of femininity constructs women simultaneously as dependent and autonomous.

By refusing to accept the logic of the prison, and by questioning its sources of legitimacy, it becomes possible to suggest new ways of seeing and critiquing punishment, imprisonment and social organization. By understanding the intellectual development of the sociology of punishment and penology, it is also possible to challenge the ideas which have been established within the discipline. In particular, by examining both those studies which have concentrated on the structural organization of the prison community, and those texts which construct the prison as a metaphor for aspects of social regulation, the criminologist can hope to retrieve the 'voice' of the prisoner and her relationship to society. Such research could answer Pat Carlen's criticism by revealing not only the relationship between specific punitive aspects of imprisonment, but also the sources of societal legitimation for penal establishments.

Notes

1   It should be stated at the outset that, beyond passing references to a small number of well-known texts for the purposes of illustration, I shall not be including any of the voluminous body of psychological literature which exists about such topics as 'coping' or 'treatment' in prison, because these texts locate agency and identity within the psychological make-up of the individual (see for example, McGurk et al. 1987; Zamble and Porporino 1988; Toch et al. 1989). In this chapter I survey studies of imprisonment in order to generalize about power and agency. My specific examples of women's expressions of resistance are set out in Chapter 5. Recent government reports on the prison service of England and Wales (Woolf 1991; Woodcock 1994; Learmont 1995), a study by the Home Office (Home Office 1992a) and a thematic review by the Prison Inspectorate (HMCIP 1997) will be considered in the following chapter.
2   Such an approach is currently defining the field of 'analytical empirical' prison studies that is best exemplified by the sequence of texts, each of which is based on empirical research in one or a number of prisons, that have been recently published in the *Clarendon Series of Criminology* (Vagg 1994; Genders and Player 1995; King and McDermott 1995; Sparks et al. 1996; Rock 1996). Although clearly critical – in intellectual and political terms – these texts ultimately prioritize a detailed analysis of particular establishments, rather than developing a conceptual apparatus with which to critique imprisonment *per se* (although see Sparks et al. 1996). As a result, it is arguable that they unintentionally reinforce the legitimacy of the prison by failing to critique its symbolic and ideological role in contemporary society. Moreover, the radical academics who have been most ideologically interested in issues of power in Britain have conducted little fieldwork inside prison following the banning of Cohen and Taylor (1976) from doing fieldwork and the forced retraction of the original version of Sim and Fitzgerald's (1982) *English Prisons* that was deemed too subversive. While critical left-wing scholars have addressed a variety of practical issues such as the establishment of prisoners' rights organizations (Ryan 1983), the effects of long-term imprisonment and prison riots (Scraton et al. 1991; Sim 1991), or the activity of the medical profession in prison (Sim 1990), their conclusions have tended to be drawn from secondary sources, from ex-prisoners, or from a series of questionnaires mailed to inmates (Scraton et al. 1991).

3   Although see Mathiesen's (1965) subtle analysis of prisoners' usage of 'censoriousness' to achieve their ends.

4   Consequently, and despite a number of historical and theoretical texts which have posed alternative models, (Rusche and Kirchheimer 1939; Garland 1990), crime and punishment largely continue to be portrayed within a causal relationship.

5   Such reformers are ironically described by Gustave de Beaumont and Alexis de Tocqueville in their nineteenth-century study of the Penitentiary System of the United States, as 'estimable men whose minds feed upon philosophical reveries, and whose extreme sensibility feels the want of some illusion. These men, for whom philanthropy has become a matter of necessity, find in the penitentiary system a nourishment for this generous passion. Starting from abstractions which deviate more or less from reality, they consider man, however far advanced in crime, as still susceptible of being brought back to virtue. They think that the most infamous being may yet recover the sentiment of honour; and pursuing consistently this opinion, they hope for an epoch when all criminals may be radically reformed, the prisons be entirely empty, and justice find no crime to punish' (de Beaumont and de Tocqueville, 1833: 48).

6   Most of the work which has engaged directly with Foucault has originated from the Edinburgh Centre for Criminology and Social and Philosophical Study of Law, with historical criminologist David Garland being central to most discussions (Garland 1985, 1990, 1992; see also P. Young 1992, and Garland and Young 1983). While some early accounts of women's imprisonment refer to *Discipline and Punish* (Carlen 1983; Dobash et al. 1986), active feminist engagement with Foucault's ideas has largely occurred outside prison studies (Diamond and Quinby 1988; Ramazanoglu 1993; McNay 1993; although see Howe 1994).

7   Foucault is also notoriously critical of the 'science' of criminology since he sees it as legitimizing the criminal justice system. In his interview 'Prison Talk', he asks: 'Have you ever read any criminological texts? They are staggering. And I say this out of astonishment, not aggressiveness, because I fail to comprehend how the discourse of criminology has been able to go on at this level. One has the impression that it is of such utility, is needed so urgently and rendered so vital for the working of the system, that it does not even need to seek a theoretical justification for itself, or even a simply coherent framework. It is entirely utilitarian' (Foucault 1980b: 47). See Garland for a refutation of Foucault's criticisms of criminology, where he points out that 'if a technique of power is supported by criminological knowledge, it can also be undermined by it' (Garland 1992: 410).

8   In fact, Bentham's own panopticon, which he himself would have directed, was never built (Bentham 1995). However, it inspired other establishments such as Stateville, Illinois (see Jacobs 1977) and the Edinburgh Bridewell. That the panopticon *per se* was not constructed as planned does not diminish its symbolic role in Foucault's analysis.

9   Unlike Foucault, Garland does include some footnotes detailing recent studies of women's imprisonment (Garland 1990: 202). He also appreciates that '[d]istinctions based upon gender differences also play an important part in structuring penal practice … In our own time, female offenders are also dealt with in gender-specific ways which reflect traditional conceptions of the female role and its pathologies … At every stage in the penal process, cultural understandings of what women are like, and how they ought to behave, operate to define the appropriate response to their misconduct and to structure the punishment of women and girls' (Garland 1990: 202). Yet, Garland himself does not spend any time considering the effects of gender.

10 Recently, Barbara Owen has published a contemporary version of these sociological accounts setting out findings from research conducted in California (Owen 1998).

11   Their obsession is best revealed by their chapter headings which include: the 'extent of homosexual behavior in prison'; the 'social-psychological bases of homosexual role differentiation'; 'the dynamics of prison homosexuality', including 'the course of the love affair' and 'the character of the love affair'; 'some implications of the homosexual adaptation of prison staff' and even 'a Methodological note on research in the area of sexual behavior'.

12   Prisons were not the only institutions that came under critique at this time. In fact, as Worrall notes, 'The 1980s was undoubtedly the decade which rendered female offenders visible and witnessed an exponential rise in interest in "women and crime"' (Worrall 1996: 68). Feminist and women-centred criminology flourished throughout this decade, as scholars explored women's experiences of probation (Worrall 1981), domestic violence (Stanko 1985; Edwards 1989), juvenile justice (Cain 1989; Gelsthorpe 1989), offending (Carlen and Worrall 1987a; Morris 1987; Carlen 1988; Morris and Wilkinson 1988), sentencing (Edwards 1984; Eaton 1986) and Mental Health (Allen 1987a).

13   Her concern with order and compliance also prefigures much of the recent work on legitimacy (see Mandaraka-Sheppard 1986: Chapter 4; see also Sparks et al. 1996).

14   In Weber's analysis, there are three types of 'legitimate domination' which, although they are never found in their 'pure form' since they have become intermingled over time, have existed throughout the 'history of civilization'. The legitimacy of domination is, in short, based on either 'rational grounds', 'traditional grounds' or 'charismatic grounds' (Weber 1968: 215–16). Characterizing 'rational grounds' as 'a belief in the legality of enacted rules and the right of those elevated to authority under such rules to issue commands', 'traditional grounds' as 'resting on an established belief in the sanctity of immemorial traditions and the legitimacy of those exercising authority under them' and 'charismatic grounds' as the belief in 'the extraordinary quality of the specific *person*', Weber clearly justifies legitimacy by people's belief in it (Weber 1968: 215).

15   See 'Evidence submitted by the Authors' to Woolf in Sparks et al. 1996: Appendix B; Woolf 1991: Annex 2E.

LIVERPOOL JOHN MOORES UNIVERSITY
LEARNING SERVICES

2 Re-evaluating Difference: The Gender of Justice, Care and Power

> If the subject is constituted by power, that power does not cease at the moment the subject is constituted, but is subjected and produced time and again. That subject is neither a ground nor a product, but the permanent possibility of a certain resignifying process, one which gets detoured and stalled through other mechanisms of power, but which is power's own possibility of being reworked. (Butler 1992: 13)

> Opinion amongst informed pressure groups and many experienced Prison Service staff is that female prisoners should be treated differently to males. (Learmont 1995: §5.38)

> *Because I am a woman in prison I am ... not catered for properly, a faceless fact, in the minority [but I am also] allowed to wear my own clothes, treated better than male prisoners (in certain respects)* (Virginia, Eleanor and Betty, HMP/YOI Drake Hall, May 1995)

Prisons confine a collection of individuals who have been convicted of an assortment of crimes and who are incarcerated for differing lengths of time. Prisoners vary in terms of their race and ethnicity, their age, their mental and physical health, their intellectual capability and education, their nationality, their class and, of course, their sex. Yet general policy statements rarely distinguish among inmates. Rather, any given establishment must somehow manage its diverse populations within the general remit set down by the Prison Service's statement of purpose:

> Her Majesty's Prison Service serves the public by keeping in custody those committed by the Courts. Our duty is to look after them with humanity and help them lead law-abiding and useful lives in custody and after release. (HM Prison Service 1996)

Although the 1993 redesignation of the Prison Service as an Agency has allowed individual prison governors some leeway in their managerial practices, ultimate authority rests with the Director-General and the Home Secretary, who are bound by the gender- and race-neutral language of the *Prison Act 1952* and the *Prison Rules 1964* (HM Prison Service 1993c; Loucks 1993; Richardson 1994).[1] Aside from the counsel of specific 'Circular Instructions', designating treatment of particular inmate groups,[2] all adult prisoners must be treated alike under the law. Consequently, the official discourse on imprisonment is posed in universalizing terms. All inmates must be governed equally according to the goals of 'justice', 'security', 'custody', 'care' and 'control'.

None the less, there is a contradiction at the heart of prison service management once women are brought into the picture, since, even though the administrative discourse of imprisonment is posed in the universal language of justice and security, documents on women in prison tend to uphold a particularist ethic of care.[3] In this chapter I shall analyse a series of recent government reports and publications in order to illuminate the manner in which the seemingly objective notions of justice, care, security/custody and control are gendered (Woolf 1991; Home Office 1992a; Woodcock 1994; Learmont 1995; HMCIP 1997). By comparing three inquiries into prison service security and operations with two contemporaneously produced documents about women in prison, I shall demonstrate that women fit uneasily into the rhetoric of justice and security. Indeed, much more so than men, women in prison are understood to require care and control. As was illustrated in the previous chapter, women prisoners have always been marginalized within the liberal, humanist discourse of rights and legitimate expectations, despite the apparent universalism of ideologies of punishment. Since the reformist zeal of Elizabeth Fry (1827), women have been defined as a separate group, exhibiting different needs and requiring care (Morris and Wilkinson 1995). Similarly, judicial and penal treatment of young women has frequently been based on a paternalistic and intrusive management ethos, which is most apparent in the literature on so-called 'status offences' (Chesney-Lind 1977; Cain 1989; Gelsthorpe 1989). Most recently, it has been suggested that adult and young female prisoners should be reallocated to a new managerial section of the Prison Service so that their particular security needs can be met more effectively (Learmont 1995: §5.89–5.94, §7.114; HMCIP 1997: §12.01).

The resultant failure to appreciate the diverse needs and characteristics of the general prison population may foster a rhetoric of austerity and control. Indeed I shall argue that in recent times, there has been a manifest shift in the language of the prison service which is apparent in the variety of ways that the *Learmont Report* ostensibly contradicts so much of the *Woolf Re-*

port. Crucially, this shift may be the natural result of excluding issues of subjectivity. For, as scholars have shown elsewhere, failing to consider the humanity of individuals in all their depth, facilitates the imposition of harsh treatment (Bauman 1989). In fact it may be concluded that Woolf excluded questions of identity in his very act of employing a liberal notion of 'justice' that was implicitly based on a normative ideal of masculinity. As a result, he neglected to ground the legitimacy of imprisonment in practical values and experiences, favouring instead a procedural justification of prison service practice.[4]

Given the severity of some of Learmont's proposals, it would appear that, once fairness of procedure has been invoked as the central legitimation of punishment, there is little safeguard against increased restrictions. When 'consistent and clear' treatment is seen to be enough, the notion of 'justice' which legitimates the practices of the prison service cannot help but disregard the impact of gender, race or class upon people's actions and judgements. Learmont and Woolf ignore the practical considerations of people's life experiences, because they do not provide sufficient means of evaluating the relationship between the material and symbolic effects of imprisonment. Ultimately, therefore, women and men are subject to the same penal regulations, and, notwithstanding women's exclusion from the discourse of justice and from many inquiries, prison law and government reports are applied uniformly to all penal establishments.

Much criminological and reformist literature criticizes the conflation of women's and men's needs, arguing instead for women's 'special circumstances' (Carlen 1990; Morris et al. 1995). In most official documents and reviews, female prisoners are characterized as a unique population requiring gender-specific treatment, in a manner which posits male prisoners as the undifferentiated norm. As a result, prison service practice is determined in part by a gender binary between the general (men) and the particular (women); that is to say, all prisoners are judged according to an implicit series of gendered assumptions about their identities. However, the 'politics of identity' underwriting the legitimacy of imprisonment is hidden. Not only is there little acknowledgement of the effect of masculinity on penal policy, but the notion of 'femininity' is rarely theorized. Because it is hidden, the gender binary has become static, meaning that administrative literature on women in prison has typically reinforced outmoded notions of passive femininity and victimization without proposing alternative explanations for women's needs and behaviour.[5] In the process of differentiating women from men, many criminologists have simply reinforced a rigid gender binary, in which female offenders are perceived as weak, passive and dependent, thereby disregarding the manner in which women constitute themselves as agents (Allen 1987b: 91–4). The subjectivity of women in prison is therefore defined according to a largely undifferentiated notion of what it means to be female, which typically excludes an appreciation of other socio-cultural phenomena like class and race.

Building on the previous chapter's discussion of agency – where I argued that appreciating prisoners as agents enables the criminologist to analyse power relations in prison – I contend that the legitimacy of imprisonment is determined, in part, according to essentialist notions of femininity and masculinity. Prisoners' actions are interpreted through a binary notion of gender, with the result being that women's needs and experiences are associated with notions of femininity. The exercise of power and the practice of imprisonment are both, in other words, always already gendered.

However, as I shall demonstrate, there are many problems with, and limitations to, the notions of subjectivity underpinning the practices of imprisonment. Specifically, it will be argued that the ideologies of femininity by which female prisoners are judged leave little room for their life experiences. In particular, socio-economic and cultural differences among women tend to be homogenized. In order to contest such a restrictive notion of subjectivity, criminologists need to devise alternative ways of understanding and theorizing how prisoners evaluate their own imprisonment. For as this chapter will demonstrate, the ability to evaluate rests on self-identity and thus can be interrogated in terms of socio-economic and cultural factors (Taylor 1985a).

The process of evaluation is ongoing, both inside and outside prison. In passing judgement or in differentiating between choices individuals must invoke constitutive elements of their sense of self. People do not, and cannot, evaluate from an 'archimedean' or purely objective viewpoint. Rather, in order to assess the legitimacy or 'justice' of a specific situation, individuals measure it in large part by what they already know and by what they already value. While normative morality plays some role in the process of evaluation – since, for example, most people would agree that murder is bad – even these values must be contextualized: if you are a soldier you will not only be expected to kill but you will be legally sanctioned to do so. The opposite is true for a battered wife, yet she may easily see herself as having few other options to escape her situation (Richie 1996).[6] The point is not that the prisoners' testimonies can illuminate the 'true' meaning of the prison, rather that their experiences and choices only make sense in relation to broader social structures.

To explore how individuals judge morality in terms of their sense of self may help to ground the pursuit and assessment of justice, without fixing or essentializing it. By examining the relationship between the constitutive elements of identity and people's framework of evaluation, it becomes possible to take the interrelated notions of race, gender and class into account. As I shall demonstrate at the end of this chapter, the notion of evaluation allows a more textured explanation of justice and power which can acknowledge the characteristics and opinions of the people passing judgement. With a deeper understanding of the process of evaluation, the criminologist becomes more capable of appreciating the meanings of gender identities and stereotypes as they are played out in prison.

The Legitimacy of Power and Punishment

The prison marks out, separates and punishes those who have broken the law by confining them in secure and frequently isolated places and by regulating their behaviour with structured rules and norms. It underwrites much of the state's moral and practical authority, and is, therefore, an institution saturated with ethical, political and instrumental power. However, neither the aims nor the effects of imprisonment are clear. The displacement of religion and moral philosophy by rationality and scientific precision in penal practices has never been total. Instead prisons have remained institutions riddled with contradictions. Their professed rationality and consistency often disguises contentious issues of morality and justice (Garland 1990: 189). As a result, the legitimacy of the prison is not assured.

Commentary on the failure of imprisonment arose during the 1970s in many academic, political and government circles. Rallying to the cry that 'Nothing Works!' (Martinson 1974), scholars and bureaucrats responded with diverse solutions and explanations. Some found sources of the crisis in the relationship of the prison to capital (Ignatieff 1978; Melossi and Pavarini 1981; Box and Hale 1985), others in its role in the establishment of modernity (Foucault 1979). A few called for its abolition (Mathiesen 1974; Scull 1977), while still others supported the development of harsher penalties and 'boot camps' (MacKenzie and Herbert 1996). Perhaps the bleakest of all suggestions was the pragmatic pessimism of those who mournfully accepted that the best option was to 'warehouse' offenders in penal establishments under conditions of 'humane containment' (King and Morgan 1980: 24; Vagg 1994; Fleisher 1989).[7] Most recently, academics and government officials have characterized the goal of imprisonment simply as incapacitation (Zimring and Hawkins 1995). The loss of confidence in the effectiveness of imprisonment by academics and practitioners alike was reinforced by a global increase in the number of riots in (male) prisons and by a rapid expansion in the size of the prison population.[8] In sum – and in the currently popular notions of penology which were outlined in the previous chapter – the prison has been suffering an ongoing 'legitimation crisis'.

Recently, in England, the sources of legitimacy of imprisonment have been explored in a series of government inquiries which were established in response to riots or escapes (Woolf 1991; Woodcock 1994; Learmont 1995). Such inquiries have shaped the practice and the discourse of the prison service.[9] Even though female prisoners did not participate in any of the breaches of security, and thus were not considered in the body of the reports (Woolf 1991: §2.18; except see Learmont 1995: §5.38–5.40), women in prison have nevertheless been affected by the policy changes (Player 1994). In fact, new restrictions on home leave, telephone calls, the spending of private cash, volumetric control of prisoners' possessions and gifts sent in from outside have had to be absorbed by the entire prison system of England and Wales. Likewise, all prisons have had to implement a system of structured incentives and privileges, and adopt increased security measures. The rhetoric of management which has been common in these reports has been posed in universalizing terms, leaving no room for difference. Therefore, the balance between security, care and justice (Woolf 1991), or, latterly, between custody, care and control (Learmont 1995), has been applied across the prison service, regardless of the race, sex or age of the confined population in question.

Custody, Security and Justice: Balancing Imprisonment

Prison riots in England and Wales increased in frequency and seriousness throughout the 1980s (King and McDermott 1990; Bottoms and Light 1987; Sim 1991). The disturbances, which spread from long-term maximum secure (dispersal) establishments to Category C establishments and to local prisons and remand centres, culminated in April 1990 when prisoners took over Manchester's local prison known as 'Strangeways'. In response, the Conservative government commissioned Lord Justice Woolf, who was later joined by Judge Tumim, to investigate the events surrounding the breakdown of control.[10] The lengthy resultant report, which was published almost a year after the Strangeways incident, is commonly held to have introduced a new style of language and a new level of conceptual apparatus into the empirical field of prison studies (Player and Jenkins 1994). Characterized by Sparks as 'standard liberal jurisprudence', the terminology and approach favoured by Woolf and Tumim was, none the less, greeted as a radical development in penal analysis by the prison service and academics alike (Sparks 1994: 20–21). In the years immediately following the publication of the *Woolf Report*, the Conservative government appeared to act on many of its key suggestions, publishing the White Paper *Custody, Care and Justice* (Home Office 1991) and passing the Criminal Justice Act (1991). Now, it was asserted, prison sentences were restricted to two kinds of offenders: those who had committed offences that outweighed other retributive penalties (CJA 1991: s. 1(2)(a)), and those who had committed a sexual or violent offence from whom it was necessary to protect the public (CJA 1991: s. 1(2)(b)). The Prison Service also vowed to increase time out of cell and meaningful activity across the prison estate (Home Office 1991: §1.34, §7.7–7.14). In 1993, the Prison Service became a semi-independent Agency and adopted a new managerialist policy which increased the autonomy of Governors within the restrictions of Key Performance Indicators and Strategic Planning (see Pilling 1992; HM Prison Service 1993b; 1993c). In sum, and in response to many of Woolf and Tumim's recommendations, during the early 1990s the prison service was rapidly modernized and reformed.

Unlike many previous government inquiries, the *Woolf Report* operated with a very wide frame of reference. The Inquiry also employed open and accountable research methods. It established a committee of independent assessors and consulted people from all sections of the prison service, including prisoners (see Woolf 1991: §2.1–2.59 and Annex 2E; Morgan 1991; for a more critical view, see Sim 1994b). As well as interviewing individuals directly involved in the rioting, Lord Justice Woolf sent letters to all prisoners and staff in the system at the time, eliciting for opinions and information about the management and direction of the prison service. Of the 4177 prisoners in the target establishments 607 replies were received, along with 603 from other prisoners (Morgan 1991: 721; Woolf 1991: Annex 2E). Only four women prisoners replied to Woolf's request and not one was personally interviewed (Woolf 1991: Annex 2E, Chapter 2, §2; see NACRO 1991b; Player 1994 and Carlen and Tchaikovsky 1996 for discussion of Woolf's exclusion of women). Moreover, although Woolf had taken a radical step by approaching prisoners for their views, his inclusiveness was compromised by the fundamental sceptism with which he received many prisoners' complaints. Sim, in particular, has underlined how 'no such qualifications [were] made with respect to the evidence given by state servants in general and prison officers in particular' (Sim 1994b: 36). Thus, despite his undeniable humanism, Woolf none the less ultimately sided with the administration.

Through their interviews with staff and inmates, Woolf and Tumim discovered that there had been a cumulative loss of faith in the operations of the Prison Service, among prisoners (§9.24–9.25), some prison officers (§13.3), as well as members of the public (§9.7). In response, the *Woolf Report* identified a widespread sense of *injustice* within the prison population and among sections of staff. Indeed, this sense of injustice was the basic cause of the prison disturbances. Overcrowding, the lack of training, education and general activity, unhygienic living areas and poor relations between staff and inmates were all designated as producing inmate dissatisfaction, while the decline in relations with managerial staff as a result of the 1987 changes to pay and employment conditions, otherwise known as 'Fresh Start', was cited as a key grievance by uniformed members of staff (see, for example, Sections 12–14). To ameliorate these dissatisfactions, the report urged that prisoners be recognized as having 'normal expectations' about the 'privileges' which are to be offered them in prison (§14.32–14.35), and that they 'be given the opportunity to make choices' (§14.14). Likewise, 'contracts' between all levels of the prison service, including establishments and prisoners, were advocated as a way to clarify, among other things, the parameters of an inmate's 'legitimate expectations' (§12.120–§12.129).

The notion of justice is implicit in each of the recommendations of the *Woolf Report*. Even when tempered by a recognition that security and control must be the other goals of the prison service (§9.19), much attention is given to refining the meaning of the notion of justice which is being advocated in the report. Yet, overall, the reader is left with a sense that Woolf's notion of justice is instrumental and aligned to the interests of the prison service, especially in the manner in which it is presented as a prerequisite for the maintenance of order in prison (see also Sparks et al. 1996: 15–22). Indeed, Woolf writes:

> A recurring theme in the evidence from prisoners who may have instigated, and who were involved in, the riots was that their actions were a response to the manner in which they were treated by the prison system. Although they did not always use these terms, they felt a lack of justice. If what they say is true, the failure of the Prison Service to act with justice created in April 1990 serious difficulties in maintaining security and control in prison. (Woolf 1991: §9.24)

In this sense, at the very basis of the Report is the belief that justice is procedural rather than normative.

Having identified justice as a central factor in the prison service management, Woolf and Tumim spend considerable energy detailing its constituent elements and requirements. In a frequently quoted passage, which is worth including here, they define justice as a prerequisite for the maintenance of order and elaborate its implications:

> *Fairness is a very important part of justice.* However, justice is a wider concept than fairness. If a prisoner is treated unfairly, then he will usually also be treated unjustly. Likewise, if he is treated unjustly, he will normally also be treated unfairly. However, justice involves more than the general requirement to act fairly in the circumstances of a particular case ... Proper structures are necessary in order to achieve justice. Within a prison in particular, it is an important requirement of justice that justice should not only actually be done but should be seen to be done. It will not be seen to be done if there is no proper procedure, if

there are no established rules, if the prisoner is not made aware of those rules and if there is not, at least in the final stage of the process, recourse to an independent element ... *If a prisoner does not perceive that he is being treated with justice, he will legitimately feel debased, he will bear grievance, and he will be a difficult prisoner to control.* (Woolf 1991: §14.296–14.298; emphasis added)

Justice, therefore, in Woolf's characterization, both delimits the boundary of 'good' imprisonment, and is its goal. It is intimately linked to a sense of 'fairness' and due process. It is prior to the good, and defines the 'legitimate' feelings and expectations of the prisoners. The prison service must pursue it as a fundamental aim.

Although the goal of attaining justice set by Woolf is complex, the suggested means of achieving it rarely rise above procedural issues. According to the *Woolf Report*, prisoners need rights, choices, responsibility and 'legitimate' or 'normal' expectations. Legitimacy is, then, closely related to justice since a 'just' establishment will acknowledge and fulfil a prisoner's 'legitimate expectations'. In Woolf's analysis inmates are presented as 'rational', reasoning men, capable of exercising their choices responsibly. There are, therefore, many similarities between the *Woolf Report* and liberal political philosophy. In particular, the relationship between justice and legitimacy which is implicit in the *Woolf Report* is reminiscent of work by philosopher John Rawls (1971).

Justice and Legitimate Expectations

Rawls first presented his vision of justice in 1958 when he wrote that 'the fundamental concept of justice is fairness' (Rawls 1958, cited in Solomon and Murphy 1990: 305). Yet it is his lengthy text, *A Theory of Justice* (1971), which is commonly heralded as initiating a renewed interest in justice and contract theory in Anglo-American political philosophy (Daniels 1975; Sandel 1982; Okin 1989; Rosenblum 1989). There have been other writers, such as John Lucas (1980), who have been influential in discussions of justice, while such commentators as Andrew von Hirsch (1976) and Nicola Lacey (1988) have examined the role of justice in sentencing and punishment. Nevertheless, Rawls, notably in his first book, remains central to any consideration of justice because of the impact of his work on philosophical debate.[11] Indeed, *A Theory of Justice* and the secondary literature which has arisen from it provide many insights into the limitations of the relationship between justice, fairness and legitimate expectations. In particular, the feminist critique which has been generated in response to Rawls may enable a critical interpretation of the *Woolf Report*.

Justice, according to Rawls, 'is the first virtue of social institutions'. Its primary subject is 'the way in which the major social institutions distribute fundamental rights and duties and determine the division of advantages from social cooperation' (Rawls 1971: §1–2, pp. 3–7). Justice depends on the fair distribution of goods, and thus a just society must strive to reduce difference between its members. Parity of access to, and ownership of, specific social and material goods are paramount. Furthermore, Rawls believes that his notion of 'justice as fairness' gives rise to 'legitimate expectations' and compliance because

> ... in a well-ordered society individuals acquire claims to a share of the social product by doing certain things encouraged by the existing arrangements. The legitimate expectations that arise are the other side, so to speak, of the principle of fairness and the natural duty of justice. For in the way that one has a duty to uphold just arrangements, and an obligation to do one's part when one has accepted a position in them, so a person who has complied with the scheme and done his share has a right to be treated accordingly by others. They are bound to meet his legitimate expectations. (Rawls 1971: §48, p. 313)

Like Woolf, in other words, Rawls perceives justice as a means to ensure social order. In a just society, individuals would adhere to shared social values and be bound by their reciprocal 'legitimate expectations'. Yet, similar to Woolf once again, Rawls provides no way of determining what realistic shared social beliefs might be, since he posits the original moment of decision making as set behind a 'veil of ignorance'. According to Rawls, 'the parties in the original position are equal, [they] all have the same rights in the procedure for choosing principles' and they are unaware of their natural attributes and endowments (Rawls 1971: §4, p.19). In this 'original position', which corresponds with the 'state of nature' in social contract theory (Rawls 1971: §3, p. 12), individuals are disembedded and disembodied, making it difficult to explain or even to imagine how their expectations might differ. Thus, to put it in more contemporary language, Rawls' society is governed by a politics of (re)distribution, rather than one of recognition (Fraser 1997).

Rawls characterizes his notion of justice as part of a theory of rational choice (Rawls 1971: §3, p. 16). Following Kant, he presumes his individuals to be endowed with rationality and to have a moral status which is irreducible. Rawls defines his rational beings as 'heads of families' (Rawls 1971: §22, p. 128), each of whom in turn is an individual who

> ... is thought to have a coherent set of preferences between the options open to him. He ranks these options according to how well they further his purposes; he follows the plan which will satisfy more of his desires rather than less, and

which has the greater chance of being successfully executed. (Rawls 1971: §25, p. 143)

Consequently, as Lucas notes, and as Michael Sandel develops in more detail, there is in fact a peculiar utilitarian aspect to Rawls' conceptualization of choice and agency (Lucas 1980; Sandel 1982: 165–7). More importantly, Rawls' characterization of rationality has been disputed for conflating the separate issues of agency and choice. The people in Rawls' vision of a just society appear to be without moral motivations or explanations for their actions. As Sandel writes:

> To arrive at a plan of life or a conception of the good simply by heeding my existing wants and desires is to choose neither the plan nor the desire; it is simply to match the ends I already have with the best available means of satisfying them. (Sandel 1982: 162–3)

Such an instrumental view of choice, resulting from Rawls' notion of rationality and his view of the determining of the boundaries of justice, precludes many of the complex factors which must always be a part of making a choice in the 'real world'.[12] Consequently, Rawls fails to consider how people evaluate justice within the frameworks available to them. According to Sandel, Rawls' failure to establish either how people make choices, and or how they differentiate between goals, demonstrates a profound weakness in a deontological theory of justice. If values are given *a priori*, in the original position, then Rawls' theory of justice can explain neither change nor difference in perceptions of the good life (Sandel 1982). Similarly, Rawls' overriding concern with 'legitimate expectations' and 'rational choice' precludes an appreciation of subjectivity, since his individuals simply act in order to maximize their efficient means of obtaining their ends. Rawlsian subjects can have little role in choosing or shaping the 'good life', or in making grounded moral decisions. In short, Rawls' notion of justice requires only agents, but not subjects.

The Injustice of Security?

Both *A Theory of Justice* and the *Woolf Report* uphold many of the central tenets of liberal political philosophy. In both texts legitimate social relations are dependent upon a collective sense of justice and fairness. While Woolf and Tumim are concerned with practical examples and displays of justice in the prison system, Rawls sets out a theoretical paradigm through which he interrogates the justice of a given society. Recently in the prison service, however, there has been an apparent shift away from such liberal understandings. Instead, issues of security and control have been presented as the primary goal of imprisonment. Even though the prison service and the Government approved many of Woolf's recommendations, making the language of 'justice' commonplace within official rhetoric and policy (Home Office 1991), it seems that a concern with justice was insufficient to stop a continuing move to austerity. Following a series of high-profile escapes and the suicide of alleged serial killer Fred West while in custody, two government inquiries have challenged Woolf's reformist intentions by demanding that issues of custody and security be given priority over justice (Woodcock 1994; Learmont 1995). In response to the perceived 'crisis' of penal policy put forward in the *Woodcock Report* and *Learmont Report*, the then Home Secretary Michael Howard introduced a formalized and restricted system of 'incentives and privileges' across the penal estate (Learmont 1995: §6.12; Bosworth and Liebling 1995), all but ended home leave, and reduced the availability of education and probation at most establishments. Consequently, the independence of establishments which arose in response to the *Woolf Report* has been curtailed. While individuals still speak of humanitarian aims and 'positive custody' (Tumim 1997: 15), the dominant rhetoric is now that of enhanced security measures, austere conditions and cutbacks (Howard 1995; Straw 1998). Why was there such a radical transformation of management procedure and belief and in such a short time? What is the ideological relationship between these recent reports?

Both the *Woodcock Report* (1994) and the *Learmont Report* (1995) criticize the prison service for security lapses and for losing control. In the words of Sir John Woodcock, the prison service is chided for letting 'the tail wag the dog' (Woodcock 1994: §9.14). As prisons institute Learmont's recommendations for enhanced security, the distribution of goods and services is bound to be disrupted for some time. Initially, therefore, as Learmont's opponents have suggested, it would seem that a concern with justice could not survive when issues of security and custody are to be emphasized so strongly (Morgan 1996). However, once the prisons and prisoners have adjusted to more regular drug testing and room searches, and once inmates become accustomed to having fewer possessions and fewer phone calls, would not the legitimacy of the prison service be assured, so long as everyone is treated with *equivalent* austerity? Since Woolf did not ground his notion of justice in the lived experiences of prisoners, does the new language of security and austerity contravene the accepted sources of legitimacy of imprisonment? In short, does Learmont's approach absolutely contradict Woolf, or is it simply the spirit of management which has shifted? What definition of justice might be used to challenge the growing support of 'less eligibility' which seems to be characterizing prison governance today (Sparks 1996; see also PRT 1997)?[13]

Like Woolf and Tumim, General Sir John Learmont acted with a wide frame of reference in his inquiry. For twelve months the prison service was buffeted by scandal.[14] Learmont was asked to head a general 'Review of Prison Service Security in England and Wales' following the publication of the *Woodcock Report* into the 'Escape of Six Prisoners from the Special Security Unit [SSU] at Whitemoor Prison' in September 1994. He also rapidly had to include a consideration of the 'Escape from Parkhurst Prison' in January 1995. While Woodcock was limited to a staff composed largely of police officers (Woodcock 1994: §1.15), Learmont was furnished with two assessors – Sir John Woodcock and Mr G. J. Dadds, a former Governor/ Area Manager and Regional Director of the Prison Service – plus three advisers, administrative staff and police officers (Learmont 1995: §1.12– 1.13). Woodcock drew comparisons with Whitemoor by visiting prisons within the British Isles (Woodcock 1994: §1.21); in contrast, Learmont held audiences in prisons as far afield as Spain, Holland and the United States (Learmont 1995: §1.14). Woodcock's conclusions were largely limited to recommendations for future practices at Whitemoor, where he suggests the prison provide a 'firm but fair' regime in the SSU (Woodcock 1994: §9.14). Learmont's proposals, on the other hand, have been used to draw conclusions for the entire prison estate.

Despite these structural and procedural differences between the reports, they are similar in their overall message and in their sentiments. In particular, they are both extremely critical of 'poor practices' within the prison service, calling for improved management in order to compensate for the service's internal and external loss of legitimacy (Woodcock 1994: §9.27; Learmont 1995: §6.4). Learmont can, therefore, be understood to speak for both inquiries when he claims that

> ... unless security measures are in place which can be managed with confidence, then any hope of progress towards humanitarian objectives is pious ... this Inquiry has starkly illustrated the need to address urgently shortcomings in leadership, operations and security. (Learmont 1995: § 6.15)

In short, the report argues, 'The Service Statement of Purpose should be clarified, *to make custody the primary purpose*' (Learmont 1995: §3.35– 3.40, §7.3; emphasis added).

Unlike the reception given to the *Woolf Report,* practitioners and academics alike responded to the *Learmont Report* with intense criticism. While the former was heralded as a constructive, intelligent and humane contribution to the study and practice of imprisonment, Learmont was excoriated for his austerity and severity (Hennessey 1996; Morgan 1996; Dockley 1996). For example, in a 'Policy Review Symposium' that appeared in the *Howard*

Journal of Criminal Justice, Sir James Hennessy wrote 'The *Learmont Report* ... marks a defining moment in the history of penal reform. For the first time in 20 years of steady progress towards more humanitarian regimes, the clock may be about to be put back' (Hennessy 1996: 345). Or, more harshly still, in the words of Professor Rod Morgan, who had previously served as one of Woolf's three assessors, 'Learmont turned out to be almost rabid, unpredictable, combative and opinionated' (Morgan 1996: 346). According to Morgan, 'Learmont's recommendation overturns the philosophy of the *Woolf Report*' by destabilizing the 'balancing act' of the prison service in favour of security and custody (Morgan 1996: 348). Thus Morgan continues, the fundamental problem with the *Learmont Report* is that 'although Learmont *talks* about "Custody, Care and Control in harmony" providing a "balanced regime" (para. 3.32), there is no reference to justice in his report and it is clear that he sees care and custody as conflicting elements' (Morgan 1996: 350).

It is my contention, however, that the new emphasis on security does not entirely subvert the earlier concern with 'justice' and that it is instead possible to see Learmont and Woolf in relationship with one another. If it is indeed the case that these two inquiries are not contradictory, but are simply at different ends of a scale, then how might criminologists reassess and redefine the notion of justice?

Undeniably, there are many distinctions between the reports. In particular, their tones diverge markedly, since Woolf adopts a conciliatory approach to the prisoners, while Learmont advocates a military style of austerity and discipline. However, there are also many similarities. First, both authors refer to a need to clarify the role of the prison service (Woolf 1991: §10.1; Learmont 1995: §3.28–3.30). Although they vary on which element in the statement of purpose is most important, they both advocate a balance of some sort between care and custody. Equally, Woolf and Learmont each suggest the introduction of in-cell television (Woolf 1991: 14.31; Learmont 1995: §6.10), personal officers and sentence plans (Woolf 1991: §14.75; Learmont 1995: §5.59), drug-free wings (Woolf 1991: §12.350; Learmont 1995: §4.16), meaningful activity (Woolf 1991: §14.137; Learmont 1995: 5.7), and a mandatory minimum entitlement to visits (Woolf 1991: §14.229–14.231; Learmont 1995: §5.77). Finally, they use similar language, since Woolf speaks of 'normal expectations' of the prisoners for humane treatment, while Learmont refers to the 'normal expectations' of the public that the prison service will be able to keep its population behind bars.

One of the key differences between the reports is organizational and concerns the number of external bodies and individuals who were consulted during the inquiry. Woolf and Tumim spoke to far more people than did Learmont. Notably, they consulted a number of academics, while Learmont limited himself to prison service and community representatives (Woolf 1991: Annex 2G, 2O; Learmont 1995: Appendix E). Of course the inquiries were established for different reasons. In 1990 the prison service had been faced with an increasing breakdown of control when many prisons erupted into riots because of a generalized feeling of unfairness, exacerbated by overcrowding and poor living conditions. In this case, the prison service was obliged to answer, or at least to acknowledge, some of the grievances of inmates. By contrast, Learmont was asked to suggest ways of preventing escapes, indicating that he was expected to address public concerns over security. Thus it is at least partially because of the different motivations for their inquiries that Woolf frequently refers to the abstract *qualities* of 'justice' and 'humanity', while Learmont is concerned with the more pragmatic *goals* of 'security' and 'custody'. So, too, Woolf emphasizes the need of prisoners to be considered as individuals with rights, responsibility, autonomy and choice, whereas Learmont is more concerned about the managerial procedures and staffing issues. Yet, given that both reports are written in a similar managerialist style, it is not clear that they are so incompatible. Specifically, they both propagate a rational, knowing, disembedded logic that does little to challenge the legitimacy of imprisonment.

Rather than placing the reports in opposition to each other, it may be more helpful to understand them as each referring to one of the twin tasks of the prison service's statement of purpose. In this case, Learmont deals with the first goal of the prison service, since he wants to ensure that it *'serves the public by keeping in custody those committed by the Courts'*, while Woolf is clearly more concerned with helping the service in its bid *'to look after [the prisoners] with humanity and help them lead law-abiding and useful lives in custody and after release'* (HM Prison Service 1996). Of course, these two goals of the prison service are meant to be integrated: hence the image of 'balance' to which Woolf and Learmont both refer. And, indeed, it is possible to criticize Learmont much more than Woolf for disregarding, or at least for minimizing, the importance of the second issue of 'humanity'. Yet, at the same time, much criminological literature argues that these two goals are incompatible or at least problematic (King and Morgan 1980; Dunbar 1985; Bottoms 1990). Moreover, there are many similarities between the two reports, arising from the priority they give to procedure over evaluation. As a result, it is unwise simply to scapegoat Learmont while idealizing Woolf. Instead, by locating the reports on a continuum, it is possible to reveal the dangers that result from measuring the legitimacy of imprisonment without first grounding the elements of care and justice in the real lives of the inmate community. Portraying prisoners as agents, without appreciating them as subjects, makes it difficult to oppose increased measures of austerity, for without a sense of how justice is experienced, it is difficult to resist the supposed rationality of administrative efficiency.[15]

If it is indeed concluded that each of the rival reports speaks the social assumptions of the day rather more than it critiques them, what might be a better approach? In the final two sections of this chapter I shall examine the related issues of subjectivity and evaluation through an assessment of the gendered nature of justice and care. Given the role of criminologists in upholding or legitimating administrative discourse it is clear that there is an urgent need to establish ways by which the current shift to austere regimes may be resisted by the academic community. Accordingly, a feminist critique of liberalism and of the official literature on women in prison will be utilized with the aim of demonstrating that any grounding of care or justice must be done carefully to avoid stereotyping of prisoners.

On the Limitations of Justice, Rights and Equality for Women

Liberal political philosophy has long occupied a contested position within feminist theory. While liberal support of individual equality and liberty was integral to much early feminism and to the legal battles for equal rights (Wollstonecraft, 1792; V. Woolf 1945), the rational, autonomous, transcendental subject has since been fiercely criticized for its masculinist, race and gender bias (Lloyd 1984; I. M. Young 1987; Pateman 1988; Collins 1990; Hekman 1990; Frazer and Lacey 1993; McNay 1993; Fraisse 1994; Mama 1995). Feminist arguments against the liberalism of thinkers such as Rawls are based upon a rejection of the autonomous, rational individual and the social contract, along with a critique of the division of society into public and private spheres. All of these qualities and arrangements are shown to be underwritten by an ideal of masculinity which excludes women. Given the parallels between Rawls and Woolf established above, feminist analyses of liberalism may be able to explain the reasons for, and the implications of, women's exclusion from administrative discourse, and their subsequent marginalization in government policy.

According to feminist philosopher Genevieve Lloyd, the pursuit of 'rational knowledge' has been a 'major strand in Western culture's definition of itself as opposed to Nature', with the result that 'femaleness' and 'woman' have been identified 'with what Reason supposedly left behind' (Lloyd 1984: 2). Consequently she claims that 'there has been no input of femaleness into the formation of ideals of Reason' (Lloyd 1984: 105). While it may be no longer generally acceptable to argue that women are naturally 'irrational',[16] the prerequisites for rational thinking – that one relinquishes subjective opinions and experiences, choosing to judge instead from an objective 'archimedean point' – require that gender, race and class be forgotten. The self must be decontextualized, so that the subject's affective ties and life experiences can be ignored. As others have recognized, because the *Woolf Report* is written in legal, rational language, it, too, disregards the impact of gender, race and class upon the measurement of justice (Sim 1994b: 39). Woolf's vision of justice ignores the motivations and knowledge which derive from prisoners' socio-economic or cultural identities, favouring instead an abstract, utilitarian notion of 'responsibility'. Similarly, although Learmont does strive to differentiate between prisoners in terms of risk assessment, he does not consider relations of socio-economic difference, since his overall goal is the pragmatic one of incapacitation. Much less is he concerned with the symbolic and material implications of such differences.

Like the notion of rationality, the theory of the social contract which Rawls resurrects in the form of the 'veil of ignorance' has also long been criticized by feminists. Because women were traditionally associated with Nature and the irrational, they were excluded from the social contract by Hobbes, Locke and Rousseau, and were instead left 'outside' positions of power (V. Woolf 1938; Pateman 1988; see Sim 1994b: 40–41). Rawls, too, does not directly mention gender, race or class in his analysis of justice. Rather, he uses the 'veil of ignorance' as an heuristic device through which to describe the basic elements needed for a just society. However, as was argued above, the disembodied figures which he deploys bear little relation to the lived experience of men and women and make his theory of justice difficult to apply to a real world. The idea of a 'social contract' or the 'original position' has been similarly criticized for de-politicizing social relationships through its implicit denial of people's differential access to power (Sim 1994b: 41). Moreover, as Frazer and Lacey point out, if 'each subject [behind the "veil of ignorance"] has exactly the same motivations and knowledge – they are in fact identical' and so there is just one individual making all the decisions and doing the choosing (Frazer and Lacey 1993: 46). Rawls' framework for choosing the principles of justice thus appears to represent the actions of a single agent, who can only be imagined as white, male and middle-class.

Significantly, the idea of a 'contract' is central to many of Woolf's recommendations and to current prison service practice (Woolf 1991: §12.120–12.129). As was outlined above, Woolf advocates contracts (or 'compacts' as they came to be called to avoid the legal implications of the former term) among the various levels of management in the prison service, as well as between the prisoner and the individual establishment. Yet, neither the contract, nor the related notion of responsibility, both of which are advocated as a means to secure compliance and justice, were applied to women because

Woolf excluded the female estate from his investigation. Indeed, as Sim notes:

> Even if women had been included, there are still some fundamental questions to be asked about the general applicability of responsibility to a group within the prison population who are systematically denied responsibility and rationality at every stage of the criminal justice process. (Sim 1994b: 40)

Like the notions of responsibility and rationality, the idea of the 'contract' is not as impartial and 'objective' as it appears but is, in fact, contingent and gendered.

Finally, Woolf, Rawls and Learmont are all compromised by their conception of the relationship between public and private. Political theorists and philosophers since Aristotle have distinguished between the two spheres of public and private life. In this dichotomy, women have been positioned in the private, domestic sphere, and have been denied – to varying degrees – the qualities, identities and responsibilities of citizenship, rationality and reason. While public or civil life has long been associated with masculine qualities and activities, the private sphere has been feminized through its association with Nature, the family, and the affective realm (Frazer and Lacey 1993: 72–6). Not only have women and children historically possessed few rights in the family – being subject to the power of the husband and the father – but the domestic realm has rarely been considered an appropriate location for discussions of justice and fairness. In the terminology of contemporary feminist theory, private life is characterized by 'care', while 'justice' belongs to the public sphere (Gilligan 1982).

Traditionally, feminists have adopted two alternative strategies to critique the polarization between public and private. They have either argued for a new appreciation of women's domestic work and private roles (Chodorow 1978), or they have illustrated the many points of connection between actions and experiences in both spheres by emphasizing women's role as socializers of children (Rosaldo and Lamphere 1974; see, more recently, Fuss 1989: Chapter 1; Fraser 1997: Chapter 7). Contemporary theoretical feminist critiques of the public-private divide are central to the valorization of difference, and mark an intellectual shift away from liberal feminist concern with equal rights. As I shall indicate below, the relationship between the public and the private is also crucial for understanding imprisonment. The usual relationship is inverted in prison since actions which were previously relegated to the private realm must all be enacted in public. It is difficult to keep anything private in prison because of the proximity of staff and other inmates. Generally this inversion is disempowering for women. However, on occasion, prisoners are able to use it to their own advantage.

The association of public and private has been an integral part of each of the government reports mentioned above. Some of Woolf and Tumim's recommendations recognize that prisoners strive to create a private space in the essentially public world of the prison. In particular, their concern over the disruptive effect of relocating inmates (Woolf 1991: §12.240–12.260), and their advocacy of allowing prisoners a variety of possessions and 'privileges' (Woolf 1991: §14.23–14.44) would seem to encourage the formation of a private realm. However, since the escapes from Parkhurst and Whitemoor, these recommendations have been all but rejected. A list of 'privileges' has been replaced by a system of 'volumetric control', where inmates' possessions must fit into a prescribed container (Woodcock 1994: §5.3–5.32; Learmont 1995: §7.61), while ideas of managing refractory prisoners have been limited to the advocacy of a 'control prison' in which all activities would be strictly monitored and curtailed (Learmont 1995: §5.41–5.52). Officers in all prisons regularly conduct searches for drugs, intimately invading prisoners' rooms and bodies with the result that prison has become even more public than before.

The ability to control the division between public and private would appear to be a crucial element of power in prison. It is frequently a point of contention and resistance. Prisoners constantly strive to retain certain activities, ideas or beliefs as private and thus as beyond the control of the administration (see also Cohen and Taylor 1972: 107–108). In this matter, Learmont can be criticized for greater harshness than Woolf, while Woodcock is the most vehement critic of all. In fact, much of the *Woodcock Report* advocates an increased publicity in prison as a means of control, since so many of the security lapses at Whitemoor's SSU seem to have been related to the prisoners' ability to 'privatize' the security unit. The prisoners achieved their privacy in both material and symbolic ways. Not only were they able to exclude officers from certain areas of the building and block their sight lines with curtains, but they also forged bonds with the officers, forcing a human recognition of their right to privacy (Woodcock 1994: §4.13–4.21, §8.57–8.65).[17]

According to feminists, women historically have been associated with the private, or domestic realm, and as a result have been excluded from many civic roles and identities. However, because the private realm is also full of domestic duties, women paradoxically have been denied any real solitude. If it is accepted that individuals are positioned differently in the public and private spheres, depending on their gender, then it becomes apparent that women in prison may be greatly disturbed by the recent intrusions into what small privacy was left for prisoners. Not only are such practices as body searches for drugs naturally more intrusive for women, but they acquire different meanings because so many women in prison have experienced sexual abuse. In order to appreciate the effect of the enforcement of publicity in prison, it is, therefore, necessary to consider the impact of gender.[18] With this in mind, it is instructive to turn to the reports which have concentrated on women in prison.

Meeting the Needs of Women in Prison: An Ethics of Care or Paternalism?

Although rehabilitative ideals are typically disavowed by the prison administration as impracticable (May 1979), much of the daily activity in women's penal institutions appears to have a therapeutic or rehabilitative purpose. Women in prison participate in a variety of pseudo-curative regimes ranging from aromatherapy and yoga to 'communication skills' (see HM Prison Service 1993a). At the same time, policy recommendations, government reports and interest-group studies underscore the hardships of the women's lives (Home Office 1992a). Despite the current climate of 'just deserts', where mitigating circumstances are more and more insignificant in the court processes (von Hirsch 1976; Hudson 1987; Thomas 1995), studies of female offenders and women in prison often emphasize the history of abuse as an influential factor in the women's patterns of offending behaviour (Chesney-Lind 1996). Likewise, as was established in the previous chapter, academic feminist studies of women in prison tend to depict a community of victims rather than a collection of victimizers (Carlen 1983, 1985, 1990; Eaton 1993). In sum, it would appear that the treatment and understanding of female prisoners rests on and reinforces a notion of dependency which, in turn, reflects an anachronistic ideal of passive femininity.[19]

Perceived as non-threatening, both in numbers and in character, women have been marginalized or ignored in most reviews of prison security (Learmont 1995), staffing (May 1979) and management (Lygo 1991). Other than *Regimes for Women* (Home Office 1992a) and the thematic review conducted by the prison inspectorate (HMCIP 1997), official publications about women's incarceration have been limited to specific aspects of women's experiences of prison such as mother and baby units (Department of Health 1992, 1994) or have been produced by semi-autonomous lobby groups (NACRO 1996; PRT 1996) and academics (Morris et al. 1995).

Published in 1992, *Regimes for Women,* appears to respond to the recommendation of the White Paper, *Custody Care and Justice* that the prison service 'prepare comprehensive guidance on regimes for establishments holding women prisoners' (Home Office 1991: §7.17). With its focus on prison service practice, it fits comfortably into the post-Woolf management ethos by concentrating on the provision of facilities and opportunities within the female estate. However, as I shall argue below, *Regimes for Women* differs significantly from the ideology of the *Woolf Report* in terms of its emphasis on care over justice.

Primarily, *Regimes for Women* stresses the unusual qualities of women and of women's prisons. It points to the small size of the population, the distance between establishments, women's child-care responsibilities, their health problems and their experiences of abuse as factors contributing to the pains of imprisonment (Home Office 1992a: §4–5).[20] It then outlines suggested 'good practice' in successfully delivering penal regimes. The 'key messages' of the report are summarized on the first page, and are reiterated on a lift-out page at the end of the review. According to this summary, the aim of the document is 'to help staff to design and deliver regimes which meet the needs of female prisoners. The key messages are: Encourage, Support, Listen, Help, Provide, Enable, Recognize, Care.' Overall, the main idea of the report seems to be that

> … some, though not all, women prisoners have real problems of low self-esteem and self confidence. *One of the most important things prisons can seek to do is to give them more self respect and to help them believe that they can cope with life* – on their own if necessary – and believe that their views matter. (Home Office 1992a: §4; emphasis added)

In short, the report argues that female prisoners need assistance in raising their self-esteem. Eschewing the language of rights, security and justice which had featured so prominently in the *Woolf Report*, *Regimes for Women* seems to promote instead a discourse of care.[21] more than men

Regimes for Women corresponds broadly to Section 14 of the *Woolf Report*. In their section on 'imprisonment', Woolf and Tumim strive to balance justice and security in order to meet the legitimate expectations of men. *Regimes for Women*, however, seems to encounter more difficulties identifying, let alone addressing, the 'legitimate expectations' of women. The document contains two contradictions. First, it is unclear whether women need to be treated similarly to or differently from men. There is a conflict between the assumption that 'women's preferences and legitimate expectations may be rather different from men's' (§2), and the belief that '[a]t the same time, a theme which runs throughout the treatment of women prisoners is the need to give them equal treatment to male prisoners in similar circumstances' (§3). Second, the report must reconcile women's treatment as responsible individuals to their apparent inadequacy and low self esteem. There is a tension between the belief that '[w]here possible governors should enable the women to take responsibility for their own lives' (§10) and the opinion that 'many women prisoners have a low opinion of themselves [so that] it is

58 Engendering Resistance

vital that initial objectives [in a sentence plan] should be ones that carry little risk of failure' (§35).

These two issues, whether women should be treated in a different manner or in the same way as men, and whether women are responsible and autonomous or passive and dependent, reveal a profound paradox both in the management of the female estate and in the ideal of femininity. In the words of criminologist Ann Worrall, 'Being a normal woman means coping, caring, nurturing, and sacrificing self-interest to the needs of others. On the other hand, it is characterized by a lack of control and dependence' (Worrall 1990: 33). Women are often assumed to be less confident, less autonomous and more passive than men. Because of greater rates of mental illness, they are typically characterized as even less rational (Fox, in Toch 1992). Overall, there is a sense that they need to be looked after rather than punished and, therefore, that they should be separated from the bureaucracy of the male estate. In many ways, women, both in prison and in the community, are trapped in a contradictory 'gender contract' in which they are always seen to be pathological and dependent (Allen 1987a).

Such a contradictory representation of women in prison occurs again in the more recent Prison Inspectorate thematic review *Women in Prison*.[22] Released in July 1997, in response to a growing concern over the treatment of female prisoners in England, the review argues that women have special needs that are often unrecognized in a system where 'many aspects of the regimes ... [have] been constructed as if male rather than female prisoners were being held' (HMCIP 1997: §1.02). In particular, the team of inspectors emphasize the different characteristics of the female population, urging the establishment of a separate managerial body for women in prison and the recognition of women's distinct needs (HMCIP 1997: §3.44–3.50). They suggest that women need prisons designed with them in mind (§3.17) and that they are 'more vulnerable and dependent ... than most adult male prisoners' (§3.47). The authors also argue that female prisoners should be allowed more space in 'volumetric control' because they have child-care responsibilities, wear their own clothes and should be 'encouraged to improve their cells as a way of increasing self-image and taking care of themselves' (§5.42–§5.45).

The stress placed on 'needs' in *Women in Prison* rests on a series of assumptions about female subjectivity which in turn legitimate an unequal gender order. While many of the recommendations denounce the failure of the prison service to acknowledge differences within its incarcerated population, this latest review often reinforces traditional stereotypes about women. Thus, for example, the prison service is criticized for its inadequate funding of education and training for women (§10.07, §10.12), while simultaneously it is claimed – without explanation – that 'Diet is such an important feature of life for women' (§9.52), that they need more hobbies (§5.45), or that they have 'low self-esteem' (§10.03). Although the review manages to recognize ethnic differences among the female population in mothering, diet, religious and property needs (§7.12–7.16, §9.49, §5.47), it is recommended without comment that women be encouraged to take pride in their appearance to help deal with their 'chaotic and depressed state of mind' (§7.04). Like *Regimes for Women*, therefore, *Women in Prison* implies that women, more than men, require care and emotional support because of their (natural) vulnerability (§11.30).

Both *Regimes for Women* and *Women in Prison* manage to reinforce the findings of a variety of studies. In particular they resonate with psychological accounts of women's self-harm and coping in prison (Maden 1996; Toch et al. 1988; Gunn et al. 1991), sociological studies of suicide (Liebling 1992: chapter 7, 1994), as well as some of the more critical feminist accounts (Carlen 1983; Shaw 1996). In many ways natural opponents, these authors unite because of a homogeneous interpretation of femininity (see Allen 1987a, 1987b; Sommers 1995: 19–20; see also Worrall 1990, Hannah-Moffat 1995 and Shaw 1995; Shaw 1996: 188–9, for a similar critique of the portrayal of female offenders). Ideas of femininity underwrite the interpretation of women in prison, indicating that agency is always already defined by subjectivity. As a result, the women's actions, needs and experiences are understood in light of gender stereotypes.

Evaluating Women's Imprisonment: Engendering Justice

According to Nicole Hahn Rafter, 'the entire history of [the US] prison system indicates [that] "equal" treatment may actually create hardships for women if male needs and programs set the standards' (Hahn Rafter 1990: 2). Much the same could be said for the situation in England and Wales. Indeed, as Elaine Player writes:

> The fact that the male and female systems vary so greatly in size and in the nature of their populations, and the fact that their respective objectives must vary to some extent, calls for management structures which enable sufficient flexibility in the development and implementation of policies to enable both services to achieve objectives which ensure equal, but not necessarily the same, treatment for men and women in prison. (Player 1994: 224)

Following the recommendations of the Inspectorate's thematic review of women in prison (HMCIP 1997: §12.01–12.160), it may well be that separate standards of governance will be applied to them. Yet, no matter what changes occur, women in prison will most likely remain subject to the same laws as their male counterparts. Most importantly, unless gender stereotypes are challenged, female offenders will continue to be managed according to restrictive norms of femininity.

The conflict between difference and equality, which seems to lie at the heart of women's treatment in the penal system, also underlies much contemporary feminist theory. Central to the debate is an expectation that women's characteristics can only be understood in comparison to men's qualities. 'Femininity' is seen to exist only in opposition to 'masculinity', meaning that gender is always situated within a binary relationship (see, for example, de Beauvoir 1953; Rosaldo and Lamphere 1974; Gilligan 1982). Recently, however, feminist theory has moved beyond this dichotomy, which has been criticized for its essentialism and for ignoring difference. Gender is no longer understood simply in relation to sex (Butler 1990), 'femininity' has been revalorized (Irigaray 1985b), and elements of class and race have been revealed as central to social relations (hooks 1982). Prison studies and government reports have, however, lagged behind much of the new literature since, as this chapter has demonstrated, women in prison have continued to be treated in terms of an outmoded ideal of passive femininity.

Clearly there is a need for a new approach. As Elaine Player argues:

> If the problem is conceived not in terms of how women can be fitted in to a system for men, but in terms of how women prisoners can be afforded an equal opportunity to minimise the unintended pains of imprisonment and to maximise their capacity for self-support outside, then the potential for different strategies and methods of organisation presents itself. (Player 1994: 221–2)

Women need to be appreciated as agents and subjects, so that their needs and experiences can be incorporated into government policy and into critique. As the previous chapter established, criminologists have long argued that prisoners themselves contribute to the maintenance of order in prison, and should thus be considered as participatory agents. Scholars have recently broadened the scope of prison studies by using the notion of 'legitimacy' to measure the negotiation of power (Sparks et al. 1996). However, they have not differentiated between prisons for women and for men. Yet, as the official literature outlined in this chapter has illustrated, women are none the less perceived to have different needs from men in prison. Despite the universal language of much prison policy, they are also managed differently. Given the primacy accorded to notions of 'care' and 'need' in *Regimes for Women* and *Women in Prison*, in contrast to the concern with 'justice' and 'security' which marked the *Woolf* and *Learmont Reports*, it is apparent that prisoners' actions may be differentially interpreted in female institutions.

Likewise, in criminological accounts, there is much evidence to suggest that women are more likely to be placed on report for minor offences against prison order (Player 1994), to receive greater amounts of medication (Carlen 1983; Smith 1996), and to perform many more acts of self-harm (Liebling 1994). What are the implications of 'difference' for the concept of justice and for the negotiation of power? How might criminologists formulate a notion of justice which was able to take into account race, gender and class?

I propose that criminologists may benefit greatly from including a reflexive notion of 'evaluation' in their analysis of justice and legitimacy. While previous studies by Sparks and Bottoms (1995) and Sparks et al. (1996) have cited work by Tom Tyler – who examined how citizens evaluated police procedures (Tyler 1988, 1990) – I advocate a different meaning of the term. Unlike Tyler, who used evaluation to measure people's satisfaction with their treatment by the police, I build on a philosophical account of evaluation which tries to explain how people rely on a sense of self to pass judgement throughout everyday life. For according to political philosopher Charles Taylor, 'what is distinctively human is the power to *evaluate* our desires, to regard some as desirable and others as undesirable' (Taylor 1985a: 15–16). People constantly distinguish between choices, and, indeed, the ability to do so is one of the characteristics of being a successful adult. Taylor differentiates between strong and weak evaluations where 'strong evaluation is concerned with the qualitative *worth* of different desires', whereas 'weak evaluation is limited to simple choice or preference' (Taylor 1985a: 16). On this view, '[s]trong evaluation is not just a condition of articulacy about preferences, but also about the quality of life, the kind of beings we are or want to be' (Taylor 1985a: 26). Given the ongoing negotiation of limited resources which characterizes prison life, such an approach may be illuminating for criminologists. Not only are there few choices of activities or goods inside, but there are also limited means of self-affirmation.

Taylor does not explore the constitutive ways in which race, gender and class create a sense of self-identity. Although his later work is directed more towards the 'politics of recognition' (Taylor 1989, 1994), his early discussion of agency does not consider socio-economic or cultural characteristics. However, as the description of *Regimes for Women* showed above, women's actions are constantly interpreted in terms of their femininity; that is to say, their needs, characteristics and desires are understood to be determined by their gender. Indeed, subsequent chapters of this book will demonstrate that race, class and gender are all significant factors in women's own evaluation of prison. In short, evaluation corresponds to a series of normative and moral beliefs which are tied to a person's identity. It is not only the prison regimes that rely upon notions of masculinity and femininity, but the prisoners who do as well.

LIVERPOOL JOHN MOORES UNIVERSITY
LEARNING SERVICES

Conclusion: Problematizing Consent, or Legitimate for Whom?

As this chapter has shown, viewing prisoners as agents without knowing them as subjects can readily lead to unequal, unjust and ultimately illegitimate treatment. In the previous chapter it was argued that prisons constantly operate with a legitimacy deficit, meaning that the prison must continually be justified to the prisoners and to the wider population. Few prisoners appreciate being locked up and, if the prison is measured by any of the standards which have traditionally been claimed for its source(s) of justification, such as individual reform, deterrence, crime reduction or even retribution, it is thought to be a particularly inefficient institution (Ignatieff 1978: 209; Foucault 1979: 277; Garland 1985, 1990: 4–10). Although many of the measures used in assessing legitimacy are shared, there are key structural differences based on sex, race and class, which influence people's consideration of power and authority. As a result, the practice of evaluation is subjective, both in terms of not being 'objective' or neutral, and because it is an appraisal which reflects an individual's identity. Introducing the concept of evaluation into prison studies may consequently enable the criminologist to appreciate the diverse needs and actions of prisoners.

Prisons are hidden institutions, which fulfil a range of conflicting social goals. It is commonly assumed that they rest upon a coherent set of values about justice and the good life because they are places of incarceration for those who have stepped outside the boundaries of socially and legally acceptable behaviour. However, as the literature review in the previous chapter indicated, the purpose and effect of imprisonment is under constant negotiation. In this negotiation, people continue to share at least nominal values and expectations. As contemporary feminist work has shown, such values will be influenced by the race, class and gender of the individuals. We are all embedded subjects. Thus, an implicit notion of feminine subjectivity governs interpretations of female agency. In order to delineate and to appreciate the effects of prisoners' identities on their negotiation of power, the criminologist must utilize a variety of sensitive research techniques. The following chapter will outline recent feminist work on research methods as a means of understanding the gendered elements within women's normative values, which the women bring with them and use to judge their experiences of imprisonment.

Notes

1   For a discussion of when the Home Secretary's authority overreaches that of the Director General, see *The Guardian's* coverage of the dismissal of Derek Lewis fol-

lowing the escapes from Whitemoor and Parkhurst (week beginning 17 October 1995). See also Lewis's own account of his dismissal and his subsequently successful legal appeal (Lewis 1997).

2   See, for example, CI 31/88 which explains the justification for mixing Young Offenders with adult prisoners in female establishments. See also CI 32/1986, for a description of the prison services' race relations policy and the display of their policy in institutions. See also Home Office (1992b, 1994) for annual reviews of 'Race and the Criminal Justice System'.

3   Such a binary corresponds with Carol Gilligan's work on justice (Gilligan 1982; Brown and Gilligan 1992; See also Larrabee 1993 for accounts of Gilligan's strengths and weaknesses).

4   Although, as Ginevra Richardson points out, Woolf hoped to establish procedural *and* substantive justice in prison, this chapter argues that the *Woolf Report* is more concerned with issues of procedure (Richardson 1994: 91–5).

5   Although see Lyon and Coleman (1996) for an attempt by the Trust for the Study of Adolescents to challenge some of the more glaring stereotypes.

6   Such an understanding of 'evaluation' differs markedly from its common usage in research literature (see for example, MacDonald 1993).

7   Criminologists Roy King and Rod Morgan gave evidence at the Home Office May Committee which was convened in response to deteriorating industrial relations within the prison service. King and Morgan argued that 'humane containment' was a more appropriate way of conceptualizing the 'aims of imprisonment' than the intangible goals of rehabilitation and reform since it could be measured and implemented by the prison service (King and Morgan 1980). Although the May Committee acknowledged that 'the rhetoric of "treatment and training" has had its day and should be replaced' (May 1979: para. 4.27), they ultimately rejected the notion of 'humane containment' in favour of the rather vague idea of 'positive custody'. (See Bottoms 1990 for a review of the main findings of the committee and McDermott and King 1995 for a contemporary reclamation of the notion of 'humane containment'.)

8   A considerable body of literature – both descriptive and analytical – exists on these riots. See, for example, PROP (1976) for a first hand account of the riot in Hull, Adams (1992) for a summary of riots throughout Britain and the United States and Scraton et al. (1991) for a critical analysis of the changing situation in British prisons. See Carrabine (1998) for an analysis of the role of discourses of masculinity in shaping the Strangeways riot. For an account of female rioting, see Hannah-Moffat's (1995) and Shaw's (1996) description of a riot in Toronto's Prison for Women in 1994.

9   See Morgan 1991, 1994 for discussion of the policy and intellectual impact of these inquiries.

10   The first half of the report was completed solely by Woolf. The recommendations for the second part, which cover more general aspects of imprisonment, were proposed jointly by Woolf and Tumim.

11   In response to the criticisms of *A Theory of Justice*, Rawls has revised some of his key concepts, most notably acknowledging that his theory of justice was valid only for members of modern democratic societies rather than being universally applicable (Rawls 1980: 554). He has also amended and expanded some of his original theory in a more recent book entitled *Political Liberalism* (Rawls 1996). In any case, the original text continues to hold a privileged place in political philosophy and is, therefore, still relevant.

12   Such a vision of rational choice has become popular in conservative criminology through the work of Ronald Clarke (1980) and James Q. Wilson and Richard Herrnstein

(1985). Rejecting the traditional interest of criminologists in causes of crime and deviance, these academics claim that criminals can be treated 'as if' they are rational, reasoning agents, so that situational crime control strategies may be enacted (Garland 1995: 191–192; see also Garland 1996).

13   It is unclear whether the New Labour government of Tony Blair will foster a different climate of penal practice. However, given their election statements and their suggestions for the treatment of young offenders (*The Guardian*, 22 May 1997: 1–2), it would appear that they will continue with the austerity of the Conservatives. While they recognize the 'causes of crime' as important, they have done nothing to stop the haemorrhaging imprisonment rate. As the current Home Secretary Jack Straw said in his summary of the current approach: 'To be effective, punishment must be fair, consistent and appropriate ... we want greater consistency in sentencing, with stricter punishment targeted at serious repeat offenders' (Straw 1998: 2).

14   As he writes in his concluding remarks: 'As 1994 drew to a close, the Prison Service should have been reeling in the aftermath of a devastating period, with the uproar over the Whitemoor escape still ringing in the ears of staff. It would not have been unreasonable to expect the whole Service to have entered 1995 with an absolute determination to apply the lessons of Whitemoor across the prison estate. The Service might also have been expected to put in place, once and for all, the proper practices already promulgated in the Manual on Security but which the *Woodcock Report* had shown to be honoured in the breach. Any such aspirations were to be short-lived for on 3rd January the Parkhurst escape occurred ... At the same time, Frederick West who was in custody at Winson Green, Birmingham, on charges of multiple murders, committed suicide; and there were riots at Everthorpe Prison on Humberside over drugs problems ... The chain of disasters has produced a Service in which morale is low, with ordinary Prison Officers feeling devastated and unfairly treated' (Learmont 1995: §6.1, §6.3).

15   As Zygmunt Bauman argues in *Modernity and the Holocaust*, the qualities of rationality and efficiency are two of the most sinister and powerful ideals of modern society (Bauman 1989: 13–20). See also Weber 1958, Adorno and Horkheimer 1972 and Giddens 1984, 1990.

16   Although the probation officer at one of the prisons informed me that male staff were initially sceptical about working with women because of an expectation that, unlike male inmates, female prisoners would constantly be either 'bawling or bleeding' and thus difficult both to understand and to control.

17   According to Woodcock, the prisoners of the SSU practised psychological 'conditioning' on the officers (§8.57–8.65) so that they were able to manipulate most of the staff on a range of issues. In an example of his criticism of the staff, Woodcock refers to an account of food shopping for the prisons 'when an inmate threw a bag of new potatoes at the officers because the potatoes were too small. A great commotion had ensued which resulted in a supervisor ordering a second visit to the shops to obtain a larger variety' (Woodcock 1994: §8.29).

18   Indeed, as the Inspectorate of prisons suggested in 1997, 'Staff should approach strip searching on the assumption that any individual might have a history of being abused' (HMCIP 1997: §5.28).

19   An alternative to this often disempowering representation of women in prison as victims can be found in contemporary criminology emerging from Canada which discusses, among other things, the possibility of developing 'feminist prisons' (see for example Shaw 1996 and Hannah-Moffat 1995). See also Gelsthorpe, 1989, for a discussion of the problems inherent in generalizing too far about the 'sexism' of official treatment practices.

20   Each of these elements also forms the basis of Pat Carlen's justification for her alternatives to women's imprisonment (Carlen 1990).

21   Notwithstanding the predominant concern about women's low self-esteem, it is stated early in the report, that 'the aim throughout the estate should be to treat women with respect ... they should not be treated in a patronising or paternalistic manner' (Home Office 1992a: §9). Similarly, there are many gestures made towards incorporating an appreciation of ethnicity into the management of female prisoners in terms of the provision of books by and about black women (§71), sports and food from different cultures (§62; §88), and support for an appreciation of foreign mothering practices (§123). However, despite the laudable intentions which are apparent in many of the recommendations, the report is also full of condescending descriptions of women's insecurities. In short, *Regimes for Women* is a contradictory document, revealing many paradoxes that characterize the governance of the female estate.

22   In its origins, this review arose from a 1995 unannounced visit to London's prison for women HMP Holloway which the Inspectorate of Prisons aborted because of poor conditions. Its eventual release in 1997 coincided with a generalized growth of interest in women's imprisonment.

3   Towards Legitimate Research Methods, or Working 'by, on, for' and *with* Women

Properly pursued, theoretical argument enables us to think about [the] real world of practice with a clarity and a breadth of perspective often unavailable to the hard-pressed practitioner. It allows us a chance to escape the well-worn thought routines and 'common-sense' perceptions which penality – like any other institution – builds up around itself like a protective shell. Theory enables us to develop analytical tools and ways of thinking which question these established habits of thought and action, and seek alternatives to them. (Garland 1990: 277)

Once women are inserted into the picture, be it as objects of social-scientific research or as subjects conducting such enquiry, established paradigms are unsettled. The definition of the *object domain* of a research paradigm, its unit of measurement, its method of verification, the alleged neutrality of its theoretical terminology, and the claims to universality of its models and metaphors are all thrown into questions. (Benhabib 1992: 178)

You're trying to find out what prison is like, our experiences ... And how it effects us (Bell and Zora: HMP/YOI Drake Hall, June 1995).

Writing and researching about people's practical and daily lives requires patience both in understanding and in retelling. Increased care is required when the research is conducted in a closed institution like a prison, where interaction is often distorted, and where honesty and openness are not guaranteed. Both the researcher and the research participants may experience alienation or hostility as a result of misinformation and, so, the social scientist must develop sensitive and reflective ways to conduct and interpret her research. The means by which she gathers information and the motivation for her inquiry must, therefore, be acknowledged and analysed. However, any such reflexive description of the research process is complicated by the undeniable tension which exists between academic theory and daily life. The dissonance between theory and practice means that social scientists risk alienating the 'real people' whose lives they seek to understand (J. Young 1992: 60). Equally, the scarcity of dialogue between academics who write 'theory' and those who 'write up' results from empirical research, risks stultifying the social sciences within two rigidly opposed camps (Downes and Rock 1988: 327–32). In this chapter I argue that reconsidering research strategies and methodological paradigms can contribute towards bridging the gap between theory and practice so that it will become easier to theorize about the meaning and effect of people's lived experiences. I shall interpret my own research techniques in light of feminist and philosophical debates concerning social science methods and methodologies (Harding 1987; Gelsthorpe and Morris 1990; Gelsthorpe 1993b; Reinharz 1992; Griffiths 1995; Foucault 1970; Ricoeur 1981; Giddens 1976; Taylor 1985a, 1985b; Rose 1989).

The three themes which have guided my work are detailed in this chapter: an advocacy of theoretically informed, qualitative empirical inquiry, an explication of the practical and intellectual problems of conducting feminist research, and an analysis of those contradictions and paradoxes associated with issues of agency and identity which I found to be central to understanding women's experiences of imprisonment. This chapter is both a description of my fieldwork and an exploration of the problems associated with writing about research. It is also an attempt to forge a dialogue between feminist theory and feminist practice through my own research experience. While I am interested in the possibility of devising alternative methods of fieldwork, this chapter is most concerned with connecting my research findings with contemporary feminist literature. By locating it at the centre of the text, I hope to demonstrate that reflecting on the research process is central to any serious criminological enterprise.

Underlying much of the analysis in this chapter is an exploration of the twin problems of legitimation and representation which any researcher must resolve in the discussion of her findings. Given that these are conceptual strands which run through this text, both in my analysis of the negotiation of power in women's prisons and in my account of the relationship between women's agency and their representation of their self-identities, it is natural that many of the matters which are raised in this chapter are discussed further elsewhere.

'Theory' is used in this chapter to suggest a responsive and flexible dialectic between criminological scholarship and the prison. The relationship between 'theory' and 'practice' is one of reflexivity, where theories of knowledge and power illuminate some of the constitutive elements of practice. It raises such fundamental questions as why we choose certain research methods, how we arrive at our topics of investigation and whom we decide to interview (Layder 1993). I follow Garland's description of 'theoretical work' as that 'which seeks to change the way we think about an issue and ultimately to change the practical ways we deal with it' (Garland 1990: 277). While such concerns undoubtedly motivate all criminological study, they are frequently left unacknowledged and are taken for granted as many scholars continue to emphasize issues of empirical validity and precision rather than ideology and reflexivity. In order to challenge the underlying and essentially scientific notion of theory which continues to define much of the discourse of criminology, it is necessary to include the innovative and formative influence of disciplines outside the boundaries of the social sciences, for these subjects are, to a greater or lesser extent, alienated from the very thinkers who theorize them (Bourdieu 1977; Giddens 1979; Skinner 1985). Indeed, in this schema, criminology often appears to be located at the end most distant from abstraction and theory. Equally, there exists much theory and knowledge about how to understand and interpret society and human motivation, yet, in this body of abstract and occasionally opaque texts, there has been little attempt at exploring the connection between ideas and real, human subjects.[1] It is not enough for charges of 'positivism' to be answered with counter-attacks of obscurity or self-indulgence when 'theorists' and 'practitioners' do battle (Downes and Rock 1988: 275). Nor is the more usual deafening silence – while each side ignores the possible contributions of the other – helpful.

This is not to say that criminologists have completely ignored theoretical issues in their practical endeavours. Indeed, there are a number of texts which outline the development of different theoretical approaches in criminology. Such a list might begin with Matza's somewhat sardonic contributions (1969) and then include the first feverish promises of the New Criminologists (Taylor et al. 1973, 1975), and their subsequent self-critique (Cohen 1988), the sober summary by Downes and Rock (1988), ex-Marxist Sumner's synopsis (1995), the feminist critiques (Smart 1976, 1995; Gelsthorpe and Morris 1988, 1990; Heidensohn 1968, 1994; Naffine 1996), and, more recently, various postmodern accounts (Gibbons 1994; Einstadter and Henry 1995; Henry and Milovanovic 1996).[2] However, it is arguable that, except for some of the later contributions to this literature, the dominant styles of criminology have evolved primarily in response to accusations of inadequate empirical validity, rather than to a critique of the legitimacy of the discipline itself. The development of different styles of criminology often appears to have been determined by a reactive stance, so that each new school is simply added when the others are perceived to be lacking in some specific quality. There is little dialogue between schools of thought and, aside from the impact of certain influential bodies of thought like functionalism, there is scarce acknowledgement of intellectual dues and precedents (Downes and Rock 1988: 3–4). In sum, there has been a poverty of theory within mainstream criminology, and such 'theory' that does exist has habitually been limited to what can be proved or disproved through empirical study.

Finally, in what might be read as a postscript to this introduction, it can be asserted that there are many aspects of the research experience in prisons which seem so important at the time of the visit, but which later do not fit easily in any analysis:[3] the morbid stench of prison corridors, of stale urine and sweat, and boiled potatoes and chips; the obligatory institutional butter yellow walls chipped and covered with graffiti, postcards, Home Office circulars,[4] advertisements for Alcoholics Anonymous, prisoner self-help groups, visiting hours and incentives lists; the noise,[5] as officers summon inmates over the loudspeakers, as women shout abuse at staff, or shout at each other with their radios turned up and competing for space, their televisions blaring, their arguments over the pool table; the difficulty of initially finding the prison, and then being shown around for the first time, the stares, the averted eyes, the provocative questions, the whispered asides. All of these sensory experiences make up the prison experience, for the researcher, as well as for the staff and inmates. Yet where do these encounters and emotions fit? They are the frame for the description of my research. They are my experiences, and in a quite basic sense they have influenced my attempt to analyse the prison.

Do Feminist Research Methods Exist?

Feminists perceive a relationship between knowledge and power in which the former is both gendered and potentially transformative (Cain 1986; Gelsthorpe and Morris 1990; Smart 1995). Furthermore, they believe that, since women and men have access to different sources of knowledge, doing research on women is a political action which recognizes the specificity of women's knowledge. In sum, feminists propose that a complex gendered relationship exists between method, methodology and epistemology. By starting from the point of view of women without recourse to the masculine standpoint, the feminist disrupts many of the traditions of knowledge and knowing because she refuses to give credence to that myth of the unitary, genderless subject which is fundamental to Western traditions of philosophy (Lloyd 1994; Code 1991). Such an approach challenges many of the intellectual premises of the social sciences, for, according to Sandra Harding: 'Traditional epistemologies, whether intentionally or unintentionally, systematically exclude the possibility that women could be "knowers" or *agents of knowledge* ... the subject of a traditional sociological sentence is always assumed to be a man' (Harding 1987: 3). As the previous chapter demonstrated in relation to prison policy, the masculine is the norm, and the feminine, or female viewpoint, is marginalized.

Feminists from all disciplines have been particularly vocal in their criticism of traditional modes of information gathering in the social and natural sciences. They have proposed the elaboration of new and specifically feminist methods which would be less hierarchical and more gender sensitive (see *inter alia* Cain 1986, 1990; Gelsthorpe 1990; Harding 1987; Harding and Hintikka 1983; Oakley 1981; Fine 1994; Reinharz 1992; Roberts 1981; Stanley and Wise 1993; Wolf 1992; Smart 1995; Naffine 1996; Maher 1997). Yet, because of the diversity of solutions offered, it remains controversial whether it is even possible to speak of such a phenomenon as 'feminist methodology'.[6] While early activists proclaimed that feminist research must be 'by, on and for' women (Stanley and Wise 1993), it is now more common to include all studies whose authors describe themselves as 'feminist' or 'pro-feminist' and who perceive their politics as influencing their research styles (Reinharz 1992).

Typically, early feminist critiques of method were concerned with the control and distribution of knowledge gained from interviewing. Epitomizing this approach was Ann Oakley's 1981 essay, 'Interviewing Women: A Contradiction in Terms?', in which she proposed that feminist researchers must befriend their interviewees and enable them to participate in the research process as agents rather than subjects. She also advocated that feminists should prioritize women's experiences, in order to challenge the 'patriarchal' control of the social sciences. With others, Oakley endeavoured to disrupt the imbalance of power and knowledge inherent in the research process and in the interview situation by calling for more 'democratic', interactive, styles of interviewing. Inevitably, however, there are many limitations to such an approach, not least because it appears to restrict feminists to analysing sympathetic, like-minded women. It also offers little advice on what action to take if rapport is unobtainable between the researcher and her subjects. For example, what happens if the interviewees belong to a different ethnic or racial group from the interviewer? What if they are native speakers in another language? What if they have very few life experiences in common? Merely targeting the interview procedure is not enough, since people bring their identities and expectations from well beyond the interview. In response to these criticisms of feminist epistemology and methodology, academics and practitioners turned to women's shared experiences of oppression, in a bid to understand more fully the implications of doing research with women.

The emphasis upon experience, so strongly advocated by the early feminists, was further developed by sociologists into what came to be known as 'standpoint epistemology' (Smith 1987; Hartsock 1983; Harding 1987). Influenced by Marxist theory, feminist standpoint epistemologists claim that women are able to understand the machinations of the patriarchy as well as its alternatives, because of their subordinated position in the gender order (Smith 1987; Hartsock 1983: 284; Jaggar 1983; Harding 1987). By occupying a subordinate position in society, women 'are forced to participate both in their own life world *and* in that of the dominant group' (Cain 1990: 125). Adopting a feminist standpoint thereby requires the researcher to start her analysis from a self-conscious position that prioritizes women's experiences. In light of the inter-feminist conflict of the 1980s, the notion of a single feminist standpoint was later expanded into plurality, thereby accommodating Black, lesbian, and/or working-class perspectives (Rice 1990; Cain 1990; Collins 1990). However, it is still unclear how recognizing one's own subjectivity and the surrounding multiplicity of realities automatically facilitates an understanding of other people operating from different positions (Naffine 1996: 45–59). Nor is it apparent how people prioritize their different standpoints in their complex daily interactions. For instance, where does a Black, working-class woman in prison choose to speak from? How can a social scientist make sense of a variety of positionalities?

Much of the early feminist work is invigorating and helpful to read before embarking on fieldwork because it is concerned with practical details: how to choose a sample, how to act in an interview, whether to answer personal questions and how to relay your personal experiences without unduly influencing the respondents' answers. Although, as I shall illustrate below, I ultimately found some weaknesses in the literature on feminist research methods, I was greatly influenced by it. For example, I deliberately chose to visit only women's prisons rather than conducting research with both sexes, since I believe that there is too little criminological literature giving priority to women's experiences. I was challenged over this decision throughout my research. People wanted to know how would I draw any 'meaningful' conclusions about imprisonment on the basis of research with women? Would I be getting the 'true story' by studying only one sex? Indeed, my harshest critics in this regard were often the women in prison themselves, since they frequently claimed that I would have to interview men to get a 'real' sense of the pains and strains of imprisonment. Yet, the decision to interview only women was not one that I made based on questions of method and validity. Rather, it was an expression of my feminism, and thus of my political, intellectual and methodological interests in women's issues and women's power and suffering. Likewise, I developed semi-structured interview schedules, specifically to encourage informal discussion. I would ask the women whether they thought that I was covering appropriate areas, and I would alter my questions accordingly. I was conscious of the existence of a deep power imbalance between us, and always ascertained whether the women were comfortable with being interviewed. If they were not, I terminated the interview.

The Tyranny of Intimacy

Research is exhausting. Being a sympathetic listener is one of the most tiring aspects of fieldwork. It is contrary to many of the normal modes of interaction, since it requires constant, yet brief and unobtrusive affirmation, so that the person speaking feels that she has a safe emotional space in which to tell her story. Many women cried in their interview. Some women were upset because of problems on the outside. Others were traumatized simply by being in prison. For still others, their emotions resulted from actually being invited to describe what they were going through, and whether they had any suggestions which they thought could change the experience of imprisonment. Many women said that they had never before been asked what they wanted and so just being solicited for their opinion upset them, although others like Elaine said that talking to me was *like having a holiday – now I've finally got an analyst*! Different emotional pressures arose from women who had not suffered poverty or violence. Such women were generally educated, middle-class and articulate. These were the women who were 'like me'. They did not necessarily require a confidante with whom to discuss the experience of homelessness or incest. They wanted a familiar individual to talk to about holidaying in France, or about favourite books or films. They required someone with whom they could be themselves, with whom they could be like the person they had been before they had come to prison, where they were surrounded by women with whom hitherto they would never have associated. For, as Betty put it, '*in here I have to live with all kinds of people I wouldn't look twice at on the outside*'.[7]

Following Mary Eaton and others (Eaton 1993: Appendix A; Gelsthorpe 1990), I realized that I needed to be well-versed in various counselling skills so that I did not leave a woman feeling more depressed afterwards than when the interview began. I also found that I had to be prepared to answer personal questions which were directed at me, about my research, as well as about my family, partner, future aspirations and so on. Finally, having built rapport with the women, I ultimately had to leave enough of the experiences of women *behind* so that it was still possible for me to get a good night's sleep. Throughout my research I found that the women's stories were often very distressing. As the criminological literature shows, many of them had survived horrific experiences of physical and sexual violence and poverty. Consequently, they were frequently very needy. Nevertheless, none of the prisons which I visited offered any regular, organized counselling or therapy.[8] Rather, they all maintained occasional sessions on 'communications', or 'anger management', or alcohol awareness, generally arranged by a combination of probation officers, personal officers, chaplains, or visitors from such outside organizations as the Salvation Army, the Samaritans and Women in Prison. Although the arrangement does work for many women, Gloria describes some of the problems of an *ad hoc* combination of counsellors:

> *The other day I wanted to talk to my personal officer, and she was like 'later, later' and then I slit my wrists then because I needed somebody to talk to and there was nobody to talk to. I think each prison should have a counsellor where you could go to at any time when you have something on your mind. Especially when you've got children ... I talk to the prisoners ...*

In order to ease the pressure on staff, the prisons also provided various versions of the 'Listeners Scheme' in which prisoners are trained by the Samaritans to counsel other inmates. Yet, very few of the women acknowledged using the Listeners Scheme, because they were concerned about anonymity. As Catherine said: '*Everything gets round this prison, no matter how minor it is. And I don't think I'd like everyone to know my business.*'

The control of knowledge in prisons is prized, and so inmates were loathe to tell others personal details in case such information became freely available. Rather, Catherine claimed, there was a belief that '*You find out who you can trust and who you can speak to*', and then you limit yourself to them. Almost all the women I spoke to demonstrated great need to confide and to describe their problems, with such detail and such volume that I often felt overwhelmed and inadequate for the task. As a result I suffered great stress and sorrow during my prison visits.

There were physical symptoms – my skin and hair quality deteriorated; I had nightmares. At one stage, near the end, I even began to have heart palpitations. There were behavioural symptoms – I smoked a lot more than usual, and drank in the evenings. I would frequently cry as I was driving away from the prison. In the periods when I would return to my books, I would block out the prison experience, leaving my cassettes to gather dust instead of transcribing them straight away. It was not until I had left the final prison and reflected on the emotional toll which my research had taken that I realized that there were two general and intellectual points inscribed within the emotional difficulties which I had faced. First, and perhaps crudely, I understand my reactions to the prisons as being a very clear sign that prisons are places of suffering. They are not – however much certain sections of the population would like to believe otherwise – 'holiday camps'. Second – and more significantly in terms of this chapter – I came to see the strains that I had encountered as a direct result of my interactive, reflexive, semi-structured, and above all *feminist* (and therefore, partisan, liberationist, critical) approach to my interviews.

Early feminist critiques of method provide few answers to the issues raised above. Rather, the definition of feminist research as non-hierarchical, qualitative, unstructured and empathetic has mainly led to such claims as, 'feminism ... means accepting the essential validity of other people's experiences. Feminists, we say, shouldn't tell other women what to be, how to be, how to behave' (Stanley and Wise 1993: 22). Although politically admirable, this provides few instrumental techniques for resolving the emotional or ethical pressures of fieldwork. It also suggests no direction for dealing with research situations, like the prison, where participants may have a particular investment in certain interpretations of their experiences because of their powerlessness or other restrictions.

In other words, despite my strongly held feminist beliefs, I came to see that there are a number of limitations to, and unintended consequences of, a commitment to feminist methodologies. As already stated, the traditional feminist advocacy of non-hierarchical, reflexive research methods provides scant recognition of the contradictions which may arise if the interviewees share vastly differing world-views from the interviewer (Acker et al. 1991). Furthermore, feminists rarely acknowledge the possible weaknesses and difficulties of pursuing empathy too far, even though the practical and emotional demands which research participants make can quickly spiral out of control. Ultimately, I discovered that I needed to supplement many of the practical suggestions with theoretical analysis taken from a range of texts, in order to make sense of the contradictions arising from my prison visits (Jaggar 1989).[9]

There was, therefore, an ongoing dialogue between my research methods and my methodology. Over a period of twelve months, I spent time in three very different penal establishments for women – an 'open' (minimum security) prison, a remand centre and a 'closed' (higher security) prison. Overall, I formally interviewed 52 women and informally spoke to many more, subsequently writing what I could remember about speaking with them. Most interviews were tape-recorded, although in some I took notes as we spoke, and in others I summarized the main points after the session. I usually let the women decide whether or not I would record the interview, although, on a few occasions, I chose to turn off the machine when I felt either that it was intrusive because the woman was extremely distressed, or because she was discussing something very personal and clearly unrelated to my immediate research needs. After each prison visit – which lasted from between three to six weeks – I returned to the theoretical literature.

Doing Time

I spent six weeks at HMP/YOI Drake Hall, three weeks at HM Remand Centre Pucklechurch and four weeks in the Women's Annex of HMP Winchester.[10] Intuitively and ideologically uncomfortable with a structured questionnaire, I sought to engage in freer and more diverse modes of information gathering. My techniques included informal discussions with individuals and groups, thematized discussion groups, standard, individual, semi-structured, questionnaire-based interviews, written question-answer sheets, as well as the habitual 'hanging out' and 'joining in' with routine activities.[11] The interviews ranged in duration from thirty minutes to almost three hours. I approached most of the women myself, only after I had spent sufficient time with them to believe that some level of rapport had been established. Generally I made the initial contact by meeting a woman in her place of work.

In order to establish my interview schedules, I explored four separate issues, each of which raised a series of distinct, yet interrelated, questions about imprisonment. These questions, many of which I developed through discussions with women in Drake Hall, uncovered a complex network of relationships between abstract concepts like justice, and women's actual experiences of poverty, abuse and family life. The women's responses and their suggestions for lines of inquiry redirected my research away from a focus upon rules and regulations, to a more complex analysis of the relationship between identity and agency. I asked questions about their *daily routine*, in order to evaluate whether they believed that they had any meaningful choices about how they spent their time in prison, and whether skills learnt inside offered any alternatives to their lives after release. I discussed *prison relationships* with the women to see how they related to each other and to the staff in comparison with how they related to people on the outside. I asked them questions about *rules and regulations*, as a means of determining the significance of women's sense of fairness and procedure in comparison with their concerns with more personal and 'domestic' issues. And, finally, we spoke about *the purpose of imprisonment*, in order to trace a relationship between the individual ways in which women made sense of their experience of incarceration and the assumption common throughout society and criminological texts, that prison is for punishment, retribution, deterrence or rehabilitation.

The transformation of my interpretation of these questions occurred following two separate events: an interview and two separate sightings of a woman. The interview happened first. In it I spoke to Betty who described her experience of imprisonment and the cause of her offending in terms of her sense of self. Images of identity, self and other appeared throughout her testimony. For Betty, the daily routine achieved meaning in comparison with her previous life on the outside, which had centred upon a strict domestic arrangement. She defined prison relationships in terms of the proximity of other inmates to her own identity. Talking about her closest friend inside she said:

> *I think the reason why we got friendly is because we both lead similar lives on the outside. We've both got children … She's wanting to get married and get a house, I'm already married with a house … we've got a lot in common really.*

Likewise Betty explained that she followed all the rules, because she was *that sort of person*. Finally, her understanding of the purpose of imprisonment and punishment centred upon personal change. As a result, Betty was very concerned about being able to readjust to her pre-prison identity. Given her previous comments about being a mother, it was understandable that she said '*The thing that worries me about coming out of here is how am I going to take to being a mother again?*' Having been separated from her children, and having been denied an active expression of her identity as a mother, she was insecure about being able to assume that identity again.

The second event was more subjective and reveals much about the contingency of actually doing research. As outlined above, it was predicated on two sightings I had of a woman one week apart. I never interviewed her, but the change in her demeanour had a great impact upon my understanding of the experience of imprisonment. The first time I saw her, she had just arrived at Drake Hall. I was based in the induction house for a day, during which time I sat in the office and observed the prisoners and the staff. When I noticed her, she was extremely upset and nervous – asking permission and direction from the staff in such a way that showed her vulnerability and confusion. One week later, as I was walking through the prison grounds, I observed the same woman again. Now she was part of a gardening team, wearing prison overalls and joking with the other women – she had completely transformed. No longer appearing to be nervous or vulnerable, she mingled with the prison community as just another inmate. The change in her presentation of self made me suddenly aware of how many women were speaking to me about 'masks', 'shields', 'putting on a face', and feeling different, ill at ease, not themselves.

Through my fieldwork I sought to add to the existing literature on imprisonment by introducing issues of agency and identity. I found that there were paradoxical similarities between women's expressions of resistance and the restrictions by which they were confined within prison and in their lives outside the walls (see Chapters 4 and 5 below). I discovered that many of these contradictions required a realignment of the current understanding of imprisonment which is frequently gender blind and configured by that vision of rationality which leaves little room for the paradoxes described by the women. If the negotiation of power is at least partially dependant upon gender, then the focus of current analyses can be extended beyond the prison walls, to examine the overall legitimacy of the prison.

Inside a Total Institution: Environmental Factors

My freedom of movement varied widely between the three establishments. Like the prisoners, I was bound by the physical arrangement of the institution. As a result, I was able to be most autonomous in the open prison where I could walk around unhindered by doors and locks. I did not ask for a set of keys in any establishment, although they were offered, because I did not want to confuse prisoners or staff about my identity. Had I carried keys I believe that I would have appeared to be allied with the staff. In each establishment I had to observe the timetable of locking and unlocking, work, classes, chapel, visits, 'free-flow', exercise, medication. I arrived each morning as classes or work began, and would remain in the prison until dinner time or occasionally until the final lock-up. I also endeavoured to come in on the weekends, although I would wait until I had established a friendship with a woman before I visited, as, even in prison, weekends are symbolically set aside as a time of rest, and I felt intrusive asking questions.

More subtly, I was also bound by the relationships which I established with the women and staff in the prisons. Prisons are exclusive and excluded places, and so anyone entering from outside must negotiate a series of complex human interactions. The hierarchy of the staff provides a primary ordering system for the outsider since it is necessary to obtain initial permission for research from the governor. However, at each subsequent point of interaction, the researcher must be able to recognize and act upon more delicate relationships among staff. I remained slightly aloof from all personnel at each prison after the first week, because I was generally physically and emotionally exhausted from my discussions with the women (for a similar description, see Heffernan 1974: 195–7). Moreover, and in retrospect perhaps unfairly, I chose to keep some distance between myself and the staff in order to ensure that the women would not identify me as on the same side as the administration and therefore mistrust me (see Mathiesen 1965: Appendix).

Criminologists tend to focus exclusively either on staff or on prisoners. Little research manages to include both social groups. Given my later conclusions about the effects of such factors as ethnicity and sexuality upon the women's sense of self and their ability to negotiate power successfully, a consideration of the role of prison officers may have stimulated new insights. Not only are staff obviously highly important regulators of prisoners' access to goods and services, but they also are crucial figures of power and authority. The prisoners commonly mentioned a gender bias towards officers, indicating a near universal preference for the male officers over the female ones. Ideas of femininity were present everywhere. Finally, many of the staff appeared to share the women's concerns with maintaining a stable sense of self, as one young officer in Winchester said '*The most important thing people said to me when I became an officer was "just be yourself". That is so true. But it is really hard.*' Future research with staff could perhaps benefit from considering these issues.[12]

In the first prison I visited, HMP Drake Hall, I arranged an 'induction' week similar to that which all new staff members complete before they commence full duties. This week enabled me to become acquainted with officers in the different sections of the prison and meant that staff later freely gave permission for me to interview women engaged in work or education.[13] Although during the induction week I was always attached to a member of staff, the orientation time often led to the most fruitful moments of contact with the women since the prisoners would talk to me while they were waiting to be dealt with by the officer. My only attempt at a 'cold' interview, where the woman was suggested by both another inmate and by a member of staff was the shortest, and least successful, discussion which I had. She clearly did not trust me, and had no desire to tell me anything very serious about her experience of imprisonment. Her first words to me when I opened the door to call her in, were '*and how old are you then?*' because she thought I looked too young to be a 'proper' researcher. Thereafter she spent the bulk of the interview talking about drugs and lesbianism in an apparent bid to unnerve me. At Drake Hall I shared an office with a Senior Officer and I was provided with a room next to the canteen in which to conduct my interviews. Because of the layout of the prison, and its management ethos, which encouraged interaction with the community, I was able to walk unhindered around most of it, including the cell blocks. I frequently came in on the weekend and sat on the lawns with the women, sunbathing and chatting.

In contrast to the ease of Drake Hall my visit to the Remand Centre was beset with problems. These difficulties had at least some of their roots in the way in which I gained access to the establishment. I was originally scheduled to visit HMP Cookham Wood, a closed prison, yet, only days before my research was meant to begin, I was suddenly denied access because a prison psychologist was concerned that my presence would 'skew' the data collection of her long-term study about staff perceptions of gender by asking general questions about women's experiences of imprisonment. This late reversal of a previously favourable decision necessitated last-minute requests to other establishments. The Governor of Pucklechurch was the only one of those approached who was prepared to agree to a research visit at such short notice. However, in what transpired to be a significant barrier to meeting staff, I was given this permission by a Governor who left before I arrived. Consequently, personnel were uninformed about my visit, and seemed to be slightly inconvenienced by it. Moreover, due to 'staffing problems',[14] and an influenza epidemic which was causing havoc among those officers who might otherwise have come to work, the women were locked in their cells for up to 23 hours a day for the duration of my visit. The situation of near 'lock-down' at Pucklechurch made it extremely difficult for me to meet any of the women, let alone to establish serious rapport with them. At one stage I was limited to introducing myself to the women through the hatch in their cell door as I accompanied a Roman Catholic nun on her parish rounds in the Hospital Wing. She was quite appreciative of my company as she was only about 4 feet tall, and had great difficulty in keeping the heavy metal flap raised while she counselled the women inside. Two cells lacked the small opening of the 'judas box' and so we had to shout our greetings through perspex. On one of those occasions both the nun and the woman inside were shorter than the height of the perspex window and so were unable even to have eye contact. Under such conditions, interviewing was almost impossible, and so I did not spend as long in Pucklechurch as I had originally intended.

At Winchester, which had only recently been added to the women's penal estate, I had complete freedom of movement and choice once again, and the staff were both numerous and friendly. Located at the back of the male local prison, in previous incarnations the Annex, now the women's prison, had housed male young offenders and Category D (low risk) men. Following substantial renovations, which had included the construction of more sanitation facilities in response to a perceived need that women require hot baths, it was reopened in April 1995 to cater for 66 long-term women who were 'hand picked' from HMP Cookham Wood and HMP Holloway. All of the higher echelons of staff, aside from one Senior Officer, were men, while almost all of the basic grade officers were young women recruited from the local area. The inexperience and youth of the female officers was a topic of much critical discussion by staff and prisoners alike. Because of the physical constraints within the prison resulting from its locks and doors, I chose to remain on the education wing and concentrate on building rapport with the twenty or so women there. For the first two weeks I based myself in the corridor outside the classes and smoked innumerable cigarettes while I became acquainted with the women. Initially they were slightly hostile to my presence, and tried to use me as a means of aggravating the staff rather than engaging with me personally. For example, they would say in extremely loud voices, so that the officer who sat slightly further down the corridor could clearly hear, various fractious comments like *'this is the worst nick I've ever been in'* or, *'it's even worse than Holloway here'*, or, *'the officers are completely useless, they don't know nothing'*. Not surprisingly, the officer would always have a 'private word' with me afterwards and warn me not to believe the women, urging that they were all liars and thieves. However, after a week of seeing me around all the time, the women became more curious about my research project, and would talk quietly and seriously to me about their experiences of imprisonment. Once the women expressed interest in my research, I started to tape-record some interviews in a more private room where we would not be disturbed either by officers or by other women.[15]

Breaking In, or Whose Side Are We On?

The phenomenon of breaking into a group is frequently discussed in sociological, anthropological and criminological literature (Becker 1963, 1967; Cohen and Taylor 1972; Wolf 1992; Maher 1997). As Mathiesen has confessed, before embarking upon research, it is very common to be anxious about one's own ability to make meaningful contact with the population under study, and thus, as he puts it, researchers 'find it especially conducive to prestige to be able to establish *rapport* with the "underdog"' (Mathiesen 1965: 234). Paradoxically, there is also considerable discussion of the opposite problem of over-identifying with the group under study and 'going native' (Becker 1963; Heffernan 1974; Fleisher 1989). Both of these issues provoke tension in the interviewer and in the research, since they require the interviewer constantly to evaluate her interactions with the research participants, rather than allowing for natural relationships to form. They are essentially issues of legitimation as they force the criminologist to question her intellectual and emotional allegiances. They are also questions of identity politics – since the researcher aligns herself, at least partially, with some women instead of others on the basis of a relationship which emerges from empathy between them.

Of the women I interviewed in each prison, I had significantly more contact with some than with others. As a result, I was able to discuss ideas with individuals whom I knew better, before taking the questions to the rest. It also meant that I built up certain relationships with women which transgressed the boundaries of my research. I became friends with some of them – or, as close as it was possible to be, under the circumstances. On other occasions, it was not so much friendship which arose, but a more intimate involvement than a purely intellectual research relationship. I remain in touch with some of these women, bound by an amalgam of guilt, sadness, happiness, interest and an abiding sense of futility about the damage which prison wreaks on people's lives. Unlike Mathiesen, who once again describes a similar situation (Mathiesen 1965: 240–1), the problem was not so much one of being 'torn between the loyalty of friendship and *the role of the scientist*' (Mathiesen 1965: 240; emphasis added), although, like him, I sometimes refrained from taking notes after a meeting with a woman I knew better than the rest because it seemed like a breach of friendship. Rather, I was less worried about the 'science' and more concerned about the emotional toll of striking up relationships with women inside. For women whom I befriended naturally made greater demands on my time. They wanted to chat about life, rather than to be interviewed. Sometimes, in violation of the prison rules, these women wanted to give me gifts. More often, they just wanted information from the outside. At Winchester, for example, with the approval of the prison, I loaned books from the University of Cambridge library to an inmate. Each weekend when I returned to Cambridge I would find new books to assist her in her writing.

In fact, it rapidly became clear to me that the 'role of the interviewer' could well be a chimera in qualitative criminological research. I spent a lot of time outside any defined role or identity as 'researcher' as we watched interminable episodes of television 'soaps' like *Eastenders*, and discussed our respective love-lives. Such 'hanging out' – known formally as 'participant observation' – led me into a number of amusing and also more poignant situations. I have memories of playing 'murder mystery' in the Education Block of Drake Hall with a group of prisoners; having my hair cut and dyed in the prison salons of Winchester and Drake Hall; taking over a class of the most 'disruptive' young women at Pucklechurch after they had been 'banged up' for a week because there were not enough trained teachers available; being taught how to 'communicate' by sharing life histories with a group of women on a pre-release course; learning how to shoplift (*'Line your bag with aluminium foil and it stops the alarms from going off'*), how to 'hot wire' a car (*'Reach under the steering wheel and pull the wires down – just attach the red to the blue and you're away'*); and, over a cup of coffee and a cigarette, hearing details about incest, rape, battering, children, drug addictions, husbands and lovers and food.

Participant observation brings into relief what one of the education officers at Drake Hall meant when she said *'It's a very fine line between us and them.'* Consequently, the researcher can risk losing her way between her 'world of emotions and ideas' (Linstead 1994: 1327) and those of the subject, because the two worlds easily overlap. In many ways the social scientist is badly equipped for the effect of messy, human emotions on her research since even qualitative researchers are taught to strive for objectivity and impartiality through practices of 'triangulation' and justification (Kleinman and Copp 1993: 2). If we reject these goals, as many practitioners do, then we are left with the problem of representing our research findings in ways which can be legitimate within the confines of our discipline (Hammersley 1995). Otherwise, we may find ourselves treading the path of 'transgression' as we go outside and beyond the discipline entirely, as has been suggested by both Maureen Cain and Carol Smart for the development of feminist analyses of crime and punishment (Cain 1986; Smart 1976). Once we accept that there are no impermeable barriers between the researcher and her informants, then the traditional goals and attributes of the social sciences become problematic and can be shown to rest upon a certain vision of the researcher as dissociated and disembodied from her research. Thus we must also find another way of representing ourselves in our own research.

Justifying My Techniques: Towards Legitimate Research Methods

Having established the basic framework of my research by describing which prisons I visited and how I interviewed the women, I shall now discuss my research methods in more depth. Immediately, however, I am faced with a choice about how to represent my research process. This problem has been named by Cohen and Taylor (1972: 32) as the 'chronological lie', which Downes and Rock describe as 'a lie which methodically misrepresents the research calendar, giving one to imagine that enquiry flowed out of a neatly framed theory, asked its questions, and returned to ponder and amend the theory that fathered it' (Downes and Rock 1988: 330). Do I acknowledge the weaknesses and the problems I faced, or do I adhere to the tradition of only mentioning the productive, successful aspects of my research? Do I quantify any of the information I gathered in order to establish whether I have interviewed sufficient numbers of women to draw any reasonable conclusions? Do I highlight or ignore differences between the establishments? Do I draw the reader's attention to the difficulties of translating the women's words precisely, because of their unusual syntax, idioms and speech patterns? Can I, in short, make any sense of my research methods, without a clear description and analysis of my methodology? I believe not. Research methods can only be fully understood if we interpret our practical strategies and techniques in terms of our theoretical drive and motivations. Therefore, in this section, I strive to highlight the contingencies of my research techniques in order to illustrate the relationship that exists between my feminist, critical epistemology and methodology and my research methods.

In retrospect, it is all too easy to fit my fieldwork experience and techniques into a traditional research schedule (Bryman 1988; Bryman and

Burgess 1994). I could present it as: the first two weeks in Drake Hall were passed 'piloting' my questionnaire, the middle two weeks were spent 'applying' my questionnaire, and the last week and a half was used to consolidate my initial data by re-interviewing some of the women about their ideas about the significance of 'gender'.[16] The next two prison visits were then periods of confirmation and development, which built upon my original findings in Drake Hall. However, I am not comfortable with labelling my research experience in that way. My fieldwork always felt fluid and at times disorganized, undirected and chaotic. I have not entered my transcripts of the interviews into any computer package; I have not 'coded' the women's answers; I am not analysing my 'data' in an 'objective' way. Rather, the women's voices are some of the many which I use to understand prisons. They are, therefore, not necessarily any more or less 'truthful' than other sources I use. However, I do not believe that meaning is wholly relative. There are, therefore, certain themes which have arisen from my work, and which I develop throughout this book, in order to critique both the practice of imprisonment and criminological perceptions of women in prison. Consequently, I am left with the twin problems of representation and legitimation, and so I must resolve how to describe, interpret and justify my research (see Wolf 1992 for a similar discussion of anthropological research; see also Geertz 1973; Denzin 1994).

There are many possibilities. I could lay the groundwork by describing a number of important characteristics of the women: their age, their colour, their marital status, their crimes, their addictions:

> The women I spoke to ranged in age from 18 to 58, and their sentences from six months to life imprisonment; only 11 had previously been imprisoned. Of the 52 women whom I interviewed, six described themselves as Black, three as 'mixed race' and two as Asian. Nineteen of the women described themselves as serious drug addicts, meaning regular alcohol, heroin or crack cocaine (ab)users. Twenty-eight of them had children, most of whom were underage and being cared for by others (generally by the extended family, although some were with foster parents) in the community. Although I did not ask any specific question about the women's experiences of sexual violence, twelve of them told me they had been raped and, for at least four of these women, the incident happened before they turned 15. One woman has a daughter from a long-term incestuous violation by her stepfather. Most of the women were multiple victims, and so those who were heroin addicts had also been raped, were in violent relationships, had been over-prescribed pharmaceutical drugs by their family doctor and so on.

Because it is the traditional discourse of a social science like criminology, the temptation to present my work in such a format is almost overwhelming. There is a sense that conclusions can only be justified with facts and figures, and that qualitative research cannot be sufficiently 'rigorous' without them (Denzin and Lincoln 1994). Similarly, given that one of the major funding bodies for criminological research is the government, the reliance upon facts and figures is further legitimated to justify state-initiated policy. Thus, a reliance upon 'objective' data is naturalized and consolidated. However, simply detailing the profile of the women does not allow for women's voices and therefore does not greatly clarify women's experiences of imprisonment (Shaw 1992: 445). Moreover, when attention is turned to the philosophy and history of the social sciences, it becomes apparent that this format may be historically contingent. The establishment of disciplines like criminology in the nineteenth century was related to developments within the natural sciences and eugenics: hence the predilection of social scientists for facts, figures and 'truth' (Foucault 1970; Rose 1989). Similarly, the ideal of objectivity which social sciences adopted from their colleagues, has disguised the manner in which 'science' may depoliticize or simplify complex human relationships by constructing a series of questions which can only be answered with seemingly unmediated information or facts. Clearly, any such facts as those listed above, can impart very little of significance without a context in which to interpret them. To contextualize the experiences and characteristics of the women inside, we need to know more about the individual establishments in which the research was conducted.

Drake Hall, Pucklechurch and the Women's Annexe at Winchester cover much of the spectrum of the types of women's prisons which exist in England. As an open prison, Drake Hall has a very high proportion of first offenders and women serving short-term sentences for fairly minor crimes. It also has extensive gardens and new cell blocks which minimize the usual claustrophobia of imprisonment. It was the largest prison I visited, with a certified normal accommodation (CNA) of 250 and between 200–240 women incarcerated while I was there. In stark contrast, Pucklechurch was filthy, and had one asphalt 'exercise yard' overlooking an industrial estate through razor wire. It was one of the few remaining penal establishments in England without integral sanitation. Its CNA was 88 and it was functioning at full capacity the entire time I was present. It had a highly volatile population of women facing charges (including some women who were already convicted and either awaiting sentence or relocation to another institution) from 'reckless driving' or non-payment of fines to murder. It has since been closed and the population has been relocated to the nearby newly built multi-purpose facility Eastwood Park.[17] Finally, Winchester is a closed 'privilege' prison. This places it in a paradoxical position of catering for long-term inmates in a secure environment with an operational ethos designed to encourage good behaviour and responsibility. Women coming to Winchester are not allowed to be on medication (although some were), nor are they meant to have a history of violent or aggressive behaviour (although some did). It is a very small unit, with a CNA of only 66 women, although, when I was there, the management was considering placing bunk beds in eleven of the larger cells that were being used as 'rewards' for particularly well-behaved prisoners. Most of the women at Winchester were serving long sentences for drug-related offences and there were a large number of foreign nationals who had been incarcerated for drug smuggling. At Winchester I met two women whom I had previously encountered (one of whom had been 'shipped out' for suspected drug dealings a few days after I arrived, the other whom I had interviewed) at Drake Hall and Pucklechurch.

Any conclusions I could draw from the differences between these establishments would require an argument about such things as the effect of environmental factors (Jacobs 1977; Home Office 1985), differences between convicted and unconvicted prisoners (Morgan 1994), the right to a minimum standard of treatment (Loucks 1993; Richardson 1994), the impact of prescribed drugs on women's experiences of imprisonment (Maden 1996; Smith 1996) and the differential effect of length of sentence (Morris et al. 1995).[18] These issues cannot be discussed without a specific theoretical vision, nor without recourse to the women's opinions. The prisoners described many differences between open and closed establishments. Those in maximum security and on remand characterized open prisons as catering for 'nonces'. In contrast, the women in Drake Hall perceived that the stress of being able to escape easily was an extra 'pain' of imprisonment, which was only partially countered by the reduction in aggression in an open prison. For, as Christine expressed it, *'When you get your frustrating letters you want to walk out the gate and say "sod it, I'll be back tomorrow".'* Yet, according to Eleanor, who had experienced both maximum and minimum secure establishments for women, *'There is a big difference between the attitude of people in an open prison, and people in a closed prison ... There's a lot less aggression here, than there is in closed prison.'*

Once again, the facts can only speak so much for themselves. Thus, I must acknowledge the way in which I gathered my 'sample' in order to clarify how the 52 women were chosen. Perhaps knowing how the women were selected will help to inscribe more meaning to the characteristics of the women and to the descriptions of the prisons listed above:

In all three penal establishments I spent most of my time in the Education Block. This meant that almost all of the women I interviewed were engaged in some form of educational course. Because of the fairly informal arrangements which existed in the education departments, I was able to become acquainted with the women over a few weeks by attending classes with them and by sitting in the corridors smoking and talking. My sample was gathered by using a 'snowball' technique since I found that once I had scheduled an interview with a women she would frequently arrive accompanied by a friend, and so I was gradually introduced to new women. In all prisons I interviewed women until I had to leave. The amount of time I spent in an establishment was determined by the prison and by my other responsibilities outside prison.

Some officers expressed concern at my reliance upon the 'girls' in education, as they felt I was not gathering a 'true cross-section' of the population. However, there were a number of reasons why I chose not to follow their advice. The most important was a practical one of time: concentrating on one location enabled me to maximize my opportunities at building rapport with the prisoners. Had I distributed myself evenly around the institutions I felt that I would have stretched myself too thinly. Furthermore, education blocks usually have spare rooms and so once a woman expressed interest at having a more intimate conversation, it was reasonably easy to find somewhere quiet to talk to her. Equally, education remains one of the more relaxed areas of a prison in terms of staff enforcement of productivity and discipline, and so the women were often allowed 'free' time, to smoke and chat and drink coffee. These were ideal moments for me to participate in group discussions and try to interest them in me and in my research.

I could explain my 'sample' by arguing that there is not such an enormous difference between the 'types' of women who enrol in courses in prison and those who are in the workshop or another location. Indeed, I could point out that, over a long sentence, women will usually move from one area to another, so my choice almost exclusively to interview those women who were enrolled in education seems unproblematical. However, this descriptive, pragmatic explanation would not acknowledge the important fact that I deliberately chose not to attempt to gather a 'representative sample'. Nor would it enable me to assert that I do not believe in such a phantasm as a 'representative sample' of human beings in any situation. In order to affirm this argument I must make recourse to theoretical notions of feminism and philosophy and show how the numbers only 'made sense' to me in so far as they could be explained by my rejection of a number of methodological assumptions central to positivist criminology. Instead, I strove for an 'appreciative' stance (Matza 1969) and 'thick' description and interpretation (Geertz 1973).

Finally, there is the difficulty of how I actually transcribe the women's testimonies. Can the reader trust my transcriptions or might they be more usefully understood as translations? Again, the starting point is to describe how I actually gathered testimonies:

Of the 52 women I interviewed, the majority had a regional accent of some sort. Six of the women had foreign accents, and/or a limited knowledge of the English language, as there were two from Nigeria, and one each from Colombia, the United States, Scotland and Egypt. Women frequently spoke in unfinished sentences and with incorrect syntax. Their language was full of prison and street jargon and expletives. Not all of the tapes are fully audible as often there is background noise. Almost all the interviews conducted in Drake Hall are truncated because the tape-recorder was faulty. Some interviews were completed without a tape-recorder and during these I wrote key words and some quotes which I later lengthened into a summary of the interview. I kept fieldwork diaries for the duration of my visits, in which I would write down phrases from the women, as well as my general sentiments and experiences of the day.

A common – yet frequently unacknowledged – problem in qualitative research is how to represent the diverse speaking styles of informants (Rubin and Rubin 1995: 271–3). The writer must choose whether to translate the idioms of the women into more comprehensible and grammatically correct modes of speech, or whether to develop some ways of imitating them. She must also decide how to represent gaps, pauses, sighs, laughter, tears and emotional shifts. As was described in the first chapter, there is a tradition within criminology of producing texts made up of lengthy transcripts of verbatim interviews (Carlen 1985; Parker 1965, 1990; Padel and Stevenson 1988). In these texts, the prisoners' 'stories' are told supposedly in their own words. Such books tend to be highly accessible and largely descriptive. Although they undeniably fill a need, particularly in the extent to which they really do 'give voice' to the inmates, they can also lapse into sensationalist descriptions of 'murder' and 'evil' (Parker 1990), and tend to disguise the complexities inherent in representing the experiences of crime and imprisonment. A further and much more insidious genre of descriptive literature can be found in the so-called 'true crime' books which litter airport bookshops and best-seller lists. These, too, are based on supposedly genuine testimonies, obtained from mass murderers, rapists and surviving victims. Although they bear no resemblance to texts like Pat Carlen's 1985 interviews with women from Holloway Prison, the 'true crime' stories represent the possible outcome of a descriptive non-analytical approach to crime and punishment, in which the 'truth' rests within the narrative of the event.

In transcribing interviews, there is the added, inevitable, problem of incomplete recordings, bad sound quality and outside noise drowning out the responses (Rubin and Rubin 1995: 126–7). The researcher must also have a plan about how to place her own words in the interview schedule: is she an invisible, omnipresent interrogator, or will she be uncovered in full, stuttering vein, of half-finished comments and leading questions? Finally, she needs to decide how to name the informants since it is common or indeed required practice to change their names so that they cannot be identified. In fact, the Prison Service has customized forms which are required to be completed by the researcher and the prisoner before using a tape-recorder. The forms are said to be legally binding, and require the researcher to maintain the anonymity of the respondent at all times. Thus the names of the women in this study are not their own. They have all been redesignated with names of famous feminists. In order to reflect the racial and ethnic mix of the respondents, the women of colour have been allocated names of feminists of colour. This naming was a purely polemical choice. I am not meaning to imply that the women were feminists themselves, although some of them were. I deal with problems of representation in the body of the text, by striving to replicate the women's words as closely as I can without creating new, phonetic, onomatopoeic words. If there is a choice of how to translate a sentence, whether it is because of language usage, or silences, or extremely truncated sentences, I strive for logical or grammatical clarity in my rendition of the woman's words.

Subjectivity, Agency and Identity: The Postmodern Turn

As should now be apparent, my practical research was directed by theoretical readings of feminism, philosophy and criminology. I sought to explore and discuss contemporary theories of subjectivity, identity and the 'self', with the women in prison in order to discover how they went through the process of judging the legitimacy of imprisonment. In particular, I was interested in whether they had developed techniques of undermining or resisting it. I relied on work by feminists (Butler 1990, 1992; Benhabib 1992; Braidotti 1991, 1994), social and critical theorists (Taylor 1989; Calhoun 1994, 1995) and philosophers of the human sciences (Foucault 1979; Rose 1989) both to devise and to interpret my interview schedule. Influencing my practical application of such theoretical work was a belief that feminist research must continue to be 'on, by and for' women (Stanley and Wise 1993), and that 'understanding' involves building a relationship between texts, subjects and my own 'horizons' (Gadamer 1975). I aimed to work with the women to reach an understanding of the experience of female imprisonment based on a combination of theoretical, textual analysis and on practical pieces of fieldwork. Moreover, I strove to combine my theoretical and practical feminist beliefs both in the design and execution of my research.

However, what do I mean when I speak of feminism? For, as was demonstrated earlier, the contributions of feminists to questions of methodology have been various and sometimes problematic (Fonow and Cook 1991). Moreover, feminism is in a state of flux. It now covers a vast range of disciplines, and refers primarily to an ideology and a strategy, rather than to a specific knowledge base. In particular, postmodern theory has greatly influenced much feminist research. The so-called 'linguistic turn' of

philosophy has introduced a number of key concepts into intellectual par-
lance, which initially appear unsuited to empirical research. Psychoanalytic
terms such as the 'imaginary', 'desire', and 'discourse' now litter philosophical studies. They have also penetrated feminist research (Flax 1990; Butler
1990, 1993; Cornell 1995). Feminist epistemology is now often as much
the theory of knowing about power through language, desire and the
unconscious as it was once about finding a women's voice (Gilligan 1982)
with which to articulate practical experiences of domestic violence, incest
or sexual harassment (see Chapters 4 and 5 below). Feminists remain concerned with uncovering the gendered nature of social life and combating
forms of oppression, which continue to exist throughout society. However,
the 1970s ideal of the 'sisterhood' holds little currency nowadays, as feminists are divided into more and more highly specialized fields of academic
inquiry and conflicting political affiliations, in a manner which can at times
be dazzling to the uninitiated and disappointing to the idealist. In particular,
the dispute over essentialism and difference (Schor and Weed 1994) has
divided many scholars from each other. Many of the current problems for
feminist epistemology rest upon the diffuse ways in which power exists and
is conceptualized in society. Where, once upon a time, it was sufficient to
critique 'patriarchy' and the unequal gender order, now feminists can no
longer be so sure of themselves. In a formal sense it appears that we have
achieved equality. There have been legislative coups and some destabilization
of cultural mores. Accompanying and reinforcing these changes, however,
has been a shift in the understanding and academic critique of power away
from a class, sex or race-based critique, to a conceptualization of power as
amorphous, omnipresent and multi-directional (Foucault 1979). Thus, the
meaning of feminism and the identities of feminists have become increasingly contested and unclear.

Similarly, what do I mean when I speak of the 'criminologist'? Is the
'criminologist' the same as the 'feminist'? Clearly, in my case, as the author
of this feminist criminological research, it is. However, not all criminologists are feminists, and indeed many may reject such an ideological position. Even those who publish critical essays and texts on female offenders
and women in prison are not necessarily feminists. In the introduction and
Chapter 1, some of the historical roots of criminology – as a vestige of
Enlightenment thought – were mentioned. As I have argued in this chapter,
there have been further limiting effects of criminology's association with
natural science upon research methods. The identity of a 'criminologist'
must somehow negotiate all these intellectual traditions. How the criminologist identifies herself will have great impact upon her research. Therefore,
when I speak of the 'criminologist', I do it in the hope of fashioning a
'critical, feminist, argumentative, self-reflective, humorous' criminologist.

Understanding and Interpreting Prisons: Is There a Method?

The relationship between inside and outside is constantly played out in the research because the researcher becomes emotionally entangled in the stories of the women. There is, therefore, a need to acknowledge and include the life history of the author:

> Fieldworkers enter the field as more than researchers. Our identities and life experiences shape the political and ideological stances we take in our research ... We must consider who we are and what we believe when we do fieldwork. (Kleinman and Copp 1993: 10–13)

The incarcerated women are not the only ones who must renegotiate their identity in prison. Uniformed staff and 'civilian' experts all spoke of the pressure they felt on their sense of self when working within a prison, and, likewise, I was not immune. I fluctuated in emphasizing specific elements of my identity – from my age, my status as a student, my status as a student at the University of Cambridge, my nationality, my feminism. All of these elements are constitutive of my identity and thus were elements which I brought to the prison. They conditioned both the contours of my research and my understanding of it.

As I have illustrated throughout this chapter, my path towards understanding the women I spoke to in prison was charted by a diverse range of texts. Rather than operating within a 'hermeneutic circle', or by following a linear empirical logic, I sought to weave a web (Griffiths 1995) of interpretation between the women's testimonies and contemporary theories of identity and agency. My threads were taken from the development of feminist epistemology and from theories of the social and human sciences.[19] The frame was the prison. The pattern will be spun over the following chapters, as I intertwine women's voices into an analysis of legitimacy, agency and identity, and aim to unveil a complex pattern of resistance and contradictions which arose from my style of theoretically motivated research. Much of what the women in prison said will be used to explore the relationship between gender and punishment. In this way, I shall constantly articulate the reflexivity of theory and practice.

Notes

1   For example, although Michel Foucault worked in the *Groupe d'information sur les prisons* (GIP) which lobbied for improved prison conditions and prisoners' rights, he did not include the voices, experiences or viewpoints of these individuals in his wide-ranging exploration of the development of disciplinary mechanisms located in the prison. Rather,

he analysed historical documents to create a 'genealogy' of the prison, which to many readers appears to be a critique of the contemporary culture of France and of the notion of punishment itself (Foucault 1979). However, it should also be acknowledged that some feminists, such as political scientist/critical theorist Nancy Fraser and criminologist Alison Young, operating at the margins of the philosophical literature on the social and human sciences, have managed to combine theory and empirical accounts in their detailed analysis of the welfare system in the United States (Fraser 1989) and their representations of the Greenham Common women in Britain (A. Young 1990).

2   For a collection of essays on the development of criminology in Britain see Rock (1988); see also Garland (1994) and J. Young (1994) in the *Oxford Handbook of Criminology*. For a more specific account of personalities within the discipline see Rock (1994).

3   A standard response to the difficulties of relating aspects of fieldwork in prison and other criminological research has been to add a 'postscript' or appendix to the study, in which the author reveals the difficulties and paradoxes she encountered without having to disrupt the logical flow of the substantive text (see for example, Sykes 1958: Appendix; Mathiesen 1965: Appendix; Heffernan 1974: Appendix A; Sommers (1995): Appendix; Sparks et al. 1996: Appendix A).

4   My favourite Home Office poster was the rather cryptic 'what's at the centre of secURity?'

5   See Gallo and Ruggiero (1991) for an analysis of the meaning of noise and 'miscommunication' in male Italian prisons.

6   See the debate in *Sociology*, 1992, between Hammersley (1992), Ramazanoglu (1992) and Gelsthorpe (1992), for a summary of the argument.

7   See Heffernan (1974: Appendix A) for a discussion of similar experiences in her research in a North American women's prison.

8   Although, according to a survey on 'groupwork' published in 1995, 50 per cent of women's prisons offer some form of groupwork (Towl and Bailey 1993, cited in Cundy 1995). However, Morris et al. found a similar result in their research on women's needs in prison, claiming that '[e]ighty four per cent of the 83 women who said they had been recently sexually or physically abused, and 89% of the 28 women who said they had been previously abused reported that they had not received any counselling while in prison' (Morris et al. 1995: iii).

9   See Kleinman and Copp (1993) for a general discussion of 'emotions and fieldwork'. Alison Jaggar offers a related theoretical discussion of the implications of giving credence to emotions rather than rationality (Jaggar 1989).

10   For a brief official description of the first two institutions see HMCIP (1994, 1995). See HMCIP (1997) for a description of Winchester.

11   See Appendix for copies of interview schedules.

12   Indeed, there is a current movement within prison studies to examine the role of management in general – which would include staff – in fostering certain gender relations (Carrabine and Longhurst 1998; see also Adler and Longhurst 1994 for a related analysis of the legitimacy of managerial practices).

13   Another woman interviewing at the same time (for a piece of Home Office-funded research) who was not given the opportunity to introduce herself to the staff, initially faced many more difficulties and resistance from them in her attempts to have women directed from work to her office. Her problems were ultimately resolved by the personal intervention of a Senior Officer who took over the task of arranging for the women to be sent directly from their workplace to the researcher's office in the Administration Block.

14   It is important to note that the 'staffing problems' appeared to denote a loss of morale resulting from the recent announcement that officers were not guaranteed their jobs once Pucklechurch was relocated (in March 1996) to a new, combined female establishment – to be called Eastwood Park – in a nearby village. Prior to 1990 Pucklechurch had been a mixed establishment, with male young offenders on one side and women on remand on the other. However, the young men were relocated after they destroyed their wing in the 1990 riots which swept the male penal estate (see Woolf 1991), and Pucklechurch never totally recovered. The tattered remains of the building which had housed the YOs was left ramshackle and unattended, casting a gloomy air over the entire establishment. Furthermore, in response to a need for a women's prison in the South West of England, Pucklechurch had long been marked to be upgraded to cater for sentenced and remanded prisoners. While I was visiting, the construction of Eastwood Park was still under way since planning had been slowed by various financial problems. It was not opened until 1 March 1996 (see HMCIP 1996 for a review of the new facility).

15   Although this was not always the case – in one particularly harrowing interview in which Jane was in tears for most of the time as she described years of domestic violence, her own alcoholism and her failings as a mother, a member of staff who was widely disliked, decided to join us for a cigarette, and thereby effectively ended the interview before either I, or Jane, had finished. Faced with a methodological problem: how to indicate that Jane and I were engaged in private conversation without alienating her, I (weakly?) chose not to complain because of her instrumental role in enabling me to interview the women during class time.

16   For this part of the research I adapted some discussion points taken from the women's self assertion course *Springboard*. I gave the women a list of sentences – 'Because I am a woman I am ... I can ... I cannot ...'; 'Because I am in prison I am ... I can ... I cannot ...'; 'Because I am a woman in prison I am ... I can ... I cannot ...' – and asked them to finish each sentence with three examples. Although initially they were fairly unenthusiastic about this 'feminist' exercise, their answers were illuminating. However, because of the limited return rate of these question and answer sheets, I only used them in Drake Hall where I was easily able to visit women in their cells and retrieve them. I handed out a number in Pucklechurch, and only managed to get one back. By the time I got to Winchester, I had dropped them entirely from my research schedule.

17   A new Young Offenders establishment is soon to be opening in the former site.

18   In their study with 200 women in prison, Morris and her colleagues find that women's needs 'were not related to the length of their prison sentence yet sentence length is often *the* factor which determines the prison system's ... response to them.' (Morris et al. 1995: 54).

19   Although strictly the 'Human' and the 'Social' Sciences do not cover precisely the same disciplines, since the Human Sciences includes such fields as History and Literature, there are sufficient similarities between them and the literature about them that they maybe discussed in tandem. Thus, I follow Foucault who claims that 'a "human science" exists, not whenever man [sic] is in question, but wherever there is analysis – within the dimension proper to the unconscious – of norms, rules, and signifying totalities which unveil to consciousness the conditions of its forms and contents' (Foucault 1970: 364).

4 Gender, Identity and the Prison: Punishing Their Bodies, Punishing Their Selves

Identity does not refer to my potential for choice alone, but to the actuality of my choices, namely to show how I as a finite, concrete, embodied individual, shape and fashion the circumstances of my birth and family, linguistic cultural and gender identity into a coherent narrative that stands as my life story. (Benhabib 1987: 89)

The notion of identity refers us to certain evaluations which are essential because they are the indispensable horizon or foundation out of which we reflect and evaluate as persons. To lose this horizon, or not to have found it, is indeed a terrifying experience of disaggregation and loss. (Taylor 1985a: 35)

Don't look at what I've done, look at who I am. (Dorothy: HMP/YOI Drake Hall, June, 1995)

A discussion of 'identity politics' has recently emerged in many academic circles as a new way of conceptualizing power relations (Benhabib 1992; I. M. Young 1990; Calhoun 1994; Gutman 1994; Taylor 1989, 1994; Braidotti 1994; Griffiths 1995; Weir 1996). In this literature, issues of 'identity' and 'subjectivity' are promoted as a critique of power relations through an appreciation of previously marginalized groups and experiences. This chapter will explore how such literature can be utilized to enhance an understanding of how power is negotiated in women's prisons by drawing attention to the ways in which women evaluate imprisonment in terms of their lived experiences of race, class and gender. As Chapter 2 demonstrated, women's actions and needs are usually already interpreted according to a restrictive notion of femininity. Without a more detailed awareness of the various

95

constitutive elements of their identity, it is difficult to establish how prisoners evaluate their experiences of imprisonment and why they comply with or resist the regime. It is not possible to comprehend the choices they have nor understand the reasons they give for the choices they make. Without knowing 'who' the prisoners are – in a deep, sociological sense – it is difficult to differentiate between inmate groups and to identify the effects of power.

Since the decline of Marxist thought in the late 1980s and early 1990s, scholars have been searching for new ways to theorize power relations (Laclau and Mouffe 1985; Laclau 1990; Fraser 1997). Previous representations of 'power' as distributed in hierarchical structures – whether they are perceived as Marxian classes or Weberian bureaucracies – have been progressively rejected in favour of viewing 'power' as relational and subject to change.[1] In particular, recent developments in feminist, communitarian and critical theory have placed the related issues of 'identity' and 'subjectivity' at the centre of a new conceptualization of power relations. In this chapter and the next, I shall use examples from the women in prison to discuss the implications of such literature for prison studies. By outlining women's descriptions of their sense of self, this chapter will demonstrate that much of the framework of prisoners' evaluation is derived from commonplace assumptions embedded in their lives outside, and that the women enter prison with a conceptual apparatus shaped by their class, race and gender. Exploring issues of identity locates the prison within the broader society, thereby enabling the criminologist to establish a critique of the prison in the prisoners' concrete, 'everyday', experiences (Goffman 1969; de Certeau 1984; Smith 1987).

In order to clarify what is meant by 'identity politics' the first section of this chapter will outline recent developments in scholarly debates outside criminology. Here there is a return to a critique of liberal political philosophy established in Chapter 2, since much of the literature on identity politics arose from a dissatisfaction with the foundationalist traditions of the Western philosophy of the subject. Such literature challenges the primacy of the (male) rational individual and brings into question who qualifies for the qualities and experiences of 'autonomy', 'responsibility', 'freedom' and 'choice'. An appreciation of the constitution of identity illustrates the powerful, albeit implicit and unspoken, ways in which these ideas underwrite many key social institutions, including the prison. In short, this chapter explores how identity is central to understanding women's experiences of imprisonment,[2] revealing that imprisonment is legitimated by, and therefore reliant on, a particular construction of (docile, feminine) subjectivity.

Yet, the concept of identity which is used in this chapter is not a stable, unchanging structure. It does not refer to the essence of a person. People transform over time, in response to differing influences so that the meaning and experience of being a 'woman in prison' is not set or uniform. While there is the obvious factor of time served in prison,[3] there are also more diffuse elements which act upon an individual's sense of self, including the collective representation of 'women in prison' in the media and in the official rhetoric of prison policy,[4] external events, religious transformations,[5] and relationships with staff and inmates inside. Indeed, as shall be argued in more detail in the following chapter, inmates strive to resist and deflect assaults on their sense of identity through a variety of practices related to their class, cultural, religious, ethnic and gendered identities. In sum, conceptualizing imprisonment through an analysis of identity introduces issues of contingency and contradiction into the field of prison studies.[6] By implication, it undermines the fixity often given to the meaning, effect and legitimacy of both femininity and imprisonment, indicating instead that each of these elements can be challenged, both by the women and by the criminologist. On a more theoretical or epistemological level, an exploration of identity politics indicates that a number of concepts which are currently at the centre of discussion in philosophy, feminist theory and sociology – including individual and collective resistance, the distinction between public and private, the politics of sexuality, and, of course, the presence of race, class and gender – help to determine the distribution of power in prison just as they do outside it. Incorporating these issues in an analysis of the prison generates a new understanding and critique of imprisonment and ultimately destabilizes the hegemony of those instrumentalist analyses outlined in Chapter 1. In conjunction with the notion of 'evaluation' which was introduced in Chapter 2, a consideration of identity may provide a new approach for prison studies.

The 'Politics of Identity': An Overview

Whether one wishes to discuss modern identity in terms of 'risk' (Beck 1992; Giddens 1991), 'ambivalence' (Bauman 1993), 'performance' (Goffman 1969; Butler 1990, 1993), or 'nomadism' (Deleuze and Guattari 1977; Braidotti 1994), or whether instead one wishes to analyse the 'body' (Foucault 1979; Cornell 1995; Grosz 1994), the 'soul' (Foucault 1979; Rose 1989), or simply the 'subject' (Barthes 1973; Derrida 1976) and 'discourse' (Lacan 1977), it is apparent that what it is to 'be' and what it is to 'feel' have become sources of great contention in the (post)modern age.[7] Following the epistemological challenges levelled by post-structuralist and feminist theorists, the subject is no longer rigidly associated with his/her 'rational self', and belief in an *a priori*, transcendental, subjectivity has dwindled. Rather, the subject is 'in process', 'constituted' by an intersection of structural and symbolic sources. S/he exists only within a specific context.

Even so, an extensive debate exists within feminist and critical race theory over the essentialist core at the heart of the new identity politics (see, for example, Spivak 1994; Fuss 1989: Chapter 6; Brown 1995: Chapter 3). Some identities, such as 'the lesbian', or 'woman', have been used as if they are static, universal notions, to the exclusion of others (Rich 1980; Daly 1974; Gilligan 1982; for a critique see Butler 1993: 226–30). While feminists like Gayatri Spivak approve of a 'strategic essentialism', in which it is allowable to speak 'as if' 'woman' were a simple, unified term, for pragmatic goals, so long as feminists acknowledge its complexity elsewhere (Spivak 1994; see also A. Young 1993), others, like Wendy Brown (1995), Diana Fuss (1989) and Judith Butler (1990, 1992, 1993), reject ever foreclosing the meaning of an identity. As Butler writes, 'Identity categories are never merely descriptive, but always normative, and as such, exclusionary' (Butler 1992: 15–16). The meaning of 'woman' is, thus, achieved in part by what it is not – man, child, girl. Rather than advocating the rejection of the term 'woman', Butler argues that the feminist task is to broaden the meaning of female identity:

> To deconstruct the subject of feminism is not, then, to censure its usage, but, on the contrary, to release the term into a future of multiple significations, to emancipate it from the maternal or racialist ontologies to which it has been restricted, and to give it play as a site where unanticipated meanings might come to bear. (Butler 1992: 16)

Without wishing to negotiate the feminist debate in too much depth,[8] the way in which identity is used in this chapter is not meant to signify a static, depoliticized experience. Rather, 'identity' refers to the intersection between the socio-economic and cultural frameworks in which we are all located – namely class, race, gender, ethnicity, sexuality – and the more diffuse and imprecise ways in which people perceive themselves. By using identity in my analysis of imprisonment, I hope to open the possibility of appreciating the effect of the dialectical relationship between socio-structural elements and the individual. In other words, like so much recent work in the social sciences, this book endeavours to articulate the relationship between agency and structure (Giddens 1984).

Such an approach has profound implications for prison studies, since, as was shown in the previous three chapters, criminological investigations of the prison remain highly influenced by the traditions of Western epistemology which have conceived of the subject as disembodied and rational. Thus, Cartesian dualities can be found both in the tendency of criminologists to conceptualize prisons in a series of polar opposites as well as in the research methods which pursued strategies of objectivity and measurement. Moreover, as Chapter 2 established, the very qualities of 'justice' and 'punishment' which the prison is meant to embody and enact depend upon an assumption of rationality and responsibility, both of which are key to the Enlightenment ideal of (male) subjectivity. Most prison studies have propagated an understanding of imprisonment based on an implicit, albeit unexplored, idealization of hegemonic masculinity (Connell 1987), which has unintentionally valorized a universalizing notion of agency and subjectivity that marginalizes, or excludes, women.[9]

In contrast to many traditions of Western philosophy, communitarians and feminists claim that the individual is both embedded and embodied (Benhabib 1992; Taylor 1989). They propose that our framework of evaluation, our sense of self and our opportunities in life, are dependent to a large extent upon a variety of factors that include race, class and gender. Similarly, they depict an individual who is relational both in her decision making and evaluation, and in her self-identity. She is an individual who can only be understood in terms of the community in which she is located. She is a 'concrete' rather than a 'generalized' Other (Benhabib 1987). Despite a number of similarities in the approach and goals of feminists and communitarians, however, they ultimately diverge sharply from one another, and must, therefore, be dealt with separately. In particular, while feminists are largely concerned with mapping how 'gender' influences perceptions and experiences of subjectivity, communitarians tend to focus more upon traditional Kantian notions of 'responsibility' and 'autonomy', since they are engaged in a specific battle to reclaim certain aspects of Enlightenment thought. In the words of Seyla Benhabib and Drucilla Cornell:

> Whereas communitarians emphasize the situatedness of the disembedded self in a network of relations and narratives, feminists also begin with the situated self but view the *renegotiation* of our psychosexual identities, and their *autonomous reconstitution* by individuals as essential to women's and human liberation ... The self is not defined exhaustively by the roles that constitute its identity; nor are social roles to be accepted uncritically. (Benhabib and Cornell 1987: 12–13)

Therefore, while the work of Taylor (1985a, 1985b, 1989) will be used in sections of this chapter, the main focus will be upon the recent contributions of feminists to the debate over identity.[10] Such literature draws attention to the 'margins', the 'intersections' and the 'context', in a bid to destabilize the primacy of rational individualism and in an attempt to uncover the implicit masculinism inherent in Western thought and institutions.

Recent theoretical discussion of 'identity' has shifted feminist theory from a position where it was stuck for some years following the nominal achievement of 'equal rights' in the law and in social discourse.[11] In particular, the theorization of 'gender' as a constitutive element of identity has enabled scholars to respond to criticism from Black and lesbian women that the notion of 'woman' was totalizing and that it marginalized difference (hooks 1982; Eisenstein and Jardine 1985). Questioning the implied universalism of the term 'woman' has facilitated an appreciation of the role of social variables such as race and class in the construction of gender identity. In short, it has become necessary to recognize that, along with gender, class, sexual orientation and so on, 'the simple matter of the color of one's skin ... profoundly affects the way one is treated, [and] radically shapes what one is allowed to think and feel about this society' (Williams 1993: 256). An appreciation of the intersection of race, gender and class, complicates but also broadens feminist vision, for 'feminist thinkers must be willing to see the female self anew, to examine how we are gendered critically and analytically from various standpoints' (hooks 1989: 110). As this chapter and the next will demonstrate, such an approach has broad implications for understanding the negotiation of power in prison.

A focus on 'identity' has also encouraged dialogue between feminist theorists and members of other schools of philosophical and psychoanalytical thought, so that the abstract level at which the idea is discussed varies enormously. For, although issues of the personal have long been central to feminism and can be identified in the early slogan that 'the personal is political', today identity is more often discussed in terms of psychoanalytic and post-structural theory (Gallop 1982; Butler 1990). Although the move towards jargon is sometimes disabling, it should not be allowed to obscure the insight that race relations, gender and sexuality constitute elements of both our self-identity and how others perceive us. In the following sections I shall establish the parameters of the contemporary debate in feminism and illustrate the interdependence of such notions as agency, choice, public/ private and autonomy. Each of these elements will first be described in terms of the theoretical literature, and then will be related to women's experiences of imprisonment.

Reconfiguring 'Woman': Agency and Subjectivity

Discussion of the constitution of (feminine) subjectivity occurs in many different fields of feminist endeavour and is a point of much dispute.[12] There is, in particular, a broad division between work by French feminists such as Hélène Cixous (1981), Julia Kristeva (1980) and Luce Irigaray (1985a, 1985b) – each of whom is greatly influenced by the psychoanalytic scholarship of Jacques Lacan (1977) – and scholars working in the United States, who often owe more to the Frankfurt School and to critical race theory (Fraser 1989, 1997; hooks 1990; I. M. Young 1990).[13] Despite these intellectual differences, however, a common theme underlying contemporary feminist literature is a critique of the disempowering effects of the universalizing notion of 'woman' as it has traditionally been conceptualized in Western culture. Whether arguing for some type of essential 'le feminin' (Irigaray 1985b),[14] or for the 'female feminist' (Braidotti 1994), or for an appreciation of race and ethnicity in women's studies (Collins 1993), or even when arguing against the categories of gender and a fixed identity altogether (Butler 1990, 1991), each of these scholars points to underlying bias in the traditions of Western political notions of identity and subjectivity.

According to many feminists, a subject is not a fixed, *a priori* 'being' but is rather 'a process of material (institutional) and discursive (symbolic) practices' (Braidotti 1994: 99). Who we are is a result of practical lived experiences, such as wealth and education, which interact with complex, dispersed ideas and 'stories' or narratives (which are both told to us and which we tell to ourselves) about masculinity, femininity, ethnicity, class and sexuality. Such ideas and 'stories' typically rest upon a division between public and private and rely on a valorization of ideals of the white, nuclear family and heterosexual monogamy. Identities are constituted in cultural venues – through the media, literature, education – and in normative ways – through the law and the family. They are also continually re-formed to some degree, following self-reflection and personal development. Like power, identity is, therefore, subject to a dialectic of control, which is both internal and externally manifest. As a result, the formation of subjectivity is understood to be continually 'in process' (Braidotti 1994: 98), and dependent upon repetitive performativity (Butler 1990).

Certainly, feminist theorists are not the only scholars to have focused upon the constitution of subjectivity.[15] A strong tradition of conceptualizing identity – which has its roots in the social psychology and symbolic interactionism of George Herbert Mead (1934) and Erving Goffman (1961, 1963, 1969) – exists in sociology, and has been highly influential in shaping the sociology of deviance (see for example Downes and Rock 1988: 94–8; Giddens 1984: 41–90; Sumner 1995: 66–70; Lemert 1993: 216–19). At the base of this tradition lies the distinction made by Mead between the 'I', the 'Self' and the 'Me'. In Mead's theory 'the "me" is the … social identity … of which the "I" becomes conscious in the course of the psychological development of the child' (Giddens 1991: 52). The 'I' is the source of agency and is thus central both to the ability of an individual to negotiate language and human interaction and to the formation of her sense of 'self'. However, as Giddens argues, the origins of the 'I' remain 'cloudy', making it difficult to use Mead to establish the constitutive elements of identity (Giddens 1984: 43, 1991: 52–3). Not only does it exclude an appreciation of such issues as race and gender from an understanding of identity, but it also posits an essentialist element of self-identity. Even so, Mead's early work prefigures much of the contemporary interest in the constitution of identity through his claim 'that all selves are constituted by the social process' (Mead 1934: 201), and through the influence his philosophical theories had on the development of sociology, most notably in the work of Erving Goffman.

Goffman has been instructive in the development of a sociological theory of self-identity. Demonstrating a rare stylishness and humour in his writings, he explored the myriad of ways in which people manage their 'presentation of self' in a variety of institutional and non-institutional settings (Goffman 1961, 1963, 1969). Many concepts can be taken from Goffman's studies of human interaction which contribute to an understanding of the importance of identity in prison. In particular, his dramaturgical metaphor of the self as a 'performance' (Goffman 1969), and his depiction of the series of 'mortifications' through which the self must pass in order to become a subject within a total institution (Goffman 1961) will be explored in greater detail in the following pages.

Finally, as was shown earlier in Chapter 1, there is a rich tradition of sociological and criminological studies of women's prisons which examine issues of identity through sex roles, or through detailed analysis of women's life experiences (Heffernan 1974; Mandaraka-Sheppard 1986; Eaton 1993; see Chapter One above). This feminist or at least women-centred literature contributes to an appreciation of issues of identity and subjectivity in criminology. Through its descriptive approach it shows how many small-scale aspects of women's lives have repercussions on their knowledge of imprisonment. However, in its reliance upon 'experience as empowerment', such literature constructs 'experience' as an infallible source of validity and truth, in which the women's stories are rarely subject to any detailed theoretical analysis. A small-scale approach contributes little to a theoretical critique of power relations, since feminists find the justification for action within the individual's experience rather than in response to broader inequalities (hooks 1989: 105–111; Scott 1992; see also Chapter 3 above).

Contemporary feminist theorists rarely delve into the 'real' world of human subjectivity (although see A. Young 1990; Fraser 1989: Chapter 7), yet their work can be used to reconceptualize many of the fundamental issues that inform empirical research. Specifically, feminists develop Mead's theory of the self by arguing that both the 'social process' and the 'self' are always gendered. Moreover, in light of recent criticisms by lesbians and women of colour (hooks 1982, 1989; Eisenstein and Jardine 1985; Collins 1990; Mama 1995), 'gender' has been further defined as 'a notion that allows us to think the interdependence of sexual identity, and other variables of oppression such as race, age, culture, class, and life-style' (Braidotti 1994: 98); that is to say, 'gender', which used to be posed as a static quality, existing only in relationship to 'sex' as 'culture' is to 'nature' (Rosaldo and Lamphere 1974), has been increasingly broadened by recent feminist authors. Indeed, in some circles, there has been a collapse of the 'certainties of gender dualism' (Braidotti 1994: 99; Butler 1990; Wittig 1992), implying, in a creative appropriation of Marx's dictum, that we choose our (gendered, sexualized, healthy) identity, but not always in circumstances of our own making. For, as Butler argues:

> I not only choose my gender, and not only choose it within culturally available terms, but on the street and in the world I am always already constituted by others, so that my self-styled gender may well find itself in comic or even tragic opposition to the gender that others see me through or with. (Butler 1987: 139–40)

These propositions, which construct gender as a contingent, constitutive element of our sense of self – and which is always in the process of formation and (mis)interpretation by oneself and others – resonate with the situation of women in prison. For, despite a gulf between the high theory of feminism and the empirical reality of prison, feminist discussions of identity, subjectivity and agency enable the criminologist to ask new questions about the experience of imprisonment by discarding the static notion of 'woman'. Once gender is understood to be both 'in process' and 'performative', it becomes possible to appreciate the women's ability to act within the confines of the prison. In sum, as the next chapter will illustrate in more detail, prisoners may express agency and resist – to some extent – despite the undeniable restrictions of their incarceration.

Institutional Constraints: Regulation of the Autonomous Self

Penal regimes strive to curtail disorder through the enforcement of a strict regulation of time and space and by encouraging the constant policing of inmate behaviour by prison officers. As has been well documented in the sociological literature, the regulation of female prisoners takes a specific, gendered form which relies upon the deployment of traditional ideals of passive, feminine behaviour (Carlen 1983; Faith 1993; see Chapter 1 above). Such 'regimes of femininity' are manifested within the employment and education typically offered in women's prisons – namely sewing, cooking, cleaning and 'mothercraft' – which are meant to shape the women's identity and their presentation of self.

In the prisons included in this study, the women were offered a limited range of work and education, much of which appeared to reflect traditional notions of femininity. Thus, at Drake Hall and Winchester, the work consisted of industrial sewing, gardening, minor repair work and cleaning.[16] Some women at Drake Hall worked in the kitchen, while at Winchester they were limited to serving the food brought over from the men's prison. Both establishments employed 'trustees' in the officers' mess. The education offered was similar – with both establishments extremely proud of their hairdressing salon. They also taught remedial language and mathematics skills and computing, while Drake Hall rotated two classes designed to enhance the women's self-esteem, one of which, called the NOW course, was self-consciously feminist, and both of which encouraged creative writing. It was perhaps in the incidental classes, many of which were run in the evening, that an outmoded idealization of femininity was most apparent. These classes in both establishments included flower arranging, silk painting, making soft toys, cooking and 'beauty'.

At the time of the research Pucklechurch was functioning with reduced staff, and so was offering very few options in either work or education. What work there was, however, was confined exclusively to the kitchens and to cleaning duties. When the women were allowed out of their cells, the education department offered an *ad hoc* selection of remedial classes, computing and sewing. The hospital wing, which catered both for women with health problems and those on Rule 43, was serviced separately from the main community, with an apparently greater emphasis on self-esteem. Classes seemed to consist largely of 'health and beauty' and extremely remedial communication skills. In short, most of the employment, education and counselling provided by the prison – with the exception perhaps of the NOW course at Drake Hall – appear to have been designed to inculcate feminine virtues in a collection of women who had stepped outside the appropriate social role of the 'good woman' through their criminal activity. Femininity was, therefore, both the goal and the form of women's imprisonment.

Many of the women interviewed recognized the gender stereotypes underlying their treatment, for as Susan said of Drake Hall:

> *You come in here and all the evening classes are like needlework and dressmaking. I mean who is to say that one of the women isn't a car mechanic on the outside? ... You get sentenced to prison and you get categorised don't you? You're a woman, so you get this. You do dressmaking, you do sewing. Because you are a woman.*

However, as Susan's confrontational tone suggests, competing notions of identity were invoked by the prisoners and by the institution. Specifically, the women rarely endorsed or practised the *passive* feminine behaviour encouraged by the establishment. Identity was, rather, under constant negotiation in prison. Although the prison had the ultimate power over the actions of the inmates, many women were able to reject their subordination. For example, Nancy and Carol used humour to reject their rejectors (Mathiesen 1965):

Mary: Do you go to any of the evening classes?
Carol: *No. Well, we've put our name down, but we've never been called up.*
Nancy: *I put my name down as soon as I came in ... people who came in after us have been going.*
Carol: *We get treated differently. They think us two wouldn't want to do it.*
Mary: Why?
Nancy: *Because we carry on. We laugh.*
Carol: *You're not supposed to laugh in prison. Because I'm from Ireland and she's from Scotland they don't know what way to take us. They don't know when we're serious and when we're joking.. so they just bang us off ... In gaol, if you laugh and joke, your gaol will go quicker. A lot quicker, and that's how we do it. So we don't get asked to go anywhere, and as for putting your name down to go to church, just forget it, I've been waiting to go to T-shirt design for 6 weeks.*
Mary: What did you put down for?
Nancy: *Flower arranging and T-shirt design! Ha ha ha.*
Carol: *So they think, 'we know what state the flowers will come out in, and as for the T-shirts, they'll do their own design, so they're not coming.'*
Nancy: *We'd do '100% guilty'! Ha ha ha.*

The women were certainly not passive, despite the restrictions imposed and images fostered by the prison. Indeed, one of the most striking aspects of women's prisons was the sense of activity, energy and emotion which pervades them.[17]

None the less, most of the prisoners did endorse aspects of an idealized femininity (see also Worrall 1990: 50–51). In particular, they cherished an ideal of motherhood. Very few of these women wished to break with a traditional binary gender order. Indeed, they drew much of their strength, agency, resistance and sense of self, from their roles outside as mothers, wives, girlfriends and daughters. Consequently, in their bid for autonomy and control, women often did not radically challenge the goals encouraged by the prison. Rather, they reinterpreted the ideals of femininity as positive attributes of their lives in the community. In doing so, they also redefined the meaning of femininity through their experiences of race, class and sexuality. For many women, being mothers and homemakers, girlfriends and wives was a source of pride and strength, which, as Olympia and Patricia complained, the prison undervalues:

Olympia: *They treat us like children.*

Patricia: *But the thing is, they don't realise that the majority of us have got children out there. You know, we cook and we clean, we run homes when we're out there, we've got families, we live just the same as everybody else. You know, it just happens to be unfortunate that we are in this position. For some of us yeah, for others no. You know? It's like they treat us like we don't know anything. Like we didn't go to school. Like we don't know how to do this or that.*

Like Patricia, many of the women appeared to define their sense of self and their needs, as well as their experience of imprisonment, in relation to their identity as mothers.

The presence of mothers behind bars has always been a controversial aspect of female imprisonment (Catan 1992; Lloyd 1992; Woodrow 1992; Department of Health 1992, 1994). A variety of studies exists which indicate that, at the sentencing stage, judges and magistrates take into account whether a female offender has children (Edwards 1984; Eaton 1986; Allen 1987a). These studies show that only certain types of mothers receive shortened sentences – specifically, those who are securely married and white (Farrington and Morris 1983). As the recent furore over housing and welfare for unwed mothers in both Britain and the US has indicated, a single woman with children – particularly if she is a member of a minority ethnic group – continues to be perceived as a threat to societal morals and to the social order (A. Young 1996: Chapter 6; Bortolaia Silva 1996). Many of the women in prison are single mothers, and those who are in heterosexual relationships are seldom in financially or emotionally secure partnerships. Although there are some middle-class mothers in prison, they are rare. There is, then, a dissonance that clearly exists between women's experiences of motherhood, and the idealization of mothering that the prison supports.[18] What is the effect of this dissonance?

Inevitably, for many of the women, the disjunction between their idea of mothering and that of the state results in their children being removed from their custody and either placed in care or adopted. One of the women I interviewed, who had sustained a long and serious heroin addiction while living on the streets, had each of her four children taken away from her, either immediately after they were born or in their infancy. For other women, the problem may not become urgent until release. Luce, for example, explained that she needed time once she left prison to adjust to life outside, and to resolve outstanding problems she had with her violent ex-husband. While she presented herself as a strong character in prison, where she was constantly in trouble with the authorities, she was clearly worried about her imminent release, which would entail an almost immediate realignment of her identity for which she felt unprepared:

Social services came up to see me a couple of weeks ago, and said that I'll be having the kids back after only a week [once I'm released]. Now, I think that that is pretty harsh. I've been on my own for a whole year, and then I come out and have the kids slammed on me, which anybody would think, 'God, you'd think you'd want the kids back', but I don't know if I can cope. A week out, and that's all they're giving me to get my head back together again, and then I've got the routine of the children. I think that's a bit too much.

For many women, their role and identity as 'mother' is interrupted while they are in prison since, like Christine, they do not tell their children of their whereabouts because prison somehow contradicts the ideals of motherhood: *'I refuse to see my kids, 'cos it would just knock 'em back. They're only just getting used to me being away … they think I'm on holiday …'*

For all of the women, the priority which the state, the prison and the general community places on their role and identity as 'mother' above their other needs and attributes, can be damaging. If women are unable to control the dominant meaning of 'motherhood' by which they are judged in the community, they will be confined and disempowered by a hegemonic idealization of maternity. While many prisons have instigated all-day visits for mothers and children to encourage family ties, there has been little consideration of alternative experiences of motherhood. Notwithstanding the recognition in both *Regimes for Women* and *Women in Prison* that establishments should expect some variety in mothering techniques from women of different nationalities (Home Office 1992a: §123; HMCIP 1997: §9.49), mothers in prison and in the community tend to be judged by an image of the white, heterosexual, homemaking mother, which is in clear disjunction with many women's real experiences.

The idealized femininity which underpins much of the daily routine of women's prisons has a contradictory outcome, for, at the same time as it firmly binds the prisoners in positions of weakness, such femininity also produces the possibility of resistance. As a result, a central effect of women's imprisonment is the construction of not just a 'disciplined', 'docile' or 'law abiding' self, but of a *feminine identity*. However, a single, uniform representation of femininity does not emerge. Rather, in a manner akin to that made plain in Judith Butler's (1990, 1991, 1993) work on 'gender performativity', women are able to construct competing feminine identities, through which they resist some of the disempowering effects of imprisonment. Although they prioritize motherhood in evaluating the special needs of female prisoners, the women frequently fail to adhere to a stereotypical image of a 'good' mother. Some, like Jane and Naomi, were neglectful, alcoholic and violent mothers. Others, like Maya and Audre left their children behind in another country. Still others, like Gloria, became involved in lesbian relationships while they were in prison. Finally, many, like Nancy, Carol and Drucilla, were multiple repeat offenders supporting expensive heroin habits. None the less, each of these women, and many others like them, perceived their identity as 'mother' to be constitutive of their identity, and thus part of their evaluations of any choices available inside and outside prison.

Identity and the 'Problem of Order'

Identity is fought over in practical and symbolic ways, becoming a primary means by which women manage the 'pains of imprisonment'. Most simply, it is an ordering mechanism of the inmate community, since the prisoners divide among themselves according to geographical origin, race, sexual orientation and types of crime. Yet, as is well known, a key aspect of a 'total institution' like the prison is that most of the divisions characteristic of the free society are destabilized within it (Goffman 1961; Foucault 1979). Once women are in prison, most distance themselves from their outside lives, following Luce's strategy in which she claims that:

> *I forget about out there, I just get on with what's going on in here. Now that I'm in here, I can't be thinking about what's going on out there. I will go right to the end, just dealing with what is going on in here, and then I'll get out, which I think will be the hard one.*

Similarly, Alice who had been in and out of prison and care since she was a child, explained the practicalities of adjusting to prison life by using a spatial, geographical metaphor:

> *When I come in here, it becomes my world. This [education block] is my school – my house [cell] is down there, my McDonalds [the prison canteen] is over there. I don't think about outside. I don't mind it in here.*

For many women, therefore, the prison becomes their entire world, even though for women with children this universalizing effect of imprisonment was clearly very complicated. As a result, daily life inside requires that actions previously confined to the private realm are enacted in public. Such disruption of the division between public and private compounds the difficulty most prisoners face in finding time and space for solitude and contemplation in prison. There is little chance for them to access their 'behind the scenes' identity, since they are always on show (Goffman 1969). The ordering of relationships in prison is, consequently, always under strain.

It has long been noted that the division between public and private, which characterizes societal organization, serves to reinforce unequal gender relations, because women have been excluded from much of the public realm (Lloyd 1984; Benhabib 1992; Fraisse 1994; see Chapter 2 above). That is to say, the use of public and private space is gendered, with women traditionally confined to the home or to segregated, 'domestic' areas of the work force (Massey 1994). Without doubt, changes to marriage laws and societal expectations have mediated some of the polarization between public and private spheres, since women are now able to have recourse to the law should their husband attack or abuse them. However, as the literature on domestic violence regularly illustrates, the home is still a problematic location for disputes of justice (Stanko 1985; Edwards 1989; Richie 1996). For example, not only has the law only fairly recently been changed in Britain to make marital rape illegal, but sufficient anecdotal evidence exists to argue that police, doctors and neighbours continue to 'turn a blind eye' to much oppression in the home (Hough and Mayhew 1982; see also Hanmer and Maynard 1987). Such anecdotal evidence was affirmed by many of the women in prison who had suffered domestic violence. For example, Elizabeth said that:

> *My father hit me, and then my husband ... I went to the doctor and he just gave me valium, and more valium and more valium. And the police as well. They'd just tell me not to worry about it ... They must've seen my broken arm, my smashed jaw, my bruises. And they did nothing.*

In another interview, she explained that the inaction of the police was a result of her marital relationship to her attacker: '*My husband raped my son. I got the police out, the police took him away. An hour later they brought him back, and said that I couldn't make a statement against him because I was his wife.*'

Elizabeth's legal and symbolic identity as a 'wife' restricted her access to 'justice'. The doctor pathologized her complaints of violence, and chose to medicate rather than to counsel her, while the police claimed that there was nothing they could do. Had Elizabeth been assaulted in public by a stranger, she would have been subject to a different legal identity, and offered the full protection of the law.

The collapse of the distinction between public and private is particularly pronounced in women's prisons through an expansion of the arena in which women's needs are discussed and monitored. By drawing private issues into public, the institution uses ideals of femininity to control the activity of the women. Thus, Maureen's despair was echoed by many others when she complained that, in Pucklechurch, she had to request the use of a safety razor in the nurse's office in order to control post-menopausal facial hair. As she appreciated, *'prison is a very public place'*. Similar experiences have been noted by criminologists who describe the shame and embarrassment experienced by menstruating women having to request sanitary items from male officers (Carlen 1983; Eaton 1993). Such archetypal feminine activities – menopause and menstruation – are typically hidden and rarely discussed in public. When they are talked about, it is generally within a women-only group, often providing a bond between the women concerned. If women are forced to bring these issues into the public arena of the prison, which is ultimately controlled by men, such feminine topics may become another means of institutional control.[19] However, as the next chapter will demonstrate, when the women initiate discussion of certain aspects of femininity in public, they can also empower themselves. Like the conflicting strengths and weaknesses which women draw from their identities as mothers, the symbolic association of women with their bodies paradoxically may both entrap and liberate them.

Within the inmates' limited ability to control the ordering of relationships in prison, ethnicity, age, religion, sexual orientation and offence become categories through which women define a prison identity. Because prisons are places in which information about others is often at a premium and it is difficult to know whom to trust, the ordering of relations between inmates is a constant source of tension. The lack of trust is a particularly difficult and long-term effect of imprisonment. According to Hester, *'You can't trust no one to the full extent ... [and] when you come out you still don't trust, not to the full extent again.'* The process of ordering relations among the inmate community is, therefore, an ongoing practice of daily prison life, despite its inevitably limited success. Moreover, as Goffman illustrated so well in his work, the ways in which individuals present themselves to one another – through the body, through language, and through cultural or ethnic practices – is key to any establishment of trust and security. According to Giddens' more recent exploration of Goffman's work on identity and the body (Giddens 1991), and to the philosophical writings of Taylor (1989), it is characteristic of modern society that the ontological security, which is prerequisite for a stable sense of self-identity, is fragile and easily disrupted. The disembedding of practices across time and space, and the restrictions placed upon choice and autonomy, both central to a sentence of imprisonment, and to much of modernity, seriously disrupt identity formation within prison (Sparks et al. 1996: 70–84).

In a closed environment like the prison, an institution that is both within and excluded from society, such discussion of 'ontological security' resonates with much daily life. Interpersonal security and trust are to a large extent suspended in prison, making it difficult to retain a strong sense of self.[20] The women are placed within a community of strangers, who are often perceived as hostile or untrustworthy, a setting which compounds their sense of personal insecurity, making it difficult to maintain a coherent self-image (Goffman 1963: 85–92). The wariness expressed by Sojourner was a constant refrain in the testimonies of all the women:

> *They're total strangers who you haven't grown up with, and you don't really know them inside out. You think they're your friends and they're not. You ... might think they are good friends, but basically they're not. And eventually you get to find that out.*

Categories of identity thus become both potential sites of resistance to the universalism of institutional control, and sites of possible conflict within the prison population. For example, in each prison, the women constantly discussed various (embellished) dramatic crimes which they had perpetrated and loudly proclaimed the allure of numerous illicit drugs, at the same time as they defined certain offences as unacceptable. Crimes against children, and drug habits which were 'out of control' and had resulted in the mental or physical damage to others, were broadly condemned by the inmate community.

Work by radical Norwegian criminologist Thomas Mathiesen (1965) is particularly instructive in this area. His subtle analysis of the largely unsuccessful ways in which male inmates in a Norwegian treatment prison resisted the strains and stresses of imprisonment indicates the important influence of the inmate community upon the prisoners' self-confidence and self-image. An inevitable effect of the prisoners' mistrust of one another was that the inmate community was weakened in relation to the power wielded by the staff.[21] Thus, while women adjust in different ways, for some the disruption of trust is overpowering. For example, Catherine said:

> *At home, I'd get on with everything, and I speak to everyone and everything and nothing gets me down. But in here everything gets me down. I find it hard to speak to people, because you don't know who you can trust.*

Inmates disguise themselves to one another, and perhaps even to themselves. Prisoners describe wearing a 'mask' or 'putting on a face' because they believe that it is necessary to 'put on a front' during their sentence. Yet, the reasons which they give for this identity charade differ. As a result, women's resistance can appear to be contradictory or inconsistent, thereby weakening their overall power in relation to staff. According to Sojourner, a mask is simply a shield behind which prisoners protect themselves:

A lot of people do put on a front when they come in, just to protect themselves really. They have to show like, an attitude, or a reputation. But to tell you the truth, if somebody does that, I don't think it lasts all that long. I think it's until they get to know who's who and who they can talk to and who they can't talk to. And who they must watch out for. So I don't think a front would last all the way through, like a whole three year period. It's just the first image you get off a person, they're letting you know what kind of person they are, or are trying to be.

Nancy, on the other hand, understood a mask to be functional both as a personal protection for oneself, and to shield others from further strains and stresses of imprisonment:

I might not feel happy inside, but I don't want to make their sentences harder. I don't want to affect everyone else. When I go into my room at night-time, that's when I feel bad. I'm with myself and I just sit and think. But during the day – I might be thinking about my daughter all the time, and laughing and carrying on – but I'm hurting inside ... but if I walked around all the time with my face tripping me up, going 'oh, I wanta see my daughter, I wanta see my daughter', people would go 'oh I'm fucking fed up with listening to her', know what I mean?

Personal disguise and the shielding of self-identity compound many of the effects caused by the breakdown of trust. Hiding one's self prevents the development of a reflexive relationship between the self and others, which, according to Giddens, is required for ontological security. Thus:

Self-identity ... is not something that is just given, as a result of the continuities of the individual's action system, but is something that has to be routinely created and sustained in the reflexive activities of the individual. (Giddens 1991: 52)

While prison would appear to provide an 'action system' and a 'routine', the fragmentation of the inmate population operates against sustaining any regular sense of self. Consequently, prisoners may become less able to resist many of the pains of imprisonment.

Wearing a mask is, of course, not limited to prisoners. As Erving Goffman so evocatively illustrated, we dissemble in many social situations because we play a variety of roles while trying to 'pass' throughout our daily life (Goffman 1969, 1963). However, the need to disguise identity takes on a new meaning in gaol, where people live, work, fight, love and hate one another in conditions of extreme confinement, often for long periods of time. Although it is impossible to generalize, it seems that presentation of self is an ongoing problem for prisoners, since, according to many of the women, hiding the pains of imprisonment from others is always difficult, no matter how many times you have been in prison.

> Mary: At this stage, after you've been in and out a few times, do you think that when you come back that it's still, does it still affect you? Is it still hard? Is it still changing you?
> Hester: *It doesn't become no easier. You still put on that front, you still – you have to, you have to put on a front when you come to prison. You still can't trust nobody.*
> Mary: Is there anywhere at all where you think that you can be yourself?
> Hester: *Be yourself by yourself. In your own room, that's about all.*

It is, in short, difficult just to 'be yourself' in prison. Consequently, the majority of the women described undergoing significant changes to their sense of identity in response to the pressures of imprisonment. Some of the changes were seen to be negative, as Olympia claimed, '*You end up giving up on things that you know you really should be fighting for*', while others, like Patricia, told of more positive effects which had helped them to become more assertive:

> *Before I came in here, I was quite a quiet person. I still am, but certain things which happen to me, or when people say things, I wouldn't have said anything, but now when I'm out there I will, because I've been here for so long, without not being able to say it, so it's when I get out there it's going to be like, 'well you don't do this, and you don't do that'. And it's not like it's a bad attitude way, but it's like I'm being very outspoken and open minded because I have now got my freedom of speech back. Where in here … You can't say things that you really want to say.*

Most importantly, the women perceived that the changes to their sense of self would last far beyond the prison walls. Such changes ranged from material issues associated with the women's reduced likelihood of finding employment, to psychological issues linked to the effect of curbing anger and frustration while incarcerated. For, as Carol said:

> *I think with gaol you get full of aggression. And I think with gaol you have to hold it in. Like mine's only been two months, but I've held aggression in for two months, so can you imagine someone who's done two years, three years. They've holded that aggression in for a hell of a long time, and when they go out there they are going to blow. And it could be a totally innocent person what you end in an argument with, and they cop the lot, because you're in an open space, you've not got a screw what's going to nick you … and you'll kick off and get all the aggression out of you. Which is wrong, a wrong person, but you do. I've done it. Every time I come out of gaol within a week I end up in a fight. The first time it*

was my brother. The next day I felt so awful, because I looked at my brother's face, and I thought 'How the hell can I do that to my own family?' But you don't think at the time. You just want to blow, you think there's no fucking screw standing behind my back, and there's no one going to drag me down the block and tell me I'm getting five fucking days, and you just let go.

The women frequently complained that the institution did not assist them to maintain ties with the outside in order that they could continue to exercise their previous roles and responsibilities which constituted their sense of self. Many of them faced a very uncertain future upon release. Often their house had been repossessed and their children placed in care – either in temporary foster homes, or with a view to more permanent adoption and often without the mother's consent – while they had been serving their sentences. For these women, being released held further difficulties since they would have to re-establish themselves on the outside, both as individuals and as mothers. Almost none of the women interviewed had realistic employment opportunities for life after prison and so Luce spoke for many when she said:

I feel that being on the outside with this criminal offence on me, I'm never going to be able to fulfil any plans I've got for the future anyway. So that's a knock back for me totally when I get out. That's knocked me for ten.

To some extent, life in prison provided a false sense of security for these women, since, as Rosi pointed out:

You adapt easily once you get into gaol. The hard part is once you get released. Adapting back to normal life is where the problems start. I mean, most girls will tell you, you don't worry about phone bills, electric, gas. The only thing you worry about is yourself and your kids if you've got kids. I mean I don't even have that problem, because I haven't got kids. But once you get back out there, and it's all slung back on your shoulders, after maybe two, three years of not having that worry, that can seem pretty hard, and really weigh you down.

For all of these reasons, women spoke at length of the difficulties they would face reasserting their autonomy and agency on the outside and expressed concern about the long-term effect of changes to their sense of self wrought by imprisonment. As Betty simply put it: '*I will not be the same person when I go out.*'

Narratives of Identity

Prison is full of competing stories, each of which constructs a narrative about self-identity:

> The self is both the teller of tales and that about whom tales are told. The individual with a coherent sense of self-identity is the one who succeeds in integrating these tales and perspectives into a meaningful life history. (Benhabib 1992: 198)

Our sense of self, or who we feel we are, is a dynamic process, and we are all implicated in the ongoing construction of our self-identity and our subjectivity. Thus, as Giddens writes, 'A person's identity is not to be found in behaviour, nor – important though this is – in the reactions of others, but in the capacity to keep a particular narrative going' (Giddens 1991: 54). However, unlike the agents of free will so cherished by early prison reformers (Howard, 1777; Bentham 1995), or those rational, reasoning agents of contract theory (Rawls 1971), individuals (within prison and outside it) both act and are acted upon. They are both free and determined.[22]

Often the women in prison are restricted by the very categories of 'criminal' with which they have been labelled. Consequently, they must find new definitions of their identity, or otherwise express different rationalizations and 'neutralizations' (Sykes and Matza 1957) of their criminal identity. For example, in Pucklechurch, I interviewed a woman who had held up a post office in Wales with an imitation weapon. She was a white, middle-aged, unemployed, single woman, with two dependent children, both of whom were suffering from chronic illnesses that required intensive medical care. She had walked into a post office, wrapped a bottle in a jacket, and demanded that they give her their money. She was easily overpowered, and had no 'real' weapon. However, she had been charged with 'armed robbery'. Allison violently objected to being called an 'armed robber'. Compounding her anxiety and frustration caused by being on remand, such a title was an identity which she eschewed, and thus a blame which she denied: '*I'm not an armed robber! ... I used to do a bit of shoplifting, cheques and things, but I couldn't believe I got so desperate I did this.*' Because of her straightened financial circumstances, caused in large part by her children's serious health problems, Allison felt entitled to more state support than she had been receiving. She wanted people to understand the exceptional nature of her action so that they would not condemn her for her crime.

Allison's story exemplifies the power differential which exists in the criminal justice system for most offenders. Although issues of identity and responsibility may be under negotiation in sentencing, it is not an equal negotiation. The women can only tell certain tales about themselves under these circumstances, and, in instrumental terms, the tale told by the judge is the one which is most important (Eaton 1986; Daly 1994).[23] While clearly Allison broke the law, the fact that she was 'not an armed robber', either subjectively – in terms of her identity – or practically – since the weapon was fake – opens the possibility for differential treatment and mercy. However, given the three-tiered belief in autonomy, responsibility and proportionality that underlies the criminal justice system, leaving little room for exceptions, Allison, in all likelihood, faced a lengthy sentence.

When prisoners do accept and are able to articulate a self-identity as a criminal, their self-description reflects a hierarchy of normative beliefs which are embedded in their lives and experiences outside. They speak in terms of morality, fairness and justice. For example, Nancy, who described herself as a 'professional thief', said:

> *Being in prison has changed my outlook. I've seen people with a lot less than me. Worser drug addicts than me. People who did a lot worse things than me. I mean I thought I was bad and evil. I mean I've met people who've mugged old women – a thing I'd never do! No matter how desperate I was. Where I wouldn't think anything of stealing a 35 year old woman in the supermarket's purse, I would never steal from a 65 or an 85. I have some guidelines that I follow. Some things that I will not do. I could never be a prostitute. I'd rather rob you, put a knife to your throat, which is probably more fierce, but I'd rather do that than be a prostitute. It's just not in my nature.*

In many ways, Nancy perceives her 'self', or, as she put it, her 'nature', in terms of widely upheld moral beliefs: she recognizes that it is 'bad' and 'evil' to be a drug addict as she is, to mug people as she does and to steal with a knife as she would. She can also differentiate herself from others by claiming that it is 'worse' to harm an old person, which she would not. In terms of identity politics, her testimony illustrates again that people are more than the sum of their actions: it is still possible to be moral – to some extent – while also being a thief. Identity is multifaceted, so that people fit into an over-arching normative structure of society in a variety of paradoxical ways.

A discussion of identity may also shed new light on the typically fraught relationship between staff and prisoners. For example, a common complaint about treatment by staff in daily life within the prison, concerned the failure of officers to distinguish among the women as individuals with specific needs and personalities. Thus Naomi and Jane bitterly said: *'We're all just prisoners to them'* and *'Once a prisoner, always a prisoner.'* As these women realized, the meaning of the identity 'prisoner' automatically disqualifies them from many qualities of social citizenship which typically characterize relationships among adults. In particular, they lose their ability – which, given their dependency on the state, was already much eroded for most of these women – to be considered as full rights-bearers (Fraser 1989: Chapter 7). Such disqualification from the discourse of rights reduces their ability to censure, or to make demands upon the staff, thereby further weakening their ability to be agents. For women in prison there is certain evidence to suggest that the gender of the officer may also have some effect upon the treatment of the inmate. Certainly, in each establishment I visited, the prisoners indicated their preference for male staff. The high levels of recorded punishments for infractions of prison rules that was mentioned above also seems to indicate that female officers may treat women in prison more punitively.[24] Given the historical division that has been propagated between women, which Anne Summers has labelled 'Damned Whores and God's Police', it would not be the first time that women in authority feel (unconsciously or otherwise) the need to differentiate themselves more starkly from the confined population with whom they share many clear ethnic, cultural and class attributes (Summers 1981).

Race, Class and Gender: Identity Formation Through Intersection

Ethnicity and class influence relationships between the prisoners and staff and within the inmate community. Although class has long been included by feminists in their analysis of gender, it has occupied a problematic role because of the failure of most male socialists to place much emphasis on gender in their critique of capitalism (Barrett 1980). The 'unhappy marriage' of feminism and socialism in the 1980s ultimately led many women to pursue a new path in psychoanalysis and to reject historical materialism (Sargent 1981). However, since the collapse of a hegemonic notion of class, it is perhaps possible to return a more reflexive version of it to a central place within feminist epistemology. It is, in any case, impossible to ignore it in a consideration of women in prison, since almost all of them belong to deprived socio-economic sections of the society. As Germaine recognized, *'Prison is a class thing ... people from working class backgrounds will be locked up more readily than people from other classes.'* Moreover, as indicated above, the similarity between the financial and social position with that of the staff may also be a large source of tension.

In England and Wales, unlike the situation in prisons in the United States (Owen 1998), class boundaries were more divisive than those of race. There appeared to be only a limited self-awareness of identity politics among the minority groups in the English prisons included in this study (see for example Díaz-Cotto 1996; Richie 1996).[25] Indeed, although there was a general acknowledgement that women of colour had some different practical needs – health, beauty or diet-related – most women did not appear to be particularly critical of, or concerned about, race relations. For the British prisoners, class was often given priority over race, partly no doubt because women from the same housing estates in Bristol or South-East London often mixed across racial and ethnic groups in their own communities. Many of these women regularly transgressed racial boundaries by cohabiting with Afro-Caribbean men and by being mothers of Black children. Differential treatment was often most apparent for these women, since as Carol explained:

> *My husband's Black. And every time my husband visits me I get a strip search. Every time. But when my sister comes I never get a search. Never. They said it's supposed to be random. But random is certain girls every week.*

Critical race scholars working in a variety of disciplines ranging through psychology (Mama 1995), literary theory (hooks 1982, 1989, 1990), sociology (Collins 1990), law (Williams 1993), literature (Walker 1982) and criminology (Richie 1996) have illustrated the importance of race and ethnicity in the formation of identity. Often critical of the failure of mainstream feminists to consider their own role in perpetuating systems of oppression based on cultural and ethnic difference (hooks 1989: 20), these women of colour have had a powerful impact on redefining the task of feminist theory. Most importantly, they have introduced an awareness of the 'interconnectedness of sex, race, and class', which as bell hooks indicates 'highlights the diversity of experience, compelling a redefinition of the terms for unity. If women do not share "common oppression", what can serve as a basis for our coming together?' (hooks 1989: 22–3). As members of ethnic, class and gender groups, people do not experience their sense of self as additive. Rather, their identities are located at the intersection of their ethnic, class and gender membership. It is impossible to disentangle these qualities from each other so that it is not enough to focus solely on gender and femininity when considering issues of identity and subjectivity. Put another way, as I shall show in the following chapter, considering gender identity requires an appreciation of the class and ethnic context in which women exist 'as women'.

Conceptualizing identity in terms of race or ethnicity adds a new political dimension to feminist concerns with subjectivity, since,

> ... for many exploited and oppressed peoples the struggle to create an identity, to name one's reality is an act of resistance because the process of domination – whether it be imperiality colonization, racism, or sexist oppression – has stripped us of our identity, devalued language, culture, appearance. (hooks 1989: 109)

However, epistemological problems arise when attempting to conceptualize the influence of race and ethnicity in prison. For, as Amina Mama argues, racial divisions and identities are themselves often a product of a racist culture (Mama 1995: Chapter 2). Early psychological and anthropological studies of African cultures employed a series of vicious stereotypes. As the recent debate in the United States over 'Blackness' and intelligence indicates, such stereotypes linger in the popular imagination (Herrnstein and Murray 1994). Although 'ethnicity' appears to be a less fraught term because it has few of the negative connotations associated with race, it also suffers from obvious limitations, since it is rarely applied to the white population, being used instead in a sleight of hand to stand for 'race' (Gelsthorpe 1993b). In fact, women from Scottish, Irish and Welsh backgrounds regularly differentiated themselves from the English prisoners, even if their family had long been resident in England. For example, Nancy who had a very heavy Glaswegian accent, recognized that her ethnicity affected her treatment and her presentation of self in prison. Although she usually managed to appear carefree in prison, she acknowledged that, with the introduction of incentives and earned privileges, her 'identity' and presentation of self were likely to become problematic:

> *I know my accent holds me back as well. It sounds harder than it actually is. The way I talk makes me sound like a hooligan sometimes – and I'm not! I mean I have a laugh and I carry on and I dance and all that ... but when I laugh, the officers think 'she's wild'. I'd get nothing, nothing [under the incentives and privileges scheme] but others would get everything. I guess it depends on who you are.*

In the new incentives scheme, which was introduced across the prison service in April 1995, prisoners' behaviour is constantly evaluated by staff, and is a key factor determining whether the inmate will be placed on 'basic', 'standard', or 'enhanced' regimes (see Liebling et al. 1997).

Issues of culture and ethnicity were also given more attention by the women from overseas since many of their life experiences were so different from those of the British women. For example, Audre who was serving an eight-year sentence for importation of drugs had been part of a polygamous household in Africa. One of four wives, she had been persuaded to smuggle drugs in an attempt to meet the expense of her husband's funeral. For her, the 'meaning' of being a woman was unlike that of either the Black British women or the white prisoners. Ethnicity was also an important issue in staffing because so few officers belonged to alternative ethnic groups – Drake Hall and Winchester each had only one minority member of staff, and Pucklechurch had none. Therefore, categories of race and ethnicity may be useful more for their denotation of subjective qualities and experiences, than as cultural absolutes. However, given the over-representation of minority women in prison, and the longer sentences being served by most of these women, it is undeniable that the colour of a woman's skin influences her experience of imprisonment.

Women in Prison: Beyond a Community of Victims

To conclude, women in prison are caught between competing expectations of values and behaviour that centred upon an implicit valorization of a passive feminine subjectivity. However, the boundaries of possible behaviour and self-expression are continually disputed as the women strive to assert themselves as agents. They challenge the idealization of passive femininity by taking pride in their achievements and responsibilities in the community. Yet, the prisoners' images of themselves as active, reasoning agents are constantly under assault by institutional constraints which encourage them to exhibit traditional, passive, feminine behaviour at the same time as denying them independent identities and responsibilities as real mothers, wives, girlfriends and sisters. The women must, therefore, negotiate discourses that valorize traditional, passive forms of femininity – epitomized by the typical work and education programmes – as well as those which encourage autonomy, agency, responsibility – found, for instance, in the idealization of motherhood.

The women evaluate their choices through a framework which is embedded in their social relationships and in their ethnic and cultural identities outside the prison. As a result, their ability to resist the pains of imprisonment does not rest entirely upon the choices which prison makes available to them. Their sense of self transgresses the prison walls, and enables them to resist much of the daily exigencies of prison life. As the next and final chapters will demonstrate, women resist the restrictions of imprisonment through enacting diverse images of femininity which, in their variety, subvert the dominant image of white, middle-class heterosexuality which is advocated by the prison and idealized in the community. The diversity of the prisoners implies that the meaning of being a 'woman in prison' is 'open to formations that are not fully constrained in advance' (Butler 1995: 135). Returning to the feminist discussion of identity with which this chapter opened, if the identity of a female prisoner is not fixed, change and resistance may be possible since, as Butler argues:

> If a term ... is not fixed, then possibilities for new configurations of the term become possible. In a sense, what women signify has been taken for granted for

too long, and what has been fixed as the 'referent' of the term has been 'fixed', normalized, immobilized, paralyzed in positions of subordination ... To recast the referent as the signified, and to authorize or safeguard the category of women as a site of possible resignification is to expand the possibilities of what it means to be a woman and in this sense to condition and enable an enhanced sense of agency. (Butler 1992: 16)

Notes

1 Although this is not the place to set forth the details of the many heated debates surrounding the post-Marxist, or 'post-socialist', critical commentary on power, it is well to remember that many of the authors who have been cited in previous chapters were central to the development of competing representations of power. In particular, the work of Foucault was exemplary (Foucault 1979, 1980a, 1980b).

2 It is instructive to recall the phenomenological study by Cohen and Taylor with maximum security men on E-Wing in Durham Prison, in which they write that the prisoners were 'peculiarly obsessive ... in their conversations about such mundane and untested matters as the passage of time, the making and breaking of friends, the fear of deterioration, *the role of self-consciousness and the loss of identity*' (Cohen and Taylor 1972: 39; emphasis added).

3 See analysis by Cohen and Taylor, Clemmer and Bettleheim of changes wrought on inmate identity according to length of time served in maximum secure gaols and concentration camps (Cohen and Taylor 1972; Clemmer 1940; Bettleheim 1960); although see also Morris et al. 1995 who claimed that sentence length was an inappropriate measure for women's needs in prison.

4 As, for example, the publicity surrounding the shackling of women in labour in January 1996, which led many prisoners in the final prison visited to question their treatment as women in the prison system (see *The Guardian*, 6 January 1996).

5 See Clear et al. (1992) for a brief discussion of the role played by religion in prisons for men in the United States.

6 A similar position has been put forward by Sim in his application of Connell's theory of masculinity to men in prison. According to Sim, in prison 'there is an everyday contestation of power and ... there is always the possibility for individual, social and historical change ... [D]espite the domineering brutalisation which underpins and reinforces the culture of masculinity inside, this culture has often been undercut by individual and collective strategies of dissent and sometimes by alternative penal policies which have provided a glimpse of the possibility for constructing social arrangements which are not built on violence and domination' (Sim 1994a: 111).

7 For a criminological discussion of the implications of some of the new theory on ideas of masculine subjectivity, see Jefferson (1994).

8 See Daly (1997) for a recent account of some of the implications of contemporary feminist literature for criminology.

9 Ironically, the ideal of masculinity has probably also marginalized aspects of the experiences of the 'real' men in prison since masculinity remains under-theorized, leading Joe Sim to point out that in general prison studies have 'concentrated on *men as prisoners rather than prisoners as men*' (Sim 1994a: 101; emphasis in original).

10 See Frazer and Lacey (1993), (especially chapter 5), for a comprehensive discussion of

the similarities and differences between feminist and communitarian literature on the 'subject'.

11   Although, of course, the extent to which parity has been achieved is inconclusive, as women continue to earn less and to occupy lower-status jobs. In terms of the criminal justice system, women also continue to suffer domestic violence and rape, and to experience greater fear of crime which restricts their social movements (Stanko 1985; 1990; Painter 1992).

12   For summaries of these feminist debates, see Fuss 1989; Nicholson 1990, Schor and Weed 1994 and Benhabib et al. 1995, Weir 1996.

13   Of course, these divisions are not absolute, since US feminists Judith Butler and Drucilla Cornell respectively synthesize Lacan with Foucault, and apply Lacanian theory to law (Butler 1990, 1991; Cornell 1995). See Braidotti 1994: 150–8 for a succinct description of the state of feminist theory.

14   Whether or not Irigaray is arguing for essentialism or not, has been a point of much dispute in feminist theory (Lacey 1997). This debate falls far outside this text, however see Schor and Weed (1994) for a summary of its content. See also A. Young (1993) and Lacey (1997) for discussions of the relevance of strategic essentialism in law.

15   At this point, I should reiterate that I shall not be drawing on the extensive body of traditional psychology or psychiatry. Although much of this literature deals with issues of the self, it often conflicts with the sociological and philosophical discussion of identity because it favours explanations which locate identity in individual psyches. This is not to say, however, that work by certain psychologists has not influenced or been shaped by sociological and philosophical concerns (Freud 1985 is the most obvious example. See also Laing 1982 and the brief discussion in Giddens 1991: 52–4). For radical feminist psychology, which incorporates a more theoretical understanding of the self, see Gilligan 1982; Ussher 1991; Brown and Gilligan 1992; Mama 1995.

16   In Drake Hall there was also a 'sheltered workshop', where women on Rule 43, or those unfit for heavy duties, assembled freezer bags and counted stamps.

17   Given the disproportionate number of women who are punished for offences against prison order and discipline, it seems that the authorities may also judge their behaviour as subversive or inappropriate, or else tend to believe that women need to be controlled more closely (Mandaraka-Sheppard 1986; Home Office 1992a: §105–106; Player 1994: 222).

18   See A. Young 1990a: 70–3 for a similar discussion of the paradoxical symbolic role played by motherhood at Greenham Common. According to Young, many of the Greenham women used the association of women with maternity to argue for women's 'special' role as peace keepers. However, as Young points out, complications usually arise from a feminism which unconditionally prizes motherhood because '[t]he "mother" and the "maternal" ... hold a place not only in a system of signification for *women*, but also within a *masculine* economy of signification. The feminism which uncritically celebrates maternity as women's ultimate natural expression can only reproduce and reinforce such an economy' (A. Young 1990: 72).

19   All three prisons visited had male Governors. Drake Hall had two female deputy governors – one of whom was on sick leave – one female principal officer and some women senior officers. Winchester had one female senior officer.

20   Again, this issue has been frequently discussed in prison studies, although it has tended to appear in studies of inmate culture (Clemmer 1940; Sykes 1958; Mathiesen 1965).

21   It also implies that the women were more akin to Mathiesen's 'disrupted' inmate population (1965: 122–36) than to Sykes' (1958) 'cohesively oriented' one (see Sparks et al. 1996: Chapter 2 for a detailed comparison of these two approaches).

22   Or, as historian E. H. Carr put it 'The fact is that all human actions are both free and determined, according to the point of view from which one considers them' (Carr 1964: 95).

23   Although, as feminist socio-legal scholars like Lucie White (1991) and Martha Fineman (1994) maintain, even the discourse of law and the courtroom may be challenged by defendants.

24   While the effect of gender upon staff in prisons has been under-researched (Carrabine and Longhurst 1998), see Heidensohn 1992 for a discussion of the gendered role of women police officers.

25   However, it is possible that the women would have discussed issues of race and ethnicity in more detail with me had I been a woman of colour. Similarly, it is also possible that the Black women who were more politicized about race/ethnicity did not come forward to be interviewed. While I tried to ensure a mix of respondents, since I mainly used a snowballing technique, it is impossible for me to know whether I missed certain types of women (see Gelsthorpe 1993b for a discussion of transferable research strategies for feminists exploring issues of race and ethnicity).

5 Voices of Agency, Voices of Resistance: Negotiating Power Relations in Prison

Of vital importance to any vision of criminological theory is a consideration of the way human agents are perceived and the nature of the social structure in which they are seen as acting ... We view humans as active agents producing their social world. This production is both continuous and continual, although not necessarily self-reflective. (Henry and Milovanovic 1994: 111)

Actions to bring about change ... empower ... Because our actions change the world from one in which we merely exist to one over which we have some control, they enable us to see everyday life as being in process and therefore amenable to change. (Collins 1991: 113)

I mean you know what girls in prison are like – they will go and have their say. Sometimes it gets them somewhere, and sometimes it don't. (Sylvia: HMP Winchester, February 1996)

This final chapter builds on the discussion of identity politics outlined above. Specifically, it explores how identity becomes a means of resistance. It does so by illustrating the ways in which women assert their agency in prison through identifying with, and transforming, aspects of that idealized femininity which is encouraged at the institution. This chapter argues that many of the women's practices which were identified in the previous chapter as assisting in identity formation – wearing a mask, discussing their roles and responsibilities on the outside, and noting the personal changes which they were undergoing as a result of their incarceration – are also the means by which the prisoners affirm their agency and autonomy.

This chapter further examines the ways in which prisoners constantly draw on aspects of their cultural identity to assert their independence from penal regimes. It finds that inmates frequently express culturally specific challenges to the homogenizing routines, by using food, dress and religion to resist the uniformity of prison. Accordingly, they refuse to eat prison food, become vegetarian, demand Halal or Kosher meat, observe days of fasting and practise cultural mores from their country of origin. Above all, this chapter proposes that women ground the symbolic language of rights and fairness in their sense of (ethnic, religious, feminine, regional, sexual) identity, indicating that the circumstances under which they recognize the legitimate authority of the staff and institution are dependent on a framework of evaluation which is tied to their sense of self.

In critical and social theory, issues of agency and choice have long been central to discussions of freedom and responsibility (Bourdieu 1977; Giddens 1984, 1991; Carr 1964; Berlin 1969). Such literature seeks to understand the paradox that individuals can constantly produce and reproduce the social world, despite being profoundly restricted by large-scale inequalities in power relations and in the distribution of economic, educational and health resources. Undoubtedly, it has become increasingly difficult to conceptualize power and power relations since the decline of Marxist theory in academic research. However, despite confusion and disaffection on the left, it is clear that there is widespread recognition of the continuing need to challenge systems of inequality and differential power relations.[1] More recently, as was illustrated in the previous chapter, feminist and critical theorists have sought to identify the specific ways in which gender, race and class define the choices and evaluative frameworks open to individuals (I. M. Young 1990; Calhoun 1994, 1995; Benhabib 1992; Bordo 1993; Braidotti 1994). According to these scholars, the capacity for agency and resistance is grounded in identity because individuals both evaluate their choices and act upon them in terms of their lived experiences. This chapter will explore whether 'resistance' and its companion theory of 'identity politics' provide a new direction for critical analyses of power through an articulation of the localized, small-scale ways that power is constantly negotiated.

Considering the manner in which individuals act and negotiate power while disempowered and vulnerable may enable criminologists to reconceptualize the prison beyond an instrumentalist concern with how to 'get things done'. As a result, it may also become easier to reveal the relationship between the symbolic and material sources of legitimate power, for acts of resistance are not always recognizable in purely material or instrumental terms. Instead, as will be demonstrated below, women invoke images on a symbolic level through their own experiences and identities to challenge their material restrictions. In spite of uniform and prohibitive prison routines, women find the means to negotiate power by articulating their differences.

Such an exploration of agency and resistance may challenge the widespread view of female offenders as victims and as poor copers. Even so, I do not underestimate Carlen's warning that

> Unfortunately, (and if, in common parlance, the word 'victim' is to retain any meaning at all) women prisoners are too frequently victims – and of more things than are usually dreamt of in either the empirical or theoretical universes of middle-class feminist criminologists. (Carlen 1994: 133)

Yet, as others have shown, a consideration of agency and resistance need not deny women's actual experiences of oppression (Worrall 1990: 10–11; 160–61; Shaw 1992, 1995). Instead, as this chapter will illustrate, the exploration of agency and resistance in prison may help to illuminate the women's ability to evaluate and negotiate power relations despite their subordination and confinement. In so doing, considering the relationship between agency and identity can serve to bridge the gap between theoretical and empirical research. Because power relations in prison are always in flux, the restrictions on choice and autonomy are neither absolute, nor distributed equally.

The capacity to define oneself as an agent is crucial to surviving imprisonment:

> It is precisely the struggle to maintain a sense of personal agency in the face of overweening institutional constraint which motivates and sustains some of prisoners' most intractable contests with the system, long after they would seem to have 'lost'. (Sparks et al. 1996: 81)

This chapter will demonstrate that the women frequently expressed great concern about the difficulties of maintaining a strong and positive self-image in the face of penal restrictions, petty disputes of the regime and an unknown inmate community. It is at this level of 'presentation of self' that they expend most of their energy in resisting the effects of imprisonment. In other words, it is through the representation of 'identity' – to other prisoners, to the staff and to themselves – that women cope with the pains of imprisonment. It is here that we may seek the sources of legitimacy of women's imprisonment, for it is here that the distribution of power is constantly contested.

Agency and Resistance: Some Definitions

The notion of 'resistance', like that of 'identity', is currently attracting much attention in theoretical circles as a means of illuminating power relations. However, like 'identity', 'resistance' has also been criticized.

Feminists, in particular, have given the idea a mixed reception. While some feminists portray it as a way of developing a critique of power through an appreciation of the everyday actions of real subjects (Collins 1991), others believe that its microscopic focus either disregards the larger power relations which lie behind the status quo or simply embroils individuals further within them (Carlen 1994). For its advocates, 'resistance' signifies a way to appropriate aspects of postmodern theory without losing a critical or partisan consciousness (Diamond and Quinby 1988; Mahoney and Yngvesson 1992; Lazarus-Black and Hirsch 1994; Griffiths 1995). In their work, resistance allows, in other words, for an appreciation of difference, and requires feminists to include socio-economic factors in their analysis. At its most useful, resistance entails a construction of power as relational rather than absolute, since by its very nature the term requires the possibility of alternative arrangements. Consequently, 'resistance' is presented as a means to continue the liberationist battle of the women's movement within a more theoretical and reflexive discourse.[2]

Recently, feminist and critical scholars in the US have applied the notion in different fields of criminological research (Arrigo 1993; Ferrell and Saunders 1995; Gagné 1996; Maher 1997; Sanchez 1999 forthcoming). Many of these criminologists have been intent on exploring the dialectical relationship between the victimization and resistance of female offenders, in order to challenge that reductive understanding of female crime and punishment which has marked much criminology (see Chapters 1 and 2 above). Lisa Maher, for example, documents women's role in the sex and drug industries of Brooklyn. In her ethnographic account she claims that, despite overwhelming (and often violent) oppression, most women find some avenues of personal agency within the drug economy (Maher 1992, 1997; Maher and Daly 1995). In a similar vein, Lisa Sanchez's account of prostitutes and dancers in a major North-West city in the United States indicates that the young women strive to retain a self-image which is strong and dynamic despite their limited choices (Sanchez, 1999 forthcoming). Both authors present their subjects in a way that appreciates the women's own power, despite its contingency and vulnerability, thus opening the possibility for change in the women's own terms.

Resistance has also been enthusiastically appropriated by postmodern and critical socio-legal scholars as a way of conceptualizing experiences and voices previously marginalized in the legal process (Merry 1990; White 1991; Yngvesson 1993). In this literature, power relations are considered as discursive and material expressions. Power is not seamless, and small acts of speaking can and do disrupt the status quo. Central to this approach is the belief that, '[a]lthough dominant groups may control the *social institutions* that regulate ... languages, those groups cannot control the *capacity* of subordinated peoples to speak' (White 1991: 55; see also Freire 1996). Thus, Lucie White describes the welfare hearing of 'Mrs. G.' who had appealed a decision that she received an overpayment on her government support:

> The lawyer had scripted Mrs. G. as a victim ... She had warned her client to play the victim if she wanted to win. Mrs. G. learned her lines. She came to the hearing well-rehearsed in the lawyer's strategy. But in the hearing, she did not play ... she abandoned their script ... She ignored the doctrinal pigeonholes that would fragment her sense of voice. Instead, ... she explained that she had used her money to meet *her own* needs. She had bought her children Sunday shoes. (White 1991: 54)

Although initially 'Mrs. G.' lost her appeal, the state later dropped their claim for money. 'Mrs. G.' managed to resist definition as a victim, but still won her case.

However, despite being currently fashionable, resistance has by no means been unanimously celebrated for conceptualizing and challenging relations of power and inequality. For example, according to one feminist critic, 'resistance by itself does not contain a critique, a vision, or grounds for organized collective efforts to enact' (Brown 1995: 49). A critic like Wendy Brown perceives the term as essentialist and de-politicizing. For that reason, she links it with the criticisms of identity politics mentioned in the previous chapter:

> Sharing with identity politics an excessively local viewpoint and tendency towards positioning without mapping, the contemporary vogue of resistance is more a symptom of postmodernism's crisis of political space than a coherent response to it ... Resistance goes nowhere in particular, has no inherent attachments, and hails no particular vision; as Foucault makes clear, resistance is an effect of and reaction to power, not an arrogation of it. (Brown 1995: 49)[3]

Brown, in attempting to construct a theory of democracy in opposition to the postmodern rejection of the Enlightenment, queries the utility of studies of resistance (Brown 1995: Introduction). For her and others, resistance is too slippery a term and an idea without sufficient critical substance. It enables the middle-class left to feel good about minority and oppressed groups without necessarily altering established injustices (Ramazanoglu 1993; Cooper 1995: 126–9; Willis 1977).

Ultimately, however, Brown's reading of Foucault and of the potential of resistance is overly negative. Although many tensions underlie Foucault's notion of resistance, Foucault himself seems to rebut Brown's pessimism by making clear that the 'plurality of resistances' which exist within any system of power relations are not 'only a reaction or rebound, forming with respect to the basic domination an underside that is in the end always passive, doomed to perpetual defeat' (Foucault 1980a: 96). Rather, resistance, like power, is everywhere. While it is often imbricated within the power structure, it can also enable change and revolution.

Given the dispute among feminists over the practicability and utility of resistance, care must be taken to demarcate its boundaries. It is right to be wary of a term which is so clearly open to abuse – given the broad range of activities which can be labelled as rebellion. Yet, resistance remains an extremely useful concept because of the way it illuminates small-scale attempts to disrupt power relations, by drawing attention to a variety of minor acts and rebellions which may otherwise escape notice. Verbal challenges, modes of dress and ethnic practices may all be seen in that light. Appreciating these subordinate acts as forms of critique demonstrates that power relations inside may not be as fixed or unchangeable as they first appear. Resistance is, therefore, not an excuse to disregard the status quo. Rather, it is precisely in people's ability, however limited, to fashion critique, that the transformation of large-scale inequalities is implied. That is why expressions of agency, particularly in restricted situations, are so important. They enable the criminologist to conceptualize resistance and the negotiation of power in terms of identity and subjectivity. Consequently, it may be possible to develop an appreciation of agency that is not locked into structural or psychological accounts.

'Agent' is used in this text to signify two different attributes of the women in prison: it denotes both their specific subject position or identity and their ability to act. To have agency is to preserve the ability to negotiate power and to resist. To be an 'agent' is to consider oneself retaining some of those practical and symbolic attributes which constitute citizenship in the community. These traits include freedom (of choice and of liberty), autonomy and responsibility. As has long been recognized, these constitutive elements of 'agency' are crucial to surviving life in prison (Sykes 1958; Mathiesen 1965), yet they are also contingent. The ability to be an agent is always under assault in prison, because imprisonment undermines people's capacity for autonomy and disqualifies them from making decisions about how to conduct their own lives. Choices are severely restricted inside, and freedom of liberty is denied. The complaints made by women to me echo many other voices of the confined:

> Eleanor: *I didn't realise when I come into prison exactly what it meant having your freedom taken away from you. Now I realise what it means, having your freedom taken away, and that's what happens here. Everything is out of your control, when you eat, when you sleep, what you can buy, what you can wear –*

Virginia: *Who you can see.*
Eleanor: *Who you can see*
Virginia: *When you can see them –*
Eleanor: *Yeah. It's all taken out of your hands, having no money in your pocket, restricted to this little area. You know, only having women to talk to. I didn't realise what it meant until you're here, and then you realise what it means. And the worst thing about it, is that it's out of your control.*

Such negation of individual agency inevitably places the prison in a paradoxical situation. For, as penal reformer Alexander Paterson recognized long ago, 'It is impossible to train men [or women] for freedom in a condition of captivity' (cited in King and Morgan 1980: 2).

Undeniably, captivity undermines self-determination. Similarly, it seems paradoxical to have agency without freedom. Yet, despite the restricted choices and opportunities that characterize all penal institutions, most prisoners find the ability to express their agency and to resist. Few prisons are run by coercion alone. Given that the ability to be an agent is usually understood to be largely dependent on choices and opportunities, how do prisoners manage to survive, let alone to resist? For women (and men) in prison can and do resist. Somehow, despite their weaknesses, they maintain the ability to be agents, demonstrating a remarkable ability to defy the universalizing effects of punishment and imprisonment.

Overall, most prisoners' non-compliance takes the form of low-level verbal challenges to the authority of the officers and to the validity of the regime. Studies of men's prisons have indicated that such challenges, which contribute to the general level of tension and disorder in any prison, can be seen as strategies by which prisoners seek to assert autonomy from the universalizing effects of imprisonment (Sykes 1958; Mathiesen 1965; Cohen and Taylor 1972; Fleisher 1989; Sparks et al. 1996); however, little literature exists which provides critical analysis of the singular ways in which women negotiate power relations inside (although see Faith 1993; Howe 1994; Hannah-Moffat 1995). Instead, criminologists must extrapolate from accounts of domestic violence (Stanko 1985; Edwards 1989; Richie 1996), feminist theory (Fraser 1989; Butler 1990, 1993; Benhabib 1992; McNay 1993; Braidotti 1994) and sociological discussions of the reflexive relationship between power and agency (Giddens 1984, 1991; Taylor 1985a, 1985b). Bolstered by an interpretative armoury derived from these diverse areas of scholarship, it becomes possible to appreciate the many moments in which women use their presentation of self – both physically in terms of appearance and more subtly in terms of their self-confidence and agency – to attempt to subvert the exigencies of daily prison life. Such small-scale acts of resistance, which echo James Scott's description of 'prosaic but constant struggle' exercised by peasant labourers in the Third World (Scott 1985: xvi), may enable a more nuanced and critical analysis of the effects of power in prison.

Freedom of Choice: Conflicting Accounts

In most liberal democracies, a rhetoric of freedom – of choice, opinion, religion and trade – drives public discourse on key issues including capital, consumerism, government and sexuality. Full of symbolic and material power, ideals of freedom are also prerequisites for agency and citizenship: one cannot fully act unless one is free. Thus freedom and liberty are determining factors of modern consciousness and social organization, and their idealization is one of the key characteristics that separates our age from what has gone before (Taylor 1985b: 319). Because prison ratifies the valorization of freedom for the law abiding community, it is necessary to investigate the meanings of these terms further.

Freedom of choice and autonomy have long been associated with the feminist movement. They have motivated campaigns for women's right to choose abortion and have inspired the establishment of rape crisis centres and women's shelters, both of which were designed to help women choose alternatives to violent relationships. Similarly, the civil rights movement in the USA aimed to increase the range of choices available to Black people in all areas of life. In particular, desegregation entailed an expansion of choices in housing and education along with a recognition of the restrictions that had previously characterized the lives of African Americans. In both these approaches, choice is portrayed as a vital prerequisite for resistance and change, as well as fundamental to the attainment of citizenship and equality.

However, more recently and in stark contrast to its use by feminists or civil rights activists, the ideology of 'freedom of choice' has been co-opted by the Right and by libertarians demanding freedom from state control. As the political arena shifted further to the Right in the 1980s, politicians and criminologists came to explain crime and social ills through an anachronistic idea of 'rational' choice. Wilfully ignoring the reality that negative freedom (Berlin 1969; Taylor 1985b: Chapter 8) has dramatically reduced all elements of choice in daily life for many sections of the population, proponents of rational choice have argued that crime can be predicted (and thus reduced or amplified) by measuring practical 'opportunities' which avail themselves to the criminal (Clarke 1980, 1983; Felson 1994).[4] This literature has had a far-reaching impact on official policies of crime control, and elements of it have recently been co-opted in prisons through the introduction of structured incentives and privileges schemes.[5]

According to rational choice theorists, whether they be philosophers (Rawls 1971) or criminologists (Clarke 1980), individuals determine the most efficient means of achieving their goals. Choice, in this theory, is not associated with resistance, but rather with responsibility. People are encouraged to take responsibility for their own actions, since everyone is judged capable of sober rationality. As a result, according to Nicholas Rose, '[i]ndividuals are to become, as it were, entrepreneurs of themselves, shaping their own lives through the choices they make among the forms of life available to them' (Rose 1989: 226; see also Garland 1997). What is lacking from a theory of 'rational choice' – and what is subsequently absent from much of the literature on crime prevention and incentives in prison – is a realistic conceptualization of *how* people choose.[6] There is no exploration of their framework of evaluation and, as a result, this literature provides no way to understand how people assess and act upon their choices. Like the coupling of 'justice' with 'fairness' in prison policy – which, as Chapter Two illustrated, precludes an appreciation of gender – the implicit relationship between 'freedom' and 'rationality' ignores the effects of difference.[7] Yet, as was shown in the previous chapter, differences in race, class, sexuality, age, nationality and religion influence many of the relationships formed in prisons. These qualities also structure women's evaluations of their prison experience. Finally, as shall be demonstrated below, the form and range of choices and opportunities available in prison differ to a large extent depending on the women's socio-economic and cultural identities.

That incarceration limits choices and opportunities for self-expression is self-evident. It is part of the meaning and expectation of a sentence of imprisonment that certain elements of social life – most obviously, freedom of movement and choice, and 'liberty' in its simplest apparent meaning – are curtailed. Significantly, while the inmates are subject to discourses of freedom, they also support them.[8] Consequently, one of their most important coping mechanisms is the development of a sense of self-determination in which prisoners perceive themselves as agents with some freedom to choose. The rhetorical power of the notion 'freedom' is clearly acknowledged and frequently invoked by the inmate community. Women in all three establishments repeatedly made such claims as that asserted by Christobel in Pucklechurch '*That they can take my liberty, but they can't take my smile*', or, as Olympia in Winchester put it, '*They can take my freedom of speech, but they can't stop me thinking.*' Although doubtlessly these claims are to some extent self-aggrandizing, they none the less indicate that some level of freedom is possible and imaginable, even in situations of great confinement.

Contingent Choices: Towards an Appreciation of Difference

There are few work options and a limited range of classes offered in any prison. Inmates are allowed only a certain number of articles of clothing and jewellery. They have no control over when their meals are served, or what they are given to eat.[9] If they dislike the designated doctor, dentist, nurse, counsellor or priest, they must make do. What few choices are available are also inconsistent. Some institutions allow regular changes of clothes to be sent in from the outside, while others do not. Certain prisoners are given extra phone calls to distant families while most are not. A course which has been advertised may suddenly be cancelled, and there is nothing the prisoners can do. The women in each prison I visited all trenchantly criticized the range of choices available to them in education and work activities. As noted in the previous chapter, paid labour was limited to industrial sewing, cleaning, gardening and kitchen work, while education mainly took the form of remedial skills, typing, sewing, cooking and hairdressing. Outside the hairdressing and typing courses, qualifications were not offered, and so most women left prison as unskilled as they arrived. Eleanor thus spoke for many when she bleakly said that *'because I am in prison, I have no choices.'*

The women in prison were also quick to criticize those choices that were made available on the basis of race and gender, indicating that choice was valued not simply on the basis of quantity, but also in terms of quality. The prisoners were deeply troubled by the kinds of activity and opportunities the prison provided. The options for work and education were frequently criticized for their outmoded assumptions about female taste. Groups of women bemoaned this:

> Eleanor: *The choice is so old fashioned, you know what I mean –*
> Zora: *Yeah, yeah.*
> Eleanor: *As if all women just want to sew, cook and clean –*
> Bell: *Iron, wash clothes, why can't they have mechanical, or carpentry ... I'd do that.*
> Eleanor: *Do some silk painting!*
> Mary: Although do some of the women like it?
> Eleanor: *Of course some of the women like it! but –*
> Zora: The majority don't
> Eleanor: *A lot of women like different things as well.*

In short, and in the words of feminist theorist Nancy Fraser in her similar discussion of women on welfare in the US, the prison service 'does not deal with women on women's terms. On the contrary, it has its own characteristic way of interpreting women's needs and positioning women as subjects' (Fraser 1989: 149). As Chapter 2 illustrated, both women's needs and their subjectivities are often interpreted in relation to now-abandoned ideals of femininity, which, as the women realize, justify such anachronistic tasks as 'silk painting'. In fact, according to research by Morris and her associates, many of the women have different needs from those that are officially acted upon (Morris et al. 1995; Morris and Wilkinson 1995). The prison service thus homogenizes the population because difference – in sexuality, religion, ethnicity and nationality – has little place inside. For women of colour and other minority groups, including lesbians and the religiously devout, the limited choices available in prison are further restricted. However, as the confrontational tone adopted by Eleanor and her friends indicates, prisoners recognize that they constitute a diverse group, few of whom conform to traditional stereotypes of femininity. These women battled to retain a sense of themselves as agents, with some sort of role in determining the form and content of their daily life.

In other words, despite their limited choices, the women in prison constantly endeavoured to resist the restrictions placed upon them inside. They frequently described themselves as having been strengthened by the experience of prison. So, for example, while conscious of the numerous difficulties inherent in re-establishing life outside, Rosi said to me that women were able to make the most of their reduced opportunities because of

> ... *the strength you find being in gaol. The things you have to take. Whereas on the out, you might have reacted violently, or screamed and shout, you hold it down more, and you either get it dealt with or you ignore it ... That lesson carries through until you get released.*

Strength of character and opinion, along with steadfastness and courage were qualities that they admired. Such attributes all challenged the disempowering images of femininity that underlay much of the daily routine. The women did not aspire to, or seem to support, the homogeneous femininity advocated by the institution and through which much criminological literature represents them. Rather, they pursued diverse gender roles through lesbian relationships and religious and ethnic practices, particularly those concerned with diet, education and dress.

A prisoner's identity structures many of her opportunities in prison. For example, the activities offered in HMP/YOI Drake Hall, HMRC Pucklechurch and HMP Winchester failed to differentiate between the needs and expectations of minority women. In response, there was sustained criticism by women of colour of the scope of choices for inmates. The absence of minority staff members, and the failure of any of the prisons to offer work and education options designed to meet specific demands and desires of inmates from different ethnic groups were particularly resented. Zora, for

LIVERPOOL JOHN MOORES UNIVERSITY
LEARNING SERVICES

example, a Black British woman in Drake Hall, argued that the already limited choices were compounded for Afro-Caribbean women, who made up a significant proportion of the prison population:

> *The only thing you could possibly say that you could come out of here and get a job with is possibly hairdressing and in there they don't cater for Afro-Caribbean hair. So basically, there's no point of anyone from an ethnic group even trying.*

However, as stated earlier, the effect of race and ethnicity on the women's experience of imprisonment was far from uniform. The intersection of race, class and nationality prevents any simple discussion of choice and oppression for minority women in prison, because women of colour do not constitute a homogenous group. As was argued in the previous chapter, the significance of racial difference among the British-born women appeared to be more dependent on class relations, rather than on a unitary sense of shared racial oppression. Prisoners often formed intimate friendships among themselves based on age and region rather than just on race, since women from the same housing estates or urban areas often already knew each other or had shared similar experiences on the outside. Therefore, women of different ethnic groups, from similar areas in London, were more likely to share horizons of evaluation than were a group of Black women from different classes and nations. To illustrate by example, I witnessed a heated discussion among a group of Black women from Nigeria, Jamaica and Britain who were disputing the propriety of a woman's practice of curtseying to the officers. While Maya explained her actions as a form of self-affirmation, because as she said it '*shows my identity*', the other women felt that her actions were dangerous because they were generalized by the officers to reinforce racist stereotypes about backward or 'uncivilized', 'simple', black women (see also Mama 1995: Chapter 1).

Many elements of evaluation were apparent in the discussion of Maya's actions. Primarily, the dispute shows that there may be irrevocable conflict between individual and collective identities: for both Maya and her opponents were right. While her actions did function as a personal reminder of her cultural heritage and thus gave her strength to serve her sentence, they also reinforced stereotypical opinions about African women. The officers all described Maya in patronizing terms, and tended to generalize from their opinions about her to the other Black women. Maya's words also raise the question whether the women consciously chose their strategies of resistance. Did she realize and plan the effects of her actions, or were they an unintended consequence?

Ultimately, the dispute cannot be interpreted without consideration of the women's lives outside the prison. For Maya not only had a different nationality, she also belonged to another class, since she came from a highly educated, ruling-class family. As a result, her framework of evaluation, the reasons which she gave for her actions, and her perceptions of her choices, were all drawn from a life unlike that of the other three women. While conscious of the problematic effects of her curtseying in terms of how she was viewed by officers and other women, she did not care. In sum, although these women each had similar practical opportunities in prison, their inter-pretation of their experiences varied widely. As a result, their expressions of agency, their ability to resist and their self-consciousness about their actions were not uniform.

In general, the Black foreign-nationals who were imprisoned for importa-tion of drugs generally held very different evaluative frameworks from those of the Black British women. As the 'war on drugs' expands across the world, an increasing number of foreign women – who are typically from developing nations – are being incarcerated in the prisons of England and Wales (Rice 1990: 61; Hudson 1993a: 17; Player 1994: 208–209; see generally Richards et al. 1995a, 1995b). They are often arrested at the airport when they enter Britain and are commonly given long sentences, which may be supplemented once they are deported home again. Often their cases are tragic, since their crimes are frequently committed under duress either in response to threats of violence or simply because of dire economic need. For example, Julia from Latin America had agreed to smuggle cocaine into Britain in an attempt to prevent the execution of her son by the militia. She failed and he was killed. Similarly Audre, who was mentioned in the previous chapter, had been co-erced into smuggling by a money lender to support her seven children. Such women – who are further disabled by their limited ability to speak English – have specific needs, and would thus like to make different choices from the majority of the prison population. Audre, despite having much better material benefits at her disposal in an English prison, wished to be deported so that she could be near her children. Foreign nationals like Audre rarely receive visits, and so are sometimes given a brief overseas phone call in lieu of their visiting rights (Home Office 1992a: §92). However, the outmoded technology of most of the communication systems in their countries of origin often necessitates multiple attempts before they succeed in gaining a connection. Therefore, these women must rely on the goodwill of the officers on duty to place the call, and to continue to try to connect when there are problems. As a result, their ability to resist publicly is diminished because they are much more dependent on the prison authorities.

Along with race, ethnicity and nationality, sexuality influenced women's expressions of agency and resistance in diverse ways. Although clearly an infringement of prison rules, and thus potentially a form of resistance to the regime, sexuality divides the inmate community because lesbian relationships in prison are accorded conflicting status. Some prisoners like Luce appreciated the opportunity to form intimate ties with other women, saying that friendships are '*a lot closer in here, because it's like you're actually living with everybody. So I mean, I would say that, all my life I have never been as close to anyone as I have been in here. Because I've never lived with a girl.*' Yet, many heterosexual women were extremely critical of any lesbian activity. They were made uneasy by same-sex relationships either because of prejudice, or for the more 'everyday' reason that lovers tended to quarrel or to be affectionate in such a way that infringed on other women's privacy. A distinction was generally drawn between 'real' lesbians, who were also lesbians on the outside, and those who developed intimate relationships with women while in gaol. 'Real' or, in Luce's words, '*full blown*' lesbians were perceived to be much more threatening than those who simply formed intimate relationships in prison. These latter women often had children and male sexual partners on the outside, to whom they planned to return, indicating that they differentiated between their internal and external identities.

The impact of lesbianism on the management of the prison was unclear, since, even though the women claimed that lesbian relationships were fairly common among the inmate community, there was no official recognition of lesbianism. While the prisons formally forbid any sexual intimacy between the women, officers commonly 'turned a blind eye' unless they felt that an older woman was 'enticing' younger inmates. Thus, lesbianism in prison was characterized by an official silence analogous to that within the broader community (Wittig 1992). Despite widespread knowledge of their existence, lesbian couples were not afforded a public identity, and thus were not given official choices. As a mode of public resistance, lesbianism was, therefore, muted in its effect. However, in terms of facilitating the construction of a private realm of emotions and sexual intimacy, it may have been more successful.

A final quality which divided the inmate community, but also provided expression for much personal strength and resistance, was religion. Women from religious groups other than those three authorized by the prison service – Roman Catholic, Church of England and Methodist – often found it difficult to practise their faith. Such restrictions were somewhat dependent on race and ethnicity. Thus, for example, Hester, who was a white convert to Islam, was treated with cynical disbelief, yet was largely left alone to practice her faith as she wished. By contrast, an Egyptian Muslim, Nawal, was characterized by the staff as a 'fundamentalist' and a 'troublemaker'. Despite being soft-spoken, educated and thoroughly conservative in her social views, Nawal was perceived as a threat to the good order and discipline of the unit. Hester managed to negotiate a relatively uncontroversial expression of her religion as long as she was prepared to accept the patronizing attitude of staff, while Nawal was in a weakened physical state because the prison was refusing her Halal meals. Rather than accept Kosher food as did Hester, Nawal was engaged in a protracted, direct confrontation to obtain all the elements she required to practise her faith.

Once again, the differences between the treatment of Nawal and Hester raise the question of self-consciousness. Was Nawal knowingly antagonizing the staff by demanding more than they were comfortable in giving? Was Hester purposely keeping a low profile? While such questions are undoubtedly significant, an answer to them must remain partial. Unless the women's testimonies are unconditionally accepted as 'true', then it is impossible to be entirely sure about the women's personal reasons. In contrast, what were very clear were the ethnic and class differences between the women. Once again, like Maya, Nawal was a foreign national and a member of the middle class. Wearing a head-scarf, and speaking with an accent, she was different not only from the staff but also from the other women. Consequently, she was marked by her identity.

The foreign-national Christian women seemed most able to negotiate religious distinctions, simply by ignoring them. Of the church services I attended at the Women's Annex of HMP Winchester, no matter which denomination, the congregation consisted of the same African women. These women did not act in typical 'English' ways during the service. Instead they laughed and giggled and danced and sang. In some ways, they appeared to take over the service, simply by virtue of their difference. Although the priest always had the support of a uniformed member of staff, who could intervene when the women became too high-spirited or irreverent, the women were able to transform the meaning and effect of the church service through their actions.

Order and Compliance in Women's Prisons: Constituting Agency and Resistance

Women's prisons are rarely perceived to be disordered, yet female prisoners often seem to be far from compliant. As was mentioned in the previous chapter, women in the prison system of England and Wales receive proportionally more punishments for offences against order and discipline than do men. Although disagreement exists whether this is a consequence of greater policing or whether it denotes more frequent levels of small-scale infractions of rules (Home Office 1992a: §105; Player 1994: 222), in neither case are women seen to constitute a significant threat to prison order. Two alternative explanations for women's compliance in prison were commonly given

by the prisoners: first, they believed that the situation had not yet degener-
ated sufficiently – although it was in the process of doing so – to warrant
large-scale disorder. In this vein Susan spoke about the introduction of the
so-called 'privileges and incentives scheme'. In it, the availability of most
material possessions in prison, as well the quantity of visits, letters and
telephone calls, is indexed to behaviour. Each institution is free to pursue its
own strategy within a general remit set down by the Home Office (Bosworth
and Liebling 1995). While popular among the 'law and order' lobby, it has
been criticized by many inmates:

> *If they're not careful – they'll push the girls too far and they'll have a riot on
> their hands. What's the point of keeping your nose clean? ... If you start taking
> things away from us in here. I mean, everybody's got a nasty side, don't they? If
> everybody decided to stick together, the officers wouldn't stand a chance.*

Second and more commonly, however, were the contradictory views that
women were either untrustworthy, fickle and weak-willed, or more sensible
and responsible for their children, so that they could not be depended upon
to unite against the staff. As Angela put it:

> *At the end of the day, right, there is only a few women who are willing to stick it
> out. And the few women who are willing to stick it out is a waste of time, because
> it's going to be either shipped out or split up. There's not enough, and the
> reason why, I think, is that a lot of the women have got kids out there and they
> consider that before, like more than men. Like men will just join together and
> don't really consider what's out there ... I'm not saying they ain't got links with
> their children but it's different with mothers, and I think that's a lot to do with it
> in the system.*

Underlying this type of criticism was a commonly held belief that somehow
women did not know how to stand up for their rights in prison. Women
appeared to judge each other by pejorative notions of femininity, thereby
reinforcing the findings of the sociological literature outlined in the first
chapter (Giallombardo 1966a). As a result, the women saw themselves as
mostly solitary and isolated, and also unmotivated. Thus Angela continued:

> *I think half the women don't know the score. You know, a lot of the men they've
> either been in, out, or they more know what's going on and they're more [willing
> to] stand up for their rights. I think the women do lack in that. There are a few of
> them that you get that's willing to do it, but it's a waste of time because if
> everyone's not willing to do it, the few what's willing to do it are only going to
> get their selfs in more trouble.*

Because many women doubted their ability to forge strong and reliable bonds of unity against the prison, there was considerable scepticism about the possibility of resistance:

> Olympia: *The thing is though that women sit and think about it where men just sort of react straight away. That's what it is. We sit and think 'well, if we go ahead and do this, it'll fall back on us at the end of the day. It'll make things worse for us, so do we do it or don't we?' So at the end of the day we don't. We don't do it. A lot of them things that men do in prison fall back on us, too. Like escapes and things like that.*
> Patricia: *Let me tell you something. They stick together. Women will not stick together.*
> Olympia: *No. We don't stick together at all.*

Such separation within the female community had a number of effects upon women's resistance and their expressions of agency. Many women found it difficult to retain a sense of agency. There were frequent examples of a certain rueful pragmatism, as the women acknowledged the superior power of the institution, whose representatives controlled release dates, work availability, visits, pay, cell changes and many other matters. For example, according to two young offenders:

> Bell: *Being in here is like being a child all over again, but even worse.*
> Beth: *'Cos instead of being slapped, or grounded, or having your pocket money taken off you, you get extra days!*

As was illustrated in the previous chapter, many women described wearing a mask and having problems trusting other inmates. For some of the women, the divisions within the inmate community dramatically exacerbated the pains of imprisonment. Thus, for example, Catherine was a very solitary figure, who found her incarceration almost unbearable. Our conversation illustrates many of the harrowing and contradictory aspects of imprisonment which have to be dealt with on a daily basis:

> Catherine: *If you're always crying, like I was, people say to you 'ooh you stupid cow, why don't you just accept it? You're going nowhere, you gotta do it, you may as well accept it'. But I think the first week is the hardest week. There's that many mixed-up feelings inside you, and you can't get your head around the system. I can't explain it, but you feel like you can't cope. Or that's how I felt anyway.*
> Mary: What changed?
> Catherine: *People saying to me 'oh stop acting so stupid, just get on with your sentence.'*
> Mary: So do you feel like you changed something about what you were thinking about it, or did you just change what you were showing people?

Catherine: *Just changed what I was showing people. I still cry now, but I do it in my own room when no one's there. Before I'd just be sitting with people and I'd be crying. When you first come in everything gets so on top of you and you just can't help it. The system is too much. I'd been in a bangup ... and the staff were just nasty ... You get grief from the inmates, they think you're a wuss if you cry. But nobody really helps you. You just have to sort out doing time.*

Mary: Do you think you've learned ways to cope that will help you on the outside?

Catherine: *No. No.*

Mary: It hasn't made you stronger?

Catherine: *Nah. I was stronger on the out than I am on the inside. I could cope better on the out.*

Mary: Do you know why that is?

Catherine: *I haven't a clue. I think it's because everything gets on top of you in here. Things never used to get on top of me at home. Maybe it's because I used to speak to my husband about it, and get things off my chest, but here I don't speak to no one. There's no way I can get in touch with him, because he can't read or write, he's dyslexic and we're not on the phone. So there's no way I can get in touch with him, unless I go home.*

For women like Catherine, often the only form of resistance available is self-harm or suicide. Seeing self-harm and suicide as expressions of agency represents a profound challenge to the paternalist perceptions of female offenders. Long characterized by male psychologists and psychiatrists as mentally unstable and suffering from 'personality disorders', women in prison have been over-medicated and pathologized (Sim 1990: Chapter 6; Smith 1996). However, little work has been conducted which specifically investigates the reasoning which women use to explain their harmful actions. While it is known that women in prison regularly cut themselves, there has been little complementary analysis of their suicides. Indeed, as work by Alison Liebling shows, there has, in fact, been a dramatic under-reporting of women's suicides since they are often classified as accidental deaths (Liebling 1994). Recently, the 'Trust for the Study of Adolescents' has formulated a guide for staffing practices which includes a section on recognizing depression and self-destructive behaviour (Lyon and Coleman 1996).

Despite the prevalence of self-harm, generally the women are not afraid to make demands on the staff. Similarly, irrespective of their lack of unity, most women appear to be far from passive in their approach to their sentence, particularly when their demands are related to life-style issues and family contact. Given their limited choices, how do the women manage to 'get what they want done' within the extremely restricted confines of a prison? Moreover, does succeeding in instrumental terms generate longer-term, symbolic power? Does their resistance 'go anywhere in particular'

(Brown 1995: 49), or can it actually entangle them further in the subordinate position of a power relation?

Although it is difficult to generalize from a few challenges that were levied at institutional authority while I was in prison, it is possible to identify two general strategies, which I believe reveal a tension in all women's expressions of agency: women either challenged prison rule through invoking ideals of 'femininity' or by appealing to the more general notion of 'humanity'. Even when these tactics had similar, successful, outcomes, they drew on qualitatively different identities, and thus represented alternative models of agency.

Resisting Identities: Strategies of Change

Despite moments of self-doubt, and frequent aspersions cast on a collective will to change, women in prison none the less value and promote self-images of control and participation. Such images are used to combat the 'pains of imprisonment' and to structure relationships with other prisoners. According to Simone:

> *A woman will try to debate everything won't she, to get what she wants? I think that's probably because, well, they say we are the fairer sex, although you do get some women who are just like men and won't. They're the opposite and are really aggressive ... I think it's not so much that a woman should be passive, even in prison, because that can be taken as a sign of weakness by the inmates, it might go down very well with the staff, but I think that ... what I've learnt from coming to prison [is] to be assertive ... Because if you're passive, you're obviously not going to stand up for yourself, you're going to be easily influenced, and led into things, and maybe into another life of crime again. Whereas, if you can be more assertive for yourself, you can stand back and say 'No I don't wish to do that, that makes me feel uncomfortable.' And be assured, and feel confident in yourself that you can turn around to that person and say 'Well, no I'm sorry but I'm not prepared to go along with this. By all means you go along with this but please don't include me, because this is where I'm coming from. I've changed. For the better.'*

Despite the undeniable restrictions they faced, most women saw themselves as rational, responsible agents. Accordingly, inmates endeavoured to present themselves as individuals with rights, deserving of justice and fair play. Angela, who was coming to the end of a six-year sentence for drug possession, and who was typical of a number of the women in prison, since she had never finished high school[10] and had been in frequent contact with the law, claimed that:

I don't wrong them, or hate no officer, but there are certain times when they try to take their little liberties with you, and I don't care, I will stand up for myself to the fullness, even if I have to go down to the block if I believe in something.

In this instance, Angela appealed to an ideal of the active, autonomous subject, who is self-sufficient and strong. She believed that she was the bearer of rights, and so should not have to endure officers 'taking liberties' with her. She also perceived herself to be fair and just, since she did not 'wrong' or 'hate' the staff. Like Angela, Simone presented herself as a fair and sober judge of character. However, her case demonstrates the limited success of such a presentation of self. Thus, she spoke of a time when, having arrived at a new prison, she was located on a wing which she found unacceptable:

I said to one of the officers, I said – how I felt basically was that I was dying inside, literally dying inside, and I thought if this goes on for any substantial time I'll die, I might be there in the flesh, but I certainly wouldn't be there in spirit. And it was frightening, to think it was going to destroy me, and that's when I told an officer that 'I've got to get put off this house, if I get put down the block, if I have to hit an officer, I will put myself down the block and be isolated, rather than put up with this.' And so I said that to her, 'I am dying inside, and you must get me off this house.'

Simone's example demonstrates the women's limited ability to rely on a rights-based idea of justice in prison. Although initially appealing to the officer's spirit of humanity and good will, Simone ultimately invoked the 'spirit of Leviathan' and the stereotype of prisoners as dangerous and potentially violent. Notwithstanding women's desire to be perceived as responsible individuals with all the rights that entails, their identity as 'inmates' constantly works against them. Ultimately, therefore, they often invoked other self-images to achieve their ends. In particular they frequently relied upon stereotypes of femininity.

Reconfiguring Identity: Femininity as Resistance

In the previous chapter it was argued that there was a slippage between the idealization of femininity by the prison authorities and the prisoners' own understanding of their identities as women. Very few of the women in prison appeared to reject feminine roles. Most of them clung to a fairly traditional gender order. In particular, most of them set great store by the role and responsibilities of motherhood, even if they themselves did not have children. As feminists have shown, particular images and stereotypes of femininity have long been identified as central mechanisms in the social control of women (Smart 1976; Carlen 1983; A. Young 1990). If the prisoners themselves associated with ideals of femininity, do their actions and beliefs signify the seamlessness of an unequal gender order, or were the women able to exert some control over the definition of their own identity? In order to answer this complex question, which really goes to the heart of this book, I shall consider the role of femininity as it featured in different events described by the women in prison. The first example will demonstrate how prisoners used specific gender stereotypes to win a dispute, while the second will document women's ability to appropriate femininity to enhance their self-confidence. The final example will describe one woman's discussion of herself as a mother. While the first two stories will indicate the ability of women to use identity politics as a means of resistance, the third will demonstrate that women themselves are able, to some extent, to redefine the meaning of femininity. Together, I argue that these examples illuminate a rich source of resistance, as well as a new way of considering gender.

In the final prison I visited, issues of femininity played an important role during a lengthy dispute about toilet paper. This small-scale dispute is perhaps typical of the types of problems in most prisons. It was a minor irritation, and a seemingly unimportant issue, but one which became endowed with huge meaning. The distribution of extremely rough and ineffective toilet paper – which inmates likened to tracing paper – motivated the women to complain for several weeks until it was replaced with more acceptable material. In their dispute, they utilized a series of different approaches, each of which represented a diverse strategy of resistance. In the final analysis, they succeeded in their dispute, by mobilizing the medicalized and pathologized image of women, in which women are associated with their bodies (Sim 1990: Chapter 6; Ussher 1991). Specifically, the prisoners complained about the inadequacy of the paper for menstruating women and for women with haemorrhoids. However, they only used this tactic after they had tried and failed with some other strategies.

First, the women simply demanded the return of the ordinary paper. They saw it as their 'right', since they had been sent to prison as a punishment, not in order to be punished. However, staff refused to listen to their complaints, and brushed aside their demands. Citing economic cut-backs, or dependency upon the central men's prison, the staff said that there was nothing that they could do. In response, the women attempted to steal softer rolls from the staff toilets, since they believed that they were entitled to the paper. At this stage, the provision of poor-quality toilet rolls was seen to epitomize their restricted choices in prison and so Olympia suggested that:

They should give us a choice then if we want to buy it. If we could buy it from the canteen, then let us buy it. You know what I mean? That's a choice. But we have no choice. We have to use it, or we'll steal it. Because the officers are still getting to use it – OUR toilet roll.

But the prison refused to sell toilet paper in the canteen, and officers soon put an end to the stealing by writing 'STAFF' on all the available rolls and punishing any prisoner caught with one.

Having tried reason and then deviance, some of the women then suggested a group demonstration. They proposed that the prisoners block the sewerage system by forcing various objects down the toilet. If everyone participated, there was hope that nobody would be punished, and the prison would be forced to change. However, this plan also failed, since an insufficient number of women agreed to participate. In the words of Patricia:

When we first came here, we had soft toilet paper, yeah? Well, now they've given us this tracing paper stuff. Well, we could stick together and say 'well, there's six landings on the whole of the prison, and there's two toilets on each of the landings', yeah? Well, what we could've done was stuff all the toilets and block them up and say 'Yeah this tissue is blocking up the toilets so we want the soft tissue back.' But they won't do it. Because they say 'Well, but then we won't be able to use the toilet because they'll be blocked up.' Rather than, you know, doing it, and letting the prison do something about it, and letting them see that we don't want to use this paper, they won't do it. So therefore we just have to leave it and put up with it.

Therefore, in the end, unless women were prepared 'to leave it and put up with it', the appeal to bodily aspects of femininity was all that remained. From this position of apparent weakness, rather than from an expression of unified strength, or deviousness, the women achieved success, by filling out numerous complaints forms, by speaking to their personal officers, and even – as Sylvia indicates below – by going to the governor:

We have to use that paper – that paper like you used to have at school, like you could sit down and write a letter on it, you know? We've been complaining about it and they don't seem to be doing anything about it, and we've had it for a fortnight now and girls that's on their period can't really use it you know, and girls with thrush … the governor's away at the moment, but when he comes back I'm going straight to his office. And I'm going to say, 'I don't know if anyone's put it to you sir, with you being a man, but when girls have got piles, thrush and are on their period, they can't use that hard toilet paper. So you're going to have to do something about it.' And hopefully he will understand.

In short, the women resisted and won by bringing issues of femininity – particularly those associated with feminine hygiene – into the public arena. Of course, as the previous chapter illustrated, many women are demoralized and disempowered by the manner in which personal issues are often forced into the public realm in prison. Yet, as some women realized, the inversion of public and private could also be deployed to their advantage.

Importantly, the dispute over toilet paper was not the only example of women using images of corporeality to achieve their ends. The provision of food – always a contested element of imprisonment – was another aspect of daily life in which women often invoked issues of feminine hygiene. Indeed, Patricia saw the two complaints as complementary when she said:

> *It's the same with the food. Because we're connected to the men's prison, it's chips every day, lots of starchy food. Women lose blood every month, we need iron, we need food to replace our iron, but we're not getting that. We have to eat what the men do. And that's not fair to us, because a lot of the women are getting run down, because they're not getting stuff to replace what they're losing.*

Finally, women's control of their appearance was understood as another means to resist. Although the regulation of women's appearance is frequently cited in criticism of the oppressive nature of femininity (Bordo 1993), according to Simone it can become a motivating force in prison, a matter that enables women to resist:

> *[In prison] you lose the shine out of your hair, your finger nails start going a funny colour. They go like a yellow-ish colour, and it's certainly not through smoking. And they soon break and become brittle. And it's all those things ... I'm not saying that you have to go around looking like we've stepped out of Hollywood, like we've stepped out of Vogue – but I think that's demeaning to a lot of the women, especially if you've been used to looking after yourself, and caring about yourself. And you still want to do that, and you still feel motivated enough to do that, even though you've come to this dreadful place. But you know in time, in time, because of these little factors which do niggle away at you, you can get to the stage where you think, 'Oh sod it! why should I bother? Why should I bother washing my hair? Why should I bother cleansing my face? Or putting face scrub on, or painting my nails?' And you can gradually just go down hill, down hill and down hill ... There've been days when I've been like that, when I've been really like that, and I've had to really gather all my power and strength together and say 'Come on, get in there, get up and fight, and look after your nails, it took you twelve bloody months to grow them!'*

Thus, in a similar way to which the women reinterpreted feminine identities as empowering, they were able to re-present aspects of a biological and passive femininity to confront and shift the administration. Women seemed to understand their identity as gendered. While they sometimes struggled against the restrictions of femininity, at other times they invoked its ideals. Their ability to resist thus appeared to rely on a paradox. Were the prisoners simply situating themselves more rigidly within a position of weakness by relying on such ideals of femininity? Or, conversely, were the women able to influence and shape the meaning of 'femininity' themselves?

Motherhood remains a crucial element of the social construction of femininity. As feminists have shown, an ideal of maternity is central to unequal gender relations (Chodorow 1978). Women are expected to be nurturers, and to stay within the private realm. However, as was mentioned in the previous chapter and as Carol Smart puts its, feminists have also portrayed motherhood as 'a source of women's strength and uniqueness, a site that is entirely feminine and that draws upon women's special qualities and knowledge' (Smart 1996: 38). Ideas of maternity, in other words, can be both pejorative and celebratory. In either case, however, motherhood has traditionally been essentialized and tied to women's 'nature'.[11]

Many women in prison felt that their identity as mothers constituted the fundamental aspects of who they were. Although there were some voices of dissent, like Luce, who was frustrated that the state was going to return her children to her so rapidly, without giving her time to sort herself out, most women prioritized their needs as mothers well above all their other needs as women. To the researcher, the apparently uniform idealization of motherhood is initially confusing, and would appear to weaken the feminist challenge to the domesticity of prison regimes. However, as will be revealed below, women's definition of their maternal identity severely challenged many of the accepted stereotypes of feminine identity.

For example, Drucilla spoke of her mothering duties and responsibilities as an unemployed, drug-dependent, white single parent in Wales. Aged 31, Drucilla had been a drug user since she was 18. Her habit had kept her involved in a constant series of illegal activity, which had recently culminated in an armed robbery of a post office, committed while under the influence of drugs. In a casual conversation, Drucilla spoke of her mothering techniques to me and to an education officer at Drake Hall. Responding to questions from the education officer – who himself had four children of a similar age to Drucilla's two daughters – about who was taking care of her children while she was incarcerated and how she maintained contact with them, Drucilla described her relationship with them. Specifically, she outlined how she dealt with her daughters' burgeoning interest in drugs, alcohol and social activity. According to Drucilla:

When she was 13 years old my eldest came and asked me, 'Mummy, can I do half a tab of acid?' and I said 'No, because you haven't finished growing yet. Perhaps when you're 16 you can have a go' ... and then I gave her a fiver to go and get drunk.

In defiance of many socially acceptable standards of parenting, and certainly to the dismay of the education officer, Drucilla appeared to condone at least some of her young daughter's illegal activity. Not only did she not entirely rule out the possibility of drug use, she enabled her young child to procure alcohol. Drucilla rationalized her approach by grounding her moral reasoning in her real life. First, she pointed out that, like any parent, she would rather know what her child was doing than have her try drugs or alcohol in secret. By being candid about her own drug habit, Drucilla strove to foster an open relationship and friendship with both her daughters. Having allowed her elder child to drink alcohol, Drucilla was then present the following day when her daughter was hungover, at which point she was able to discuss the pitfalls of drinking too much. Finally, by allowing one illegal activity, Drucilla felt empowered to refuse her daughter other, more dangerous and debilitating drugs.

There are many issues implicit in Drucilla's story and in my usage of it. I propose that the importance of her story lies in the ways in which, within her very restricted choices and opportunities – that were in turn determined by her drug problems, her unemployment, her violent relationship with her ex-husband and her poverty – Drucilla none the less had some control, and exercized some authority and power. It is not that Drucilla's parenting skills were ideal, or somehow more natural. Rather, they were different, and they were different *because* of social-structural conditions: namely her economic and domestic arrangements. Moreover, when describing her actions, Drucilla located them within a gendered identity of motherhood. She, too, relied on an ideal of femininity to legitimate her actions. Because of the discomfort her parenting skills inspired – in me and in the education officer, both of us clearly representatives of a middle-class élite – Drucilla's story disclosed the hidden class bias which underpins the ideals of femininity. By claiming for herself the identity of a 'good mother' – along with so many of the other women in prison – in defiance of a common-sense, normative understanding of mothering, Drucilla challenged gender stereotypes. Her story should not be understood to mean that there are as many 'good mothers' as women with children, rather it reveals that the idealization of femininity, which has been shown to underpin so many social structures, including the prison, rests on a false universalism, which may be disrupted.

Femininity as Resistance: Repoliticizing Prison Studies

The women in prison challenged the unitary notion of femininity in a variety of ways. Most obviously, they used their cultural and ethnic identities to broaden the meaning of 'woman'. That is to say, the prisoners' gendered identity intersected with many other factors, including their nationality, race, class, sexual orientation and age. Consequently, the prisoners did not represent a uniform image of hegemonic (white, heterosexual, passive) femininity. Rather, they displayed numerous variations on a theme. Although many of their practical choices in prison were restricted by their ethnicity and sexuality, it was also through their (cultural, ethnic and sexual preference) variety that women managed to challenge some of the restrictions of the universalizing effects of imprisonment. Therefore, while the inmates' identities as 'women in prison' appeared to be defined by the closed walls of the prison, their alternative interpretations of the meaning of the material and symbolic choices open to them gave them some possibility of resistance.

Of course women's ability to redefine femininity is not guaranteed. Class, race and sexuality can be limiting factors which appear to be all but inescapable. Thus, for example, Audre's ability to perceive herself as, or to gain any strength from, her identity as a mother, was almost entirely restricted by her socio-economic, cultural and geographical status. Her distance from her children – who were left without a care-giver – coupled with her identity as a woman from a developing country and a member of a traditional polygamous household, made it almost impossible for her to appeal to a recognizable notion of 'mother' in a British context. As a result, she was very dependent on the prison authorities.

If women are drawing on similar images and identities by which they are oppressed, to what extent can they liberate themselves? Does interpreting femininity through race, class, sexuality and culture destabilize it – by refusing to accept a single definition – or does it rather strengthen it by expanding its possible meaning and terrain? Are the women in prison resisting, or are they merely trapping themselves further?

Clearly, one way of interpreting the women's actions would be to claim that they suffer from 'false consciousness', that they promote and adhere to certain stereotypes of femininity because they have internalized their own oppression. However, this understanding of women's actions demeans the prisoners' power and initiative. On this view, women become victimized and are disempowered. Yet, despite the numerous and apparently overwhelming restrictions which were fundamental to their prison sentences, the women saw themselves as interacting with one another and with the institution, thereby shaping their daily lives. As has been demonstrated on many occasions, they frequently portrayed themselves as agents, controlling at least some aspects of their lives. The observer who dismisses their under-standing so completely risks misrepresenting the women themselves.

An alternative interpretation might be to celebrate women's power as women. In this view, the task would be to invert the current pejorative definition accorded to 'womanliness' – the qualities of passivity, emotion, irrationality which were discussed in Chapter 2 – in order to redefine femininity as worthwhile. This approach has been favoured in much radical lesbian feminism, and forms the basis for some of the identity politics of new social movements (Rich 1980; Daly 1978; Gutman 1994). However, inverting the current definition of femininity does not destroy it, but rather re-establishes it in a new form. Such essentialism thereby traps women in an idealized form of femininity yet again (Schor and Weed 1994).

In contrast to the two suggestions above, I would argue that the women's interpretation of femininity through their race, class and sexuality allows the prospect of a new understanding of gender. If femininity is not singular, but rather is differentiated along race and class lines, for example, then it can no longer be understood as one side of a binary. Following Butler, it may be that the women's potential for 'agency' is located in their ability to vary the repeated performance of their identity as 'women in prison' (Butler 1990: 145, 1991). If identity is constituted by, among other factors, a variety of socio-economic and cultural attributes, change both in the discourse and practice of imprisonment is possible. For, according to Worrall:

> While much of the women's resistance is individualistic, inconsistent, and, in some senses, self-destructive, it has the important effect of undermining the authority of official discourses and keeping open the possibility of the creation of new knowledge about them – both as women and as [prisoners]. (Worrall 1990: 163)

Resisting Imprisonment: Some Conclusions

The concepts of identity and resistance enable the criminologist to develop a feminist theoretical critique of imprisonment which can acknowledge the specificity of different experiences of punishment rather than constructing another normative, generalizing analysis. Given the scarcity of texts which include an analysis of gender in any discussion of imprisonment or punishment, such an exercise will contribute an important dimension to criminological scholarship. It will extend the current boundaries of studies of legitimacy through its appreciation of an alternative, smaller-scale analysis of the effects of the distribution of power inside in such a way as is concomitant with recent developments in much feminist theory.

Significantly, however, it is important to acknowledge that practices of resistance are often 'read' in different ways by the individual woman concerned, by the inmate community, and by the staff – indicating the contingent nature of 'discursive consciousness' (Giddens 1984; Merry 1990). As the examples of Maya's curtseying and that of lesbianism illustrated, the effects of class, sexuality, gender and race often divide the prisoner community even as they unite them. Any contradictions or shifting alliances prompted by these qualities do not necessarily limit their utility in analysing the prison. For the task is not to identify a rigid distribution of power, but rather to appreciate its complexity. In avoiding the temptation to begin research with a unitary notion of what a 'woman in prison' is, needs, or feels, the researcher fosters a deeper understanding of the complexity of power. Examining women's testimonies about how prison has changed their sense of identity helps to destabilize the seeming immutability of the treatment of women in prison. It illuminates the finer details of the effects of imprisonment, and uncovers the conflicting ways that regimes of femininity both undermine and bolster the women's sense of identity. For, as the women themselves recognized, if only they could be considered as agents, there were many more alternative possible choices and expressions of agency than those which are commonly conceptualized in penal practice and analysis:

Eleanor: *I don't think the choices are broad enough, and I don't think the choices are in the right things … you know, when you look at the facts at what type of women are in prison, a lot of the women who are in prison, about 99 per cent of them have been sexually abused – either raped or sexually abused –*
Zora: *Mentally unstable basically –*
Eleanor: *But not mentally unstable. It's women who, through their experience, what's happened to them they could become counsellors. They could become drug counsellors, rape counsellors –*
Bell: *It's true, it's true –*
Eleanor: *Child abuse counsellors –*
Betty: *Something that they know about … turn the tables on their bad experiences –*
Bell: *'Cos judges they've never had any experience of offending, they all come from well-off families, they've never been skint, so if someone …*
Eleanor: *… Probation officers, all of those types of jobs. A lot of the women would be more than capable of doing them.*

Notes

1   Of course, many of these intellectual difficulties predate the historical events of 1989/ 91, going back at least to 1968, or perhaps to the growing disaffection of the left with communism following the 1956 Soviet invasion of Hungary (see for example, E.P. Thompson 1978; Rowbotham 1979: 21–42). For some recent attempts to reconceptualize ideology and power by ex-Marxist feminists, see Fraser 1997. See also Laclau and Mouffe's classic *Hegemony and Socialist Strategy: Towards a Radical Democratic Politics*, (1985) and I.M. Young's critique of Fraser's new approach (1997).

2   In particular, resistance has been used to recast the history of slavery in America. According to Laura Fishman – who is also known for her work with the wives of US prisoners – 'resistance was carried off both overtly in the form of slave rebellions, and overtly in the form of indirect attacks on the system through resistance to the whip, feigning illness, conscious laziness and other means of avoiding work and impeding production' (Fishman 1995: 37; see also Fox-Genovese 1988, 1990). As Toni Morrison's disturbing novel *Beloved* demonstrates so powerfully, infanticide was perhaps the ultimate form of resistance exercised by some women (Morrison 1988).

3   Here Brown is referring to Foucault's discussion of power in Volume One of *The History of Sexuality*. Although Foucault says 'where there is power, there is resistance', he then proceeds to query whether acts of resistance challenge power relations (Foucault 1980a: 95). For a variety of feminist applications of Foucault's notion of resistance, see the edited collection by Diamond and Quinby (1988).

4   See Wright and Decker's (1994) study of residential burglars which challenges the validity of rational choice models.

5   See Bottoms et al. 1990 and Sparks et al. 1996: Chapter 2 for an exploration of theories of situational and social crime prevention in men's prisons.

6   See Sandel (1982: Chapter 4) for a similar criticism of Rawls' articulation of choice. According to Sandel, 'Rawls' limited account of agency and reflection are implausible in themselves, incapable of making sense of what choice and deliberation could possibly consist in' (Sandel 1982: 161).

7   For a similar argument, see I.M. Young's criticism of the primacy accorded to 'impartiality' in modern theories of morality and justice (I.M. Young 1990: Chapter 4). According to Young, 'The ideal of impartial moral reason corresponds to the Enlightenment ideal of the public realm of politics as attaining the universality of a general will that leaves difference, particularity and the body behind in the private realms of the family and civil society' (I.M. Young 1990: 97).

8   See Foucault (1979: 231–56) for a discussion of the symbolic role played by the prison in reinforcing the ideal of liberty.

9   Although prisoners were able to request vegetarian, vegan, Halal and Kosher meals, their requests for special diets were often not met (see below).

10   Due in large part to a learning difficulty which was only belatedly identified in prison.

11   It is this association which Smart challenges in her article 'Deconstructing Motherhood' (Smart 1996). By indicating the historical and sociological assumptions implicit in ideas and practices of maternity, Smart points to the ways in which discourses of motherhood are used to police all women (Smart 1996: 46–56).

Conclusion
Women's Imprisonment:
Conclusions and New Directions

The deliberate infliction of pain on another person – that is what punishment inexorably is – should require an anxious concern for its purposes and some knowledge of its effects. (Morris 1994: vii)

We need to make a space for an understanding of self-identity and autonomy which will not clash with our conviction that individuals must be understood as embedded, embodied, localized, constituted, and fragmented, as well as subject to forces beyond our control. We need to understand ourselves clearly as actors capable of learning, of changing, of making the world and ourselves better. (Weir 1995: 263)

Now they're sending more and more people to prison as well. They're not giving people an option. (Hester: HMP Winchester, February 1996)

The twin issues of agency and identity have been the central organizational and intellectual motifs of this book. They have provided both the means of critique and the mechanisms of analysis. I have used them to re-examine criminological accounts of imprisonment and women in prison. Building on the traditions of prison studies, I have demonstrated that power relations in prison are continually contested. I have argued that prisoners, in defiance of their limited choices and opportunities, strive to present themselves as independent agents. In particular, I have shown that women manage their experiences of imprisonment by drawing on their sense of self which they ground in their (feminine) identities as mothers, wives, girlfriends and lovers. In short, I have argued that identity plays a key role in women's management of the pains of imprisonment and in their ability to resist.

However, since most constitutive elements of the prisoners' self-image are destabilized or derogated, there is an asymmetrical negotiation of identity and behaviour in prison. Autonomy, agency and choice are all restricted, and (sexual, ethnic, age) difference is homogenized under a universalizing penal regime. Moreover, the women arrive in prison already carrying 'spoiled' and 'stigmatized' identities – both as offenders and as victims – so that their individual autonomy and power have already been destabilized (Goffman 1963). Once incarcerated, the women have had their vulnerability compounded by the triple practice of 'infantilization, medicalization, and domesticization' which characterizes their treatment by the authorities (Carlen 1983; 1985). In short, they are cast in roles as ineffective, disempowered, feminine subjects. Under these circumstances, the women's opportunity to be, and to perceive themselves as, agents is greatly reduced.

Nevertheless, or perhaps because of these contradictions, identity remains a crucial site of the negotiation of power in prison. In particular, much of the battle in women's prisons is fought in terms of femininity. Despite the prison's ostensibly greater power of definition – given that it has the weight of the law behind it – the women resist homogeneity. As in White's account of 'Mrs. G.' (White 1991), the women in prison may act unexpectedly and in contrast to the received wisdom about their 'low self-esteem' and poor coping. Instead they may, like Simone, present themselves as assertive. Or else, like Maya, they may affirm their cultural traditions, even when they realize that others do not fully understand them. They may claim – as Drucilla did – the identity of a 'good mother', despite failing to conform to societal expectations of appropriate behaviour. Although a hegemonic notion of passive femininity continues to underpin much of the management and criminological assessment of female imprisonment, thereby appearing as both the goal and the form of women's punishment, it does not pass unchallenged. Rather, as this text has demonstrated, women co-opt elements from the dominant notion of 'femininity' to reinforce their own sense of self, and to challenge aspects of the penal regime.

In light of this situation, it becomes possible to suggest future directions for criminological thinking about imprisonment. I contend that a consideration of agency, identity and resistance can provide the basis for a new analysis of the prison, since together they reveal that the relationship between power and punishment is always shaped by that between gender, ethnicity and class. Such an approach, moreover, bridges the gap between theoretical explorations of punishment and practical descriptions of imprisonment by demonstrating the grounded nature of all configurations of power; illuminating how the legitimacy of the prison is constantly being negotiated by the prison population. Furthermore, it reveals how the ability to resist in circumstances of confinement is to some extent dependent on a coherent sense of self rather than simply on instrumental choices or opportunities. A full understanding of how prisoners evaluate their experiences of imprisonment is impossible without knowing who the prisoners are in a sociological or socio-cultural way. Without such knowledge, it becomes difficult to recognize motivation or desire, or even to imagine alternatives. Finally, examining the relationship between agency, identity and resistance introduces fresh ideas into prison studies, thereby justifying Sparks, Bottoms and Hay's belief that '[i]t may well be that the most illuminating perspectives on prisons actually originate elsewhere, in the study of other institutions, or in more general theoretical debates' (Sparks et al. 1996: 33).

Resisting Identities: Formulating a Gendered Understanding of Power

The interrelated notions of identity, agency and resistance can establish a new 'criminological imagination' and a strategy of critique by encouraging criminologists to engage with literature outside the discipline. As I have shown, there is a major resonance between women's accounts of prison and aspects of the discussion of agency and subjectivity in the feminist and critical theoretical literature on identity politics, since so many of the metaphors used by the women when speaking about the effect of imprisonment relate to subjectivity and identity. While criminologists and prison service administrators have long acknowledged that prisoners should be considered as agents within the ongoing negotiation of daily life inside, there has been little corresponding attempt to represent the prisoners in other than psychological ways. It is arguable that such lack of attention to identity has marginalized ethnicity and gender in analyses of punishment and imprisonment. Although there have been studies of the effect of prison on women since Elizabeth Fry transformed the prisoners at Newgate by a combination of prayer and education, most discussions of imprisonment and punishment have rarely considered women. Similarly, even though minority and female prisoners have been a topic of sociological analysis since the 1960s, contemporary criminologists routinely exclude a detailed appraisal of gender or ethnicity from mainstream prison studies. Finally, despite the introduction of masculinity to criminology, gender is rarely considered in relation to men's prisons. All in all, it is necessary to look beyond criminology for an account of the relationship between agency and identity.

According to Braidotti and others, 'identity' has become the central point of analysis for contemporary feminist theory (Braidotti 1994). Although much dispute surrounds the essentialism at the heart of 'identity politics', it is generally agreed that the 'politics of recognition' have given new life to a series of social movements and to feminist research. The analysis of subjectivity has enabled feminists to respond to criticisms of the implicit racism and heterosexism of the women's movement. Thus, as Braidotti writes, 'feminist analyses of the gender system show that the subject occupies a variety of possible positions at different times, across a multiplicity of variables such as sex, race, class, age lifestyles, and so on' (Braidotti 1994: 157). Moreover, and more radically, feminist work on identity has fractured the stability previously accorded to subjectivity by psychologists and philosophers:

> The challenge for feminist theorists today is how to invent new images of thought that can help us think about change and changing constructions of the self. Not the staticness of formulated truths or readily available counteridentities, but the living process of transformation of self and other. (Braidotti 1994: 157)

In other words, if identity is always in process, then resistance and change may be possible both in our understanding and in the practices of gender. By implication, if we accept that constitutive elements of identity influence people's access to power, it may be that there is greater cause for optimism about social change than previously thought.

Ethnicity, sexuality, age, experiences of abuse and a sense of alienation, all help to determine women's lives in the community and in prison. As Howe writes:

> The woman imprisoned in a Western penal institution is not a stable subject. She is constituted as part of a highly diversified population of long- and short-term prisoners, ethnically and racially mixed, heterosexual and lesbian women. (Howe 1994: 170)

Consequently, identity can be a disruptive influence as well as a unifying one. Mapping the constitution of prisoners' identities lays bare the influence of socio-economic and cultural factors on the form and experience of punishment. For some prisoners, like the foreign nationals, or the Black British women, the significance of ethnicity and class are readily apparent. Practical choices and opportunities for these women are further reduced in prison, since few institutions cater for different language or culture groups. Because of racial stereotypes which are implicit within both the criminal justice system and throughout society, these women will also have to negotiate a series of implicit and explicit expectations about their behaviour and identities. The colour of a woman's skin is a determining factor of her experience of imprisonment. However, as has been asserted above, the women in the prisons I visited did not arrange themselves solely in terms of their ethnicity. Rather, class was often of greater organizational force. Elements of identity intersect with each other, meaning that no single aspect is constantly prioritized (Daly 1997).

Offences are another category of association since crimes are given differential status. Most commonly, women serving sentences for child abuse, or for other morally deplored crimes, are forced into a community. Thus, for example, in HMRC Pucklechurch the women on the hospital wing, many of whom were on Rule 43 for their own protection, formed a distinct group which was entirely separate to the women on the other landings. On occasion, class and offence intersect to forge specific identities. For example, at HMP/YOI Drake Hall the women who had stolen money from their employers formed a separate group. These middle-class women like Betty and Hélène rarely associated with the mainstream incarcerated population, and instead organized themselves into a small band of law-abiding and rule-following inmates. The other prisoners were often extremely critical of these women, accusing them of greed and snobbery.

Along with race/ethnicity and class, gender also provides the grounds for group and personal identification in prison. As feminists have long argued, ideals of femininity are crucial to women's self-identities inside and outside prison. Such ideals have typically been characterized as key factors in the oppression of women in prison (Carlen 1983). However, as I have indicated in this text, women themselves often invoke the ideals of femininity in order to resist the pains of imprisonment. Crucially, they lay claim to traditional feminine identities *despite failing to adhere to many of the key norms associated with those identities*. Thus, for example, they identify themselves as 'good mothers' even though their children may have been removed from their care by the state. They take great pains over their physical appearance even though they see the same people on their prison wing every day for months at a time. They insist on their biological needs, despite being (hetero)sexually inactive for long periods of time. In all these ways, women in prison rely on ideals of femininity to reinforce their sense of self as purposeful and strong. Do their actions simply entangle them more comprehensively in subordinate positions, or in fact are the women utilizing femininity in order to empower themselves?

Undoubtedly, a hegemonic notion of femininity does exist. Yet few women in prison adhered to it. For example, although the dominant ideal of a 'good mother' in Western society is a heterosexual, married, white, middle-class woman, many, or even most, of the prisoners do not exhibit any of the socio-economic or cultural characteristics of such an ideal type. None the less, the women still claim for themselves the qualities, such as domesticity, care, reassurance and responsibility, which are implicit within the ideal of maternity. Does their adherence to these values mean that the prisoners are totally oppressed? Or, rather, can the women's alternative interpretations and representations be understood as expanding the meaning of 'motherhood'? That is to say, can alternative definitions of identity be harnessed by the women or by the criminologist to challenge the received wisdom about femininity, punishment or the prison? Or is change and resistance impossible?

The Paradox of Resistance: New Directions?

As should by now be clear, women's experiences of imprisonment are configured by a series of paradoxes: women in prison are both victims and victimizers. They have special needs, yet defining them solely by these needs can be disempowering. Perhaps most surprisingly, women draw strength from similar ideals of femininity to those which oppress them. Their ability to be agents and thus to negotiate power appears to rest on qualities other than those present within the prison. For, despite their restricted choices and opportunities inside, they manage to resist. However, it is necessary to be careful not to overstate the case, since many of the women in prison are extremely vulnerable and may feel that they are left with no options other than cutting up (Liebling 1992, 1994).[1] The ability to resist oppression or inequality only makes sense in terms of evaluation, indicating once again that issues of identity must always be recognized.

Finally, it is necessary to acknowledge the contradiction that, although many of the key pains of imprisonment are a result of the prison's assault on women's sense of self, the prison can provide opportunities for the prisoners to review their outside identities. A number of women claimed that being inside had enabled them to question their lives and roles on the outside. For example, Betty queried her role as homemaker, by planning to go back to university: '*I've been studying on the [NOW] course [at Drake Hall] and I've been getting good marks in what I've done and I've proved to myself I can do it.*' Angela was harshly criticized by the other women for her involvement with an abusive man, and resolved to change her lifestyle once she was released. Both she and Hester believed that they would finally be able to give up drugs. In Hester's words: '*I've decided that I want to go off the drugs, because I've had enough of the drugs. Enough of having nowhere to live that I've got off my back side, that I've decided "yes, I don't want to come back to prison again".*' Like the women in Eaton's study, these three prisoners were able to re-evaluate to some degree their lives and their selves in prison (Eaton 1993).[2] What are the implications of these paradoxes? Can they form the basis for a new, theoretically driven, feminist criminology?

Criminologists rarely consider the symbolic effects of prisoners' abilities to devise counter-hegemonic acts of interpretation, however contingent. Instead, according to feminist criminological studies, female offenders' divergence from 'appropriate' mothering usually has dire effects – increasing their likelihood of receiving a custodial sentence and the possibility that their children will be removed from their care by the state (Eaton 1986). Such critical work has been of great importance for challenging the supposed 'objectivity' of magistrates' and judges' sentencing. Supported by convincing statistical proof, its substantive findings are unassailable. However, I would contend that there are other ways of appreciating women's alternative expressions of motherhood, or of sexuality, appearance and deference. In particular, I believe that women's attachment to the same ideals that are typically seen to oppress them indicates that there may be a liberationist potential within them. For, if we listen to the prisoners' voices, and give them sufficient space, it becomes possible to discern the boundaries of the current dominant definition. Many women in Britain experience a range of not dissimilar economic hardships as the women in prison since ethnicity and sexuality define choices, opportunities and identities throughout society. Why should criminologists and others insist on writing as if there is only one important way of being a woman? Instead, might it not be possible that a series of alternative definitions exist, simultaneously challenging and reinforcing a dominant definition of femininity?

Women in prison who identify themselves as 'good mothers', despite being unable to provide economically for their children, despite living outside a monogamous heterosexual unit, or having a drug problem, or engaging in differential ethnic practises of parenting, contradict the constitutive elements of the dominant values associated with motherhood. They may denaturalize its 'common sense' associations (Smart 1996). If they are given full weight and consideration, the women's representations of their identities can, therefore, be profoundly challenging. Yet, women in prison need to be considered as agents instead of victims if their stories are to be heard and considered. Thus the meaning of 'agency' needs to be recast to include symbolic and small-scale acts of resistance instead of simple, instrumental ability 'to get things done'. 'Resistance' is an evocative term that enables the criminologist to include many actions previously excluded from an analysis of power. As a result, power is shown to be relational rather than fixed or hierarchical. And once it is viewed that way, change is always possible.

Towards a New Criminological Imagination

Women in prison have recently become the object of much official and popular attention in Britain. Throughout February and March 1997, a discussion of female imprisonment featured regularly in the newspapers, in Parliament and on radio. Articles on women's prisons even appeared in

162   *Engendering Resistance*

Sainsbury's The Magazine (Hennessey 1997). Issues under debate have included: health and safety and time in cell at HMP Holloway (*The Guardian*, 19 December–21 December 1995), cell sizes at HMP/HMRC Eastwood Park (HMCIP 1996), the practice of shackling pregnant women in hospital and the high number of suicides in Scotland's only prison for women, HMP Cornton Vale (Galloway 1997). While these last two situations in particular have forced a reappraisal of women's psychological, medical and emotional treatment inside, the others have demonstrated an urgent need for renewal of the fabric of much of the women's estate. Finally, the completion of the Prison Inspectorate's thematic review (HMCIP 1997) appears to have inspired the formation of a new managerial section within the prison service, designed to concentrate on women's needs (Prison Service, March 1997).

Looking simply at the critical, public attention which has been given to these issues, it might be tempting to believe that women's prisons are about to alter in a drastic way. It could almost be possible to imagine that the decarceration movement of the 1980s is about to be reborn (Carlen 1990). At the very least, it might seem reasonable to hope that there will be some pragmatic improvements – more counselling, more time out of cell and less reliance upon medication. In reality, however, there are few grounds for optimism. Rather, within the rhetoric of austerity which characterizes prison service policy today, there is scant likelihood for change either for women or men. Despite the *possibility* of transformation, it is probable that women will simply continue to be situated uneasily within the official discourse of punishment. Their treatment will be excused – as it always has been – because of their small numbers, the limited establishments available and the difficulties caused by their mental health problems.

In England and Wales, prison numbers are up and, indeed, are rising faster than ever before. No matter whether or not 'prison works', its legitimacy seems to be assured. In the overall dramatic increase of prison numbers, the population of women in prison has been increasing at double the rate of men (PAC 1996). New female establishments are being opened with increased frequency since female overcrowding has reached such an extent that former male prisons are being 're-roled' to cater for women. Notwithstanding the fact that women in prison continue in great majority to serve short sentences for minor crimes, and often have no previous convictions, for the most part they appear to have been adversely affected by the new sentencing practices. Despite all the public criticisms, and regardless of its manifest failure to 'solve' the crime problem through reform or rehabilitation, the prison continues to serve as one of the most common forms of punishment for all law-breaking. There is little reason to hope for amendment – unless it is possible to develop new ways of thinking critically about imprisonment. In sum, there is a clear need for a new 'criminological imagination'.

Following Worrall, I believe that, '[a]lthough women offenders are subject to a matrix of controlling and oppressive mechanisms, they do not respond totally passively. They do find ways of eluding control and of challenging professionals' (Worrall 1996: 74). Thus, despite the rigour of the prison regimes and the overwhelming power of the institution, most of the women I interviewed were not completely incapacitated. They found ways to express their religious beliefs, their sexuality and their creativity. They even were able to fight and win disputes with the establishment. In order to challenge both the understanding and the treatment of women in prison, the criminologist ought to listen and respond to the prisoners. For, as Patricia and Olympia point out, the women themselves have much to offer.

> Patricia: *[Prison] makes you stronger. It definitely makes you stronger. Because every time they put you down and you get back up, it seems like a test. Like they're testing you ... And every time you overcome that test, you feel it in yourself, you feel 'well yes, I overcame that. I didn't kick off like they wanted me to, or like they expected me to I held it down, I got on with it.' You don't realise it when you're in here. I only realised it when I went home for five days on a home leave. That is when I really noticed it. Because in here you don't really see it and in the end you won't really notice it until you leave. But it does, it makes you stronger as a person. It makes you stronger as to when you get out you can deal with certain situations quite easy, whereas people on the out are all like 'oh my God what do I do, what do I do?'*
> Olympia: *But that's not giving them credit. That's us, that's us. In ourselves, our own strength.*
> Patricia: *That's us yeah.*
> Olympia: *That's giving ourselves credit.*

Yet, if their resistance is, ultimately, to 'go anywhere in particular' (Brown 1995), they must be recognized and heard. For that to occur, criminologists must speak out, both on practical and conceptual issues.

Notes

1　While attention is more commonly given attempted suicides among young men in custody, a spate of deaths in the Scottish establishment Cornton Vale in 1996/97 tragically proved that women in prison are also severely at risk (Galloway 1997). Indeed, as work by Alison Liebling has suggested, women in prison commit suicide as frequently as men, yet often their deaths are classified differently (Liebling 1994).

2　However, fundamental problems obviously remain. For example, almost all the women claimed that the prison ought to provide a more supportive environment, with more counselling, so that women would be able to consider options. Furthermore, many women felt that they had reconsidered and decided to change, and still had a long time left to serve, during which period they became progressively more aggressive or frustrated. Finally, external factors often intervene, such as when a flat is repossessed by the council, or a child is adopted without the mother's consent. Under all these circumstances, personal change was impeded regardless of the women's intentions.

Appendix

Prison questionnaire

General

1. How old are you?
2. Where are you from?
3. How would you describe your ethnic origin?
4. Is this your first time in prison?
5. Were you in another prison before you were sent to here? How did they differ?

Routine Activities

6. How do you spend a normal weekday in here?
7. What is there to do on the weekends?
8. What do you think about the work/education/activities which are offered here? What do you think they are trying to teach you? What kinds of other things do you think they should offer, if any?
9. What sorts of needs do you think women in prison have? Do you think Drake Hall/Winchester/Pucklechurch meets these needs?

Relationships

10. How do the women get along with each other here? Is Drake Hall/Winchester/Pucklechurch different to any other prisons you've been to?
11. Do women tend to hang out with a small number of other women, or is everyone friendly with everybody else?
12. Is there any tension between different groups of prisoners?
13. What kinds of things do you value in your friendships with the women in Drake Hall/Winchester/Pucklechurch?

14.   Do you feel that the friendships you have on the inside are different to the ones you have outside? If so, how?
15.   How do the women get along with the staff in here?
16.   Do you feel that the staff treat all prisoners equally?
17.   In what ways does being in prison change the ways you deal with people and situations?

Choices

18.   Do women go along with the main rules and regulations of Drake Hall/Winchester/Pucklechurch? If so, why? And which rules do they break?
19.   Are the rules and regulations applied fairly and consistently?
20.   What do you do if there is something upsetting you, or something that you want to change in here?
21.   Do you feel like your ability to plan and act to fulfil your plans has changed over the time that you have been in prison? What institutional factors seem to affect planning or choice?

Aims and Effects of Imprisonment

22.   Do you think that your time in prison has changed you in any way?
23.   Can you remember how you felt when you first arrived? How did you change or adapt to prison life in the first few weeks?
24.   Where can you feel most 'yourself' in here?
25.   Can you think of anything about being in prison that is different for women than for men?
26.   Are the Black or Asian women treated any differently in here to the other women?
27.   What aspects of prison create the greatest demands on you? What skills and behaviours have you learnt in order to deal with prison?
28.   Has your time in prison helped you to develop any alternatives to your life outside?
29.   What do you think prison is for, and do you think it works? If not, why do you think we still have prisons?
30.   What alternatives to prison do you think there should be?

References

Acker, J., Barry, K. and Esseveld, J. (1991) 'Objectivity and Truth: Problems in Doing Feminist Research' in Fonow, M. M. and Cook, J. A. (eds) *Beyond Methodology: Feminist Scholarship as Lived Research*, Bloomington: Indiana University Press.

Adams, R. (1992) *Prison Riots in Britain and the U.S.A.*, London: Macmillan.

Adler, M. and Longhurst, B. (1994) *Discourse, Power and Justice: Towards a New Sociology of Imprisonment*, London: Routledge.

Adorno, T. and Horkheimer, M. (1972, 1979) *Dialectic of Enlightenment*, London: Verso.

Allen, H. (1987a) *Justice Unbalanced*, Milton Keynes: Open University Press.

Allen, H. (1987b) 'Rendering Them Harmless: The Professional Portrayal of Women Charged with Serious Violent Crimes' in Carlen, P. and Worrall, A. (eds) *Gender, Crime and Justice*, Milton Keynes: Open University Press.

Arrigo, B. (1993) *Madness, Language and the Law*, Albany, NY: Harrow and Heston.

Barrett, M. (1980, 1988) *Women's Oppression Today: The Marxist/Feminist Encounter*, London: Verso.

Barthes, R. (1973) *Mythologies*, St Albans: Paladin.

Bartky, S. (1988) 'Foucault, Femininity, and the Modernization of Patriarchal Power' in Diamond, I. and Quinby, L. (eds) *Feminism and Foucault: Reflections on Resistance*, Boston: Northeastern University Press.

Bauman, Z. (1989) *Modernity and the Holocaust*, Cambridge: Polity Press.

Bauman, Z. (1993) *Postmodern Ethics*, Oxford: Blackwell.

Beck, U. (1992) *Risk Society: Towards a New Modernity*, London: SAGE Publications.

Becker, H. (1963) *Outsiders*, New York: Free Press.

Becker, H. (1967) 'Whose Side Are We On?', *Social Problems*, 14: 239–47.

Beetham, D. (1991) *The Legitimation of Power*, London: Macmillan.

Benhabib, S. (1987) 'The Generalized and the Concrete Other: The

Kohlberg-Gilligan Controversy and Feminist Theory' in Benhabib, S. and Cornell, D. (eds) *Feminism as Critique*, Cambridge: Polity Press.

Benhabib, S. (1992) *Situating the Self: Gender, Community and Postmodernism in Contemporary Ethics*, Cambridge: Polity Press.

Benhabib, S., Butler, J., Cornell, D. and Fraser, N. (1995) *Feminist Contentions: A Philosophical Exchange*, New York: Routledge.

Benhabib, S. and Cornell, D. (eds) (1987) *Feminism as Critique*, Cambridge: Polity Press.

Bentham, J. (1787, 1995) *The Panopticon Writings*, London: Verso.

Berlin, I. (1969) *Four Essays on Liberty*, Oxford: Oxford University Press.

Bettleheim, B. (1960) *The Informed Heart*, Glencoe: Free Press.

Bordo, S. (1993) *Unbearable Weight: Feminism, Western Culture and the Body*, Berkeley, CA: University of California Press.

Bortolaia Silva, E. (ed.) (1996) *Good Enough Mothering? Feminist Perspectives on Lone Mothering*, London: Routledge.

Bosworth, M. (1998) 'The Imprisoned Subject: Agency and Identity in Prison', *Social Pathology: A Journal of Reviews*, 4(1): 48–54.

Bosworth, M. and Liebling, A. (1995) *Incentives in Prison Regimes: A Review of the Literature*, London: HMSO.

Bottoms, A. E. (1990) 'The Aims of Imprisonment' in Garland, D. (ed.) *Justice, Guilt and Forgiveness in the Penal System*, Edinburgh: University of Edinburgh Centre for Theology and Public Issues.

Bottoms, A. E. (1995) 'The Philosophy and Politics of Punishment and Sentencing' in Clarkson, C., and Morgan, R. (eds) *The Politics of Sentencing Reform*, Oxford: Clarendon Press.

Bottoms, A. and Light, R. (eds) (1987) *Problems of Long-Term Imprisonment*, Aldershot: Gower.

Bottoms, A., Hay, W. and Sparks, R. (1990) 'Situational and social approaches To the Prevention of Disorder in Long-Term Prisons', *The Prison Journal*, 70: 83–95.

Bourdieu, P. (1977) *Outline of a Theory of Practice*, Cambridge: Cambridge University Press.

Box, S., and Hale, C. (1985). 'Unemployment, Imprisonment and Prison Overcrowding', *Contemporary Crises*, 9: 209–28.

Braggins, J. (1998) 'Twelve Months of Labour', *Prison Service Journal*, 117: 10–11.

Braidotti, R. (1991) *Patterns of Dissonance: A Study of Women in Contemporary Philosophy*, Cambridge: Polity Press.

Braidotti, R. (1994) *Nomadic Subjects: Embodiment and Sexual Difference in Contemporary Feminist Theory*, New York: Columbia University Press.

Brown, L. M. and Gilligan, C. (1992) *Meeting at the Crossroads: Women's Psychology and Girls' Development*, New York: Ballantine Books.

Brown, W. (1995) *States of Injury: Power and Freedom in Late Modernity*, Princeton, NJ: Princeton University Press.

Bryman, A. (1988) *Quantity and Quality in Social Research*, London: Unwin Hyman.

Bryman, A. and Burgess, R. G. (eds) (1994) *Analyzing Qualitative Data*, London: Routledge.

Burgess, R. (1990) *Reflections on Field Experience*, London: JAI Press Inc.

Burgess, R. G. (1984) *In the Field*, London: Allen and Unwin.

Butler, J. (1987) 'Variations on Sex and Gender: Beauvoir, Wittig and Foucault' in Benhabib, S. and Cornell, D. (eds) *Feminism As Critique*, Cambridge: Polity Press.

Butler, J. (1990) *Gender Trouble: Feminism and the Subversion of Identity*, New York: Routledge.

Butler, J. (1991) 'Imitation and Gender Subordination' in Fuss, D. (ed.) *Inside/Out: Lesbian Theories, Gay Theories*, New York: Routledge.

Butler, J. (1992) 'Contingent Foundations: Feminism and the Question of "Postmodernism"' in Butler, J. and Scott, J. (eds) *Feminists Theorize the Political*, London: Routledge.

Butler, J. (1993) *Bodies That Matter: On the Discursive Limits of 'Sex'*, New York: Routledge.

Butler, J. (1995) 'For a Careful Reading', in S. Benhabib et al. (eds) *Feminist Contentions: A Philosophical Exchange*, New York: Routledge.

Cain, M. (1986) 'Realism, Feminism, Methodology and Law', *International Journal of the Sociology of Law*, 14(3/4): 255–67.

Cain, M. (1989) *Growing Up Good: Policing the Behaviour of Girls in Europe*, London, SAGE.

Cain, M. (1990) 'Towards Transgression: New Directions in Feminist Criminology', *International Journal of the Sociology of Law*, 18(1): 1–18.

Calhoun, C. (ed.) (1994) *Social Theory and the Politics of Identity*, New York: Blackwell.

Calhoun, C. (1995) *Critical Social Theory: Culture, History and the Challenge of Difference*, Oxford: Blackwell.

Campbell, A. (1981) 'Interviewing Women: A Contradiction in Terms?' in Roberts, H. (ed.) *Doing Feminist Research*, London: Routledge and Kegan Paul.

Caplan, P. (1987) *The Cultural Construction of Sexuality*, London: Tavistock.

Carlen, P. (1983) *Women's Imprisonment: A Study in Social Control*, London: Routledge and Kegan Paul.

Carlen, P. (ed.) (1985) *Criminal Women: Autobiographical Accounts*, Cambridge: Polity Press.

Carlen, P. (1988) *Women, Crime and Poverty*, Milton Keynes: Open University Press.

Carlen, P. (1990) *Alternatives to Women's Imprisonment*, Milton Keynes: Open University Press.

Carlen, P. (1992) 'Criminal Women and Criminal Justice: The Limits to, and Potential of, Feminist and Left Realist Perspectives' in Matthews, R. and Young, J. (eds) *Issues in Realist Criminology*, London: SAGE Publications Ltd.

Carlen, P. (1994) 'Why Study Women's Imprisonment? Or Anyone Else's? An indefinite article', *British Journal of Criminology*, 34 (Special Issue on Prisons): 131–40.

Carlen, P. (1995) 'Virginia, Crime and the Antisocial Control of Women' in Blomberg, T. G. and Cohen, S. (eds) *Punishment and Social Control: Essays in Honor of Sheldon L. Messinger*, New York: Aldine de Gruyter.

Carlen, P. and Tchaikovsky, C. (1996) 'Women's Imprisonment at the End of the Twentieth Century: Legitimacy, Realities and Utopias' in Matthews, R. and Francis, P. (eds) *Prisons 2000: An International Perspective on the Current State and Future of Imprisonment*, London: Macmillan Press Ltd.

Carlen, P. and Worrall, A. (eds) (1987a) *Gender, Crime and Justice*, Milton Keynes: Open University Press.

Carlen, P. and Worrall, A. (1987b) 'Introduction: Gender, Crime and Justice' in Carlen, P. and Worrall, A. (eds) *Gender, Crime and Justice*, Milton Keynes: Open University Press.

Carpenter, M. (1872) *Reformatory Prison Discipline*, London: Longman.

Carr, E. H. (1964) *What is History?* Harmondsworth: Penguin.

Carrabine, E. (1998) *Power, Discourse and Disorder: An Analysis of Strangeways Prison Riot*, Ph.D. Thesis, Department of Sociology: University of Salford.

Carrabine, E. and Longhurst, B. (1998). 'Gender and Prison Organisation: Some Comments on Masculinities and Prison Management', *The Howard Journal*, 37(2): 161–76.

Carroll, L. (1974) *Hacks, Blacks and Cons: Race Relations in a Maximum Security Prison*, Lexington, DC: Heath and Company.

Catan, L. (1992) 'Infants with Mothers in Prison' in Shaw, R. (ed.) *Prisoners' Children: What Are the Issues?*, London: Routledge.

Cavadino, M. and Dignan, J. (1992) *The Penal System: An Introduction*, London: Sage.

Chesney-Lind, M. (1977) 'Judicial Paternalism and the Female Status Offender: Training Women to Know their Place', *Crime and Delinquency*, 23: 121–30.

Chesney-Lind, M. (1996) 'Sentencing Women to Prison: Equality Without Justice' in Schwartz, M. and Milovanovic, D. (eds) *Race, Gender, and Class in Criminology: The Intersection*, New York: Garland Publishing.

Chodorow, N. (1978) *The Reproduction of Mothering: Psychoanalysis and the Sociology of Gender*, Berkeley: University of California Press.

Christie, N. (1993) *Crime Control As Industry*, London: Routledge.

Cixous, H. (1981) 'The Laugh of the Medusa' in Marks, E. and de Courtivron, I. (eds) *New French Feminisms: An Anthology*, Brighton: The Harvester Press.

Clarke, R. (1980) 'Situational Crime Prevention: Theory and Practice', *British Journal of Criminology*, 20: 136–47.

Clear, T., Stout, B., Dammer, H., Kelly, L., Hardyman, P. and Shapiro, C. (1992) 'Does Involvement in Religion Help Prisoners Adjust to Prison?', *NCCD Focus*, November.

Clemmer, D. (1940, 1958) *The Prison Community*, New York: Holt, Rinehart and Wilson.

Code, L. (1991) *What Can She Know? Feminist Theory and the Construction of Knowledge*, Ithaca: Cornell University Press.

Cohen, S. (1992) *The Evolution of Women's Asylums Since 1500: From Refuges for Ex-Prostitutes to Shelters for Battered Women*, New York: Oxford University Press.

Cohen, S. (1985) *Visions of Social Control*, Cambridge: Polity Press.

Cohen, S. (1988) *Against Criminology*, New Brunswick, NJ: Transaction Books.

Cohen, S. and Taylor, L. (1972) *Psychological Survival*, Harmondsworth: Penguin.

Cohen, S. and Taylor, L. (1976) *Prison Secrets*, London: Penguin Books.

Cohen, S. and Taylor, L. (1978) *Escape Attempts: The Theory and Practice of Resistance to Everyday Life*, Harmondsworth: Penguin Books.

Collins, P. H. (1990) *Black Feminist Thought: Knowledge, Consciousness and the Politics of Empowerment*, Boston: Unwin Hyman.

Collins, P. H. (1991) 'Learning from the Outsider Within: The Sociological Significance of Black Feminist Thought' in Fonow, M. M., and Cook, J. A. (eds) *Beyond Methodology: Feminist Scholarship as Lived Research*, Bloomington: Indiana University Press.

Collins, P. H. (1993) 'Towards a New Vision: Race, Class and Gender as Categories of Analysis and Connection', *Race, Sex and Class*, 1(1): 3–11.

Connell, R. (1987) *Gender and Power*, Cambridge: Polity Press.

Cook, D. and Hudson, B. (eds) (1993) *Racism and Criminology*, London: SAGE Publications.

Cooper, D. (1995) *Power in Struggle: Feminism, Sexuality and the State*, Buckingham: Open University Press.

Cornell, D. (1995) *The Imaginary Domain: Abortion, Pornography and Sexual Harassment*, London: Routledge.

172   *Engendering Resistance*

Cundy, S. (1995) *An Evaluation of Anger Management Groupwork With Women Prisoners*, East Anglia Area Psychology Unit.
Daly, K. (1994) *Gender, Crime, and Punishment*, New Haven: Yale University Press.
Daly, K. (1997) 'Different Ways of Conceptualizing Sex/Gender in Feminist Theory and their Implications for Criminology', *Theoretical Criminology*, 1(1): 25–51.
Daly, M. (1978) *Gyn/Ecology: The Metaethics of Radical Feminism*, Boston: Beacon Press.
Daniels, N. (ed.) (1975) *Reading Rawls: Critical Studies on Rawls' 'A Theory of Justice'*, Oxford: Basil Blackwell.
de Beaumont, G. and de Tocqueville, A. (1833; 1970) *On the Penitentiary System in the United States and Its Application in France*, New York: Augustus M. Kelley.
de Beauvoir, S. (1953) *The Second Sex*, London: Pan Books Ltd.
de Certeau, M. (1984) *The Practice of Everyday Life*, Los Angeles: University of California Press.
Deleuze, G. and Guattari, F. (1977) *Capitalism and Schizophrenia: The Anti-Oedipus*, New York: Viking.
Denzin, N. (1994) 'The Art and Politics of Interpretation' in Denzin, N. and Lincoln, Y. (eds) *Handbook of Qualitative Research*, London: SAGE Publications.
Denzin, N. K. and Lincoln, Y. S. (eds) (1994) *Handbook of Qualitative Research*, London: SAGE Publications.
Department of Health (1992) *Inspection of Facilities for Mothers and Babies in Prison: A Multi-Disciplinary Inspection by the Department of Health*, London: HMSO.
Department of Health (1994) *Inspection of Facilities for Mothers and Babies in Prison*, London: HMSO.
Derrida, J. (1976) *Of Grammatology*, Baltimore: The Johns Hopkins University Press.
Diamond, I. and Quinby, L. (eds) (1988) *Feminism and Foucault: Reflections on Resistance*, Boston, MA: Northeastern Press.
Díaz-Cotto, J. (1996) *Gender, Ethnicity and the State: Latina and Latino Prison Politics*, Albany, NY: SUNY Press.
DiIulio, J. J. (1987) *Governing Prisons: A Comparative Study of Correctional Management*, New York: Free Press.
DiIulio, J. J. (1991) *No Escape: The Future of American Corrections*, New York: Basic Books.
Ditchfield, J. (1990) *Control in Prisons: A Review of the Literature*, London: HMSO.

Dobash, R. O., Dobash, R. E. and Gutteridge, S. (1986) *The Imprisonment of Women*, Oxford: Basil Blackwell.

Dockley, A. (1996) 'What Did Learmont say? Some "On the Ground" Views of the Learmont report', *The Howard Journal of Criminal Justice*, 35(4): 353–62.

Donziger, S. R. (ed.) (1996) *The Real War on Crime: The Report of the National Criminal Justice Commission*, New York: HarperCollins Publishers.

Downes, D. and Rock, P. (1988) *Understanding Deviance: A Guide to the Sociology of Crime and Rule Breaking*, Oxford: Clarendon Press.

Dunbar, I. (1985) *A Sense of Direction*, London: HMSO.

Durkheim, E. (1964) *The Rules of Sociological Method*, New York: Free Press.

Eaton, M. (1986) *Justice for Women?*, Milton Keynes: Open University Press.

Eaton, M. (1993) *Women After Prison*, Buckingham: Open University Press.

Edwards, S. (1984) *Women On Trial*, Manchester: Manchester University Press.

Edwards, S. (1989) *Policing 'Domestic' Violence: Women, the Law and the State*, London: SAGE.

Einstadter, W. and Henry, S. (1995) *Criminological Theory: An Analysis of its Underlying Assumptions*, Fort Worth, TX: Harcourt, Brace.

Eisenstein, H. and Jardine, A. (eds) (1985) *The Future of Difference*, New Brunswick, NJ: Rutgers University Press.

Elias, N. (1978) *The Civilizing Process: Volume One – The History of Manners*, Oxford: Oxford University Press.

Faith, K. (1993) *Unruly Women: The Politics of Confinement and Resistance*, Vancouver: Press Gang Publishers.

Farrington, D. and Morris, A. (1983) 'Sex, Sentencing and Reconvictions', *British Journal of Criminology*, 23(3): 229–48.

Feeley, M. and Simon, J. (1992) 'The New Penology', *Criminology*, 39(4): 449–74.

Felson, M. (1994) *Crime and Everyday Life*, London: Pine Forge Press.

Ferrell, J. (1995) 'Urban Graffiti: Crime Control and Resistance', *Youth and Society*, 27(1): 73–92.

Ferrell, J. and Sanders, C. (eds) (1995) *Cultural Criminology*, Boston: Northeastern University Press.

Field, X. (1963) *Under Lock and Key: A Study of Women in Prison*, London: Max Parrish.

Finch, J. (1993) '"It's Great to Have Someone to Talk to": Ethics and Politics of Interviewing Women' in Hammersley, M. (ed.) *Social Research: Philosophy, Politics, and Practice*, London: SAGE Publications.

Fine, M. (1994) 'Working the Hyphens: Reinventing Self and Other in Qualitative Research', in Denzin, N. and Lincoln, Y. (eds) *Handbook of Qualitative Research*, London: SAGE Publications.

Fineman, M. A. and Thomadsen, N. S. (eds) (1991) *At the Boundaries of Law: Feminism and Legal Theory*, New York: Routledge.

Fineman, M. L. A. (1994) 'Feminist Legal Scholarship and Women's Gendered Lives' in Cain, M. and Harrington, C. (eds) *Lawyers in a Postmodern World: Translation and Transgression*, Buckingham: Open University Press.

Fishman, L. (1995) 'Slave Women, Resistance and Community: A Prelude to Future Accommodation', *Women and Criminal Justice*, 17: 35–65.

FitzGerald, M. and Marshall, P. (1996) 'Ethnic Minorities in British Prisons: Some Research Implications' in Matthews, R. and Francis, P. (eds) *Prisons 2000: An International Perspective on the Current State and Future of Imprisonment*, London: Macmillan Press Ltd.

Fitzgerald, M. and Sim, J. (1982) *British Prisons*, Oxford: Basil Blackwell.

Flax, J. (1990) *Thinking Fragments: Psychoanalysis, Feminism and Postmodernism in the Contemporary West*, Berkeley: University of California Press.

Fleisher, M. (1989) *Warehousing Violence*, Newbury Park, CA: SAGE Publications.

Fonow, M. M. and Cook, J. A. (eds) (1991) *Beyond Methodology: Feminist Scholarship as Lived Research*, Bloomington: Indiana University Press.

Foucault, M. (1967) *Madness and Civilisation: A History of Insanity in the Age of Reason*, London: Tavistock.

Foucault, M. (1970) *The Order of Things: An Archaeology of the Human Sciences*, London: Routledge.

Foucault, M. (1979) *Discipline and Punish: The Birth of the Prison*, London: Penguin Books.

Foucault, M. (1980a) *The History of Sexuality, Volume 1: An Introduction*, New York: Random House.

Foucault, M. (1980b) *Power/Knowledge: Selected Interviews and Other Writings, 1972–1977*, London: The Harvester Press.

Foucault, M. (1991a) 'Questions of Method', in Burchell, G., Gordon, C. and Miller, P. (eds) *The Foucault Effect: Studies in Governmentality*, Chicago: University of Chicago Press.

Foucault, M. (1991b) 'Governmentality' in Burchell, G., Gordon, C. and Miller, P. (eds) *The Foucault Effect: Studies in Governmentality*, Chicago: University of Chicago Press.

Fox-Genovese, E. (1988) *Within the Plantation: Black and White Women of the Old South*, Chapel Hill: The University of North Carolina Press.

Fox-Genovese, E. (1990) 'Strategies and Forms of Resistance: Focus on

Slave Women in the US' in Hine, D. C. (ed.) *Black Women in American History: From Colonial Times Through the Nineteenth Century, Vol. 2*, Brooklyn, NY: Carlson Publishing Inc.

Fraisse, G. (1994) *Reason's Muse: Sexual Difference and the Birth of Democracy*, Chicago: Chicago University Press.

Fraser, N. (1989) *Unruly Practices: Power, Discourse and Gender in Contemporary Social Theory*, Minneapolis: University of Minnesota Press.

Fraser, N. (1997) *Justice Interruptus: Critical Reflections on the 'Postsocialist' Condition*, New York: Routledge.

Frazer, E. and Lacey, N. (1993) *The Politics of Community: A Feminist Critique of the Liberal-Communitarian Debate*, London: Harvester Wheatsheaf.

Freedman, E. B. (1981) *Their Sisters' Keepers: Women's Prison Reform in America, 1830–1930*, Michigan: University of Michigan Press.

Freire, P. (1996) *Pedagogy of the Oppressed*, New York: The Continuum Publishing Company.

Freud, S. (1985) *Civilization, Society and Religion: Group Psychology, Civilization and its Discontents and Other Works*, London: Penguin Books.

Fry, E. (1827) *Observations on the Visiting, Superintending, and Government of Female Prisons*, London: John and Arthur Arch.

Fuss, D. (1989) *Essentially Speaking: Feminism, Nature and Difference*, London: Routledge.

Gadamer, H.-G. (1975) *Truth and Method*, London: Sheed and Ward.

Gagné, P. (1996) 'Identity, Strategy, and Feminist Politics: Clemency for Battered Women Who Kill', *Social Problems*, 43: 77–93.

Gallo, E. and Ruggiero, V. (1991) 'The "Immaterial" Prison: Custody as a Factory for the Manufacture of Handicaps', *International Journal of the Sociology of Law*, 19: 273–91.

Gallop, J. (1982) *The Daughter's Seduction: Feminism and Psychoanalysis*, Ithaca, NY: Cornell University Press.

Galloway, J. (1997) 'Forsaken on Romeo Block', *The Guardian Weekend*, February 8: 21–29.

Garfinkel, H. (1967) *Studies in Ethnomethodology*, Englewood Cliffs, NJ: Prentice-Hall, Inc.

Garland, D. (1985) *Punishment and Welfare: A History of Penal Strategies*, Aldershot: Gower.

Garland, D. (1990) *Punishment and Modern Society: A Study in Social Theory*, Oxford: Clarendon Press.

Garland, D. (1992) 'Criminological Knowledge and its Relation to Power: Foucault's Genealogy and Criminology Today', *British Journal of Criminology*, 32(4): 403–22.

Garland, D. (1994) 'Of Crimes and Criminals: The Development of

Criminology in Britain' in Maguire, M., Morgan, R. and Reiner, R. (eds) *The Oxford Handbook of Criminology*, Oxford: Oxford University Press.

Garland, D. (1995) 'Penal Modernism and Postmodernism' in Blomberg, T. G. and Cohen, S. (eds) *Punishment and Social Control: Essays in Honor of Sheldon L. Messinger*, New York: Aldine de Gruyter.

Garland, D. (1996) 'The Limits of the Sovereign State: Strategies of Crime Control in Contemporary Society', *The British Journal of Criminology*, 36(4): 445–71.

Garland, D. (1997) '"Governmentality" and the Problem of Crime: Foucault, Criminology, Sociology', *Theoretical Criminology*, 1(2): 173–214.

Garland, D., and Young, P. (eds) (1983) *The Power to Punish: Contemporary Penality and Social Analysis*, London: Heinemann Educational Books.

Geertz, C. (1973) *The Interpretation of Cultures: Selected Essays*, New York: Basic Books.

Gelsthorpe, L. (1986) 'Towards a Sceptical Look at Sexism', *International Journal of the Sociology of Law*, 14(2): 125–52.

Gelsthorpe, L. (1989) *Sexism and the Female Offender*, Aldershot: Gower.

Gelsthorpe, L. (1990) 'Feminist Methodologies in Criminology: A New Approach of Old Wine in New Bottles?' in Gelsthorpe, L. and Morris, A. (eds) *Feminist Perspectives in Criminology*, Buckingham: Open University Press.

Gelsthorpe, L. (1992) 'Response to Martyn Hammersley's paper "On Feminist Methodology"', *Sociology*, 26(2): 213–18.

Gelsthorpe, L. (ed.) (1993a) *Minority Ethnic Groups in the Criminal Justice System*, Cropwood Conference Series No. 21. Cambridge: Institute of Criminology.

Gelsthorpe, L. (1993b). 'Approaching the Topic of Racism: Transferable Research Strategies?' in Cook, D. and Hudson, B. (eds) *Racism and Criminology*, London: SAGE Publications.

Gelsthorpe, L. and Morris, A. (1988) 'Feminism and Criminology in Britain' in Rock, P. (ed.) *A History of British Criminology*, Oxford: Clarendon Press.

Gelsthorpe, L. and Morris, A. (eds) (1990) *Feminist Perspectives in Criminology*, Milton Keynes: Open University Press.

Genders, E. and Player, E. (1987) 'Women in Prison: The Treatment, the Control and the Experience', in Carlen, P. and Worrall, A. (eds) *Gender, Crime and Justice*, Milton Keynes: Open University Press.

Genders, E. and Player, E. (1989) *Race Relations in Prisons*, Oxford: Clarendon Press.

Genders, E. and Player, E. (1995) *Grendon: A Study of a Therapeutic Prison*, Oxford: Clarendon Press.

Giallombardo, R. (1966a) *Society of Women: A Study of a Women's Prison*, New York: John Wiley and Sons, Inc.

Giallombardo, R. (1966b) 'Social Roles in a Prison for Women', *Social Problems*, 13(3): 268–88.

Gibbons, D. C. (1994) *Talking about Crime and Criminals: Problems and Issues in Theory Development in Criminology*, Englewood Cliffs, NJ: Prentice Hall.

Giddens, A. (1976) *New Rules of Sociological Method: A Positive Critique of Interpretative Sociologies*, London: Hutchinson and Co. (Publishers) Ltd.

Giddens, A. (1979) *Central Problems in Social Theory: Action, Structure and Contradiction in Social Analysis*, Berkeley: University of California Press.

Giddens, A. (1984) *The Constitution of Society: Outline of the Theory of Structuration*, Cambridge: Polity Press.

Giddens, A. (1990) *The Consequences of Modernity*, Cambridge: Polity Press.

Giddens, A. (1991) *Modernity and Self-Identity: Self and Society in the Late Modern Age*, Cambridge: Polity Press.

Gilligan, C. (1982) *In a Different Voice: Psychological Theory and Women's Development*, Cambridge MA: Harvard University Press.

Gilligan, C. (1983) 'Do the Social Sciences Have an Adequate Theory of Moral Development?', in Haan, N. (ed.) *Social Science as Moral Inquiry*, New York: Columbia University Press.

Goffman, E. (1961) *Asylums: Essays on the Social Situation of Mental Patients and Other Inmates*, London: Penguin Books.

Goffman, E. (1963) *Stigma: Notes on the Management of Spoiled Identity*, London: Penguin Books.

Goffman, E. (1969) *The Presentation of Self in Everyday Life*, London: Allen Lane.

Gorelick, S. (1991) 'Contradictions of Feminist Methodology', *Gender and Society*, 5(4): 459–77.

Griffiths, M. (1995) *Feminisms and the Self: The Web of Identity*, London: Routledge.

Grosz, E. (1994) *Volatile Bodies: Towards a Corporeal Feminism*, Bloomington: Indiana University Press.

Gunn, J., Maden, T. and Swinton, M. (1991) *Mentally Disordered Offenders*, London: HMSO.

Gutman, A. (ed.) (1994) *Multiculturalism: Examining the Politics of Recognition*, Princeton, NJ: Princeton University Press.

Habermas, J. (1976) *Legitimation Crisis*, London: Heinemann.

Hahn Rafter, N. (1990) *Partial Justice: Women, Prisons and Social Control*, New Brunswick, NJ: Transaction Publishers.

Hammersley, M. (1992) 'On Feminist Methodology', *Sociology*, 26(2): 187–206.

Hammersley, M. (ed.) (1993) *Social Research: Philosophy, Politics and Practice*, London: SAGE Publications.

Hammersley, M. (1995) *The Politics of Social Research*, London: SAGE Publications.

Hanmer, J. and Maynard, M. (eds) (1987) *Women, Violence and Social Control*, Atlantic Highlands, NJ: Humanities Press, International Inc.

Hannah-Moffat, K. (1995) 'Feminine Fortresses: Women-Centered Prisons?' *The Prison Journal, Special Issue: Women in Prisons and Jails*, 75: 135–64.

Harding, S. (ed.) (1987) *Feminism and Methodology: Social Science Issues*, Milton Keynes: Open University Press.

Harding, S. and Hintikka, M. B. (eds) (1983) *Discovering Reality: Feminist Perspectives on Epistemology, Metaphysics, Methodology and Philosophy of Science*, Dordrecht: D. Reidel Publishing Company.

Hartsock, N. (1983) 'The Feminist Standpoint: Developing the Ground for a Specifically Feminist Historical Materialism', in Harding, S. and Hintikka, M. (eds) *Discovering Reality*, Boston: D. Reidel Publishing Company.

Hay, W. and Sparks, R. (1991) 'Maintaining Order in the English Dispersal System' in Bottomley, A. K. and Hay, W. (eds) *Special Units for Difficult Prisoners*, Hull: University of Hull.

Hay, W., Sparks, R. and Bottoms, T. (1990) 'Control Problems and the Long-Term Prisoners', Unpublished report submitted to the Home Office and Planning Unit by the Cambridge University Institute of Criminology.

Heffernan, E. (1974) *Making it in Prison: The Cool, the Square and the Life*, New York: Wiley.

Hegel, G. W. F. (1953) *Reason in History*, New York: Bobbs-Merrill.

Heidensohn, F. (1968) 'The Deviance of Women: A Critique and An Enquiry', *British Journal of Sociology*, 19(2): 160–75.

Heidensohn, F. (1985) *Women and Crime*, London: Routledge and Kegan Paul.

Heidensohn, F. (1992) *Women in Control? The Role of Women in Law Enforcement*, Oxford: Oxford University Press.

Heidensohn, F. (1994) 'Gender and Crime', in Maguire, M., Morgan, R. and Reiner, R. (eds) *The Oxford Handbook of Criminology*, Oxford: Clarendon Press.

Hekman, S. (1990) *Gender and Knowledge*, Cambridge: Polity Press.

Hekman, S. J. (1995) *Moral Voices, Moral Selves: Carol Gilligan and Feminist Moral Theory*, Cambridge: Polity Press.

Hennessey, M. (1997) 'Where's the Justice?' *Sainsbury's The Magazine*, February: 52–57.

Hennessy, Sir J. (1996) 'The Learmont Inquiry', *The Howard Journal of Criminal Justice*, 35(4): 340–46.

Henry, J. (1952) *Women in Prison*, New York: Doubleday and Company, Ltd.

Henry, S. and Milovanovic, D. (1994) 'The Constitution of Constitutive Criminology: A Postmodern Approach to Criminological Theory', in Nelken, D. (ed.) *The Futures of Criminology*, London: SAGE Publications.

Henry, S. and Milovanovic, D. (1996) *Constitutive Criminology: Beyond Postmodernism*, London: SAGE Publications.

Herrnstein, R. J. and Murray, C. (1994) *The Bell Curve: Intelligence and Class Structure in the United States*, New York: Free Press.

HMCIP (1994) *HMP and YOI Drake Hall: Report of an Unannounced Short Inspection*, London: HMSO.

HMCIP (1995) *HM Remand Centre Pucklechurch: Report of an Unannounced Short Inspection*, London: HMSO.

HMCIP (1996) *HM Prison Eastwood Park: Report of an Unannounced Short Inspection*, London: HMSO.

HMCIP (1997) *Women in Prison: A Thematic Review by HM Chief Inspector of Prisons*, London: HMSO.

HM Prison Service (1993a) *Women's Prisons Gazetteer*, London: HMSO.

HM Prison Service (1993b) *We Are Now An Agency*, London: HMSO.

HM Prison Service (1993c) *Corporate Plan, 1993–1996*, London: HMSO.

HM Prison Service (1996) *Annual Report and Accounts, April 1994–March 1995*, London: HMSO.

HM Prison Service (1997) *Prison Service News*, Vol. 15, No. 152.

HM Prison Service (1998) *Prison Service News*, Vol. 16, No. 164.

Hobbes, T. (1960) *Leviathan*, Oxford: Blackwell.

Home Affairs Committee (1993) *The Prison Service Minutes of Evidence*, Monday, 19 April 1993, London: HMSO.

Home Affairs Committee (1997) *The Management of the Prison Service (Public and Private)* Second Report, London: HMSO.

Home Office (1967) *Studies of Female Offenders*, Home Office Studies in the Causes of Delinquency and the Treatment of Offenders, No. 11, London: HMSO.

Home Office (1972) *Girl Offenders Aged 17 to 20 Years*, Home Office Research Unit Report, No. 14, London: HMSO.

Home Office (1976) *Further Studies of Female Offenders*, Home Office Research Study, No. 33, London: HMSO.

Home Office (1984) *Managing the Long-Term Prison System*, Report of the Control Review Committee, London: HMSO.

Home Office (1985) *New Directions in Prison Design: Report of a Home Office Study of New Generation Prisons in the USA*, London: HMSO.

Home Office (1986) 'Race Relations', *Circular Instruction*, 32/1986.

Home Office (1987) *Special Units for Long-Term Prisoners: A Report by the Research Advisory Group on the Long-Term Prison System*, London: HMSO.

Home Office (1988) 'Age Mixing in Female Establishments', *Circular Instruction*, 31/88.

Home Office (1991) *Custody, Care and Justice: The Way Ahead for the Prison Service of England and Wales*, London: HMSO.

Home Office (1992a) *Regimes for Women*, London: HMSO.

Home Office (1992b) *Race and the Criminal Justice System*, London HMSO.

Home Office (1994) *Race and the Criminal Justice System*, London: HMSO.

hooks, b. (1982) *Ain't I a Woman? Black Women and Feminism*, London: Pluto Press.

hooks, b. (1984) *From Margin to Center*, Boston: South End Press.

hooks, b. (1989) *Talking Back: Thinking Feminist – Thinking Black*, London: Sheba Feminist Publishers.

hooks, b. (1990) *Yearning: Race, Gender and Cultural Politics*, Boston: South End Press.

Hough, H. and Mayhew, P. (1982) *The British Crime Survey: First Report*, Home Office Research Study, No. 76, London: HMSO.

Howard, J. (1777) *The State of the Prisons*, 1929 edn, London: J. M. Dent and Sons Ltd.

Howard, M. Rt Hon. (1995) 'Speech to 100th Conservative Party Conference', Winter Gardens, Blackpool, *Conservative Party News*, London: Conservative Central Office.

Howe, A. (1994) *Punish and Critique: Towards a Feminist Analysis of Penality*, London: Routledge.

Hudson, B. (1987) *Justice Through Punishment: A Critique of the 'Justice' Model of Corrections*, New York: St Martin's Press Ltd.

Hudson, B. (1993a) *Penal Policy and Social Justice*, London: The Macmillan Press Ltd.

Hudson, B. (1993b) 'Penal Policy and Racial Justice', in Gelsthorpe, L. (ed.) *Minority Ethnic Groups in the Criminal Justice System*, Cropwood Conference Series, No. 21, Cambridge: Institute of Criminology.

Ignatieff, M. (1978) *A Just Measure of Pain: The Penitentiary in the Industrial Revolution 1750–1850*, London: Penguin Books.

Immarigeon, R. and Chesney-Lind, M. (1992) *Women's Prisons: Overcrowded and Overused*, San Francisco: NCCD.

Irigaray, L. (1985a) *Speculum of the Other Woman*, Ithaca: Cornell University Press.

Irigaray, L. (1985b) *This Sex Which is Not One*, Ithaca: Cornell University Press.

Irwin, J. (1970) *The Felon*, Englewood Cliffs, NJ: Prentice-Hall, Inc.

Irwin, J. and Austin, J. (1994) *It's About Time: America's Imprisonment Binge*, Belmont, CA: Wandsworth.

Irwin, J. and Cressey, D. (1962) 'Thieves, Convicts and the Inmate Culture', *Social Problems*, 10.

Jack, R. (1992) *Women and Attempted Suicide*, Hove: Lawrence Erlbaum and Associates.

Jacobs, J. (1977) *Stateville: The Penitentiary in Mass Society*, Chicago: Chicago University Press.

Jaggar, A. (ed.) (1983) *Feminist Politics and Human Nature*, Brighton: Harvester.

Jaggar, A. (1989) 'Love and Knowledge: Emotion in Feminist Epistemology', in Jaggar, A. and Bordo, S. (eds) *Gender/Body/Knowledge: Feminist Reconstructions of Being and Knowing*, New Brunswick, NJ: Rutgers University Press.

Jefferson, T. (1994) 'Theorising Masculine Subjectivity', in Newburn, T. and Stanko, B. (eds) *Just Boys Doing Business? Men, Masculinities and Crime*, London: Routledge.

Jefferson, T. and Carlen, P. (eds) (1996) 'Special Edition on Masculinities, Social Relations and Crime', *British Journal of Criminology*, 36(3).

Kelley, J. (1967) *When the Gates Shut*, London: Longmans.

Kemp, Sir P. (1996) 'The Next Steps Approach', *The Howard Journal of Criminal Justice*, 35: 336–40.

King, D. (1988) 'Multiple Jeopardy, Multiple Consciousness: The Context of Black Feminist Thought', *Signs: Journal of Women in Culture and Society*, 14(1): 42–72.

King, R. D. (1994) 'Order, Disorder and Regimes in the Prison Services of Scotland, England and Wales', in Player, E. and Jenkins, M. (eds) *Prisons After Woolf: Reform Through Riot*, London: Routledge.

King, R. and Morgan, R. (1980) *The Future of the Prison System*, Aldershot: Gower.

King, R. D. and McDermott, K. (1990) 'My Geranium is Subversive: Some Notes on the Management of Trouble in Prisons', *British Journal of Sociology*, 41(4): 445–71.

King, R. and McDermott, K. (1995) *The State of Our Prisons*, Oxford: Clarendon Press.

Kleinman, S. and Copp, M. A. (1993) *Emotions and Fieldwork*, London: SAGE Publications.

Kristeva, J. (1980) *Desire in Language: A Semiotic Approach to Literature and Art*, New York: Columbia University Press.

Lacan, J. (1977) *Ecrits: A Selection*, New York: Norton.

Lacey, N. (1988) *State Punishment: Political Principles and Community Values*, London: Routledge.

Lacey, N. (1997) 'On the Subject of "Sexing" the Subject ...', in Naffine, N. and Owens, R. J. (eds) *Sexing the Subject of Law*, Sydney: Sweet & Maxwell.

Laclau, E. (1990) *New Reflections on the Revolution of Our Time*, London: Verso.

Laclau, E. and Mouffe, C. (1985) *Hegemony and Socialist Strategy: Towards a Radical Democratic Politics*, London: Verso.

Laing, R. D. (1958) *The Divided Self*, Harmondsworth: Penguin.

Larrabee, M. J. (ed.) (1993) *An Ethic of Care: Feminist and Interdisciplinary Perspectives*, London: Routledge.

Layder, D. (1993) *New Strategies in Social Research*, Cambridge: Polity Press.

Lazarus-Black, M. and Hirsch, S. F. (1994) *Contested States: Law, Hegemony and Resistance*, New York: Routledge.

Learmont, J. (1995) *Review of Prison Service Security in England and Wales and the Escape from Parkhurst Prison on Tuesday 3rd January 1995*, Cmnd 3020, London: HMSO.

Lemert, C. (ed.) (1993) *Social Theory: The Multicultural and Classic Readings*, Boulder: Westview Press.

Lewis, D. (1997) *Hidden Agendas: Politics, Law and Disorder*, London: Hamish Hamilton.

Liebling, A. (1992) *Suicides in Prison*, London: Routledge.

Liebling, A. (1994) 'Suicides Amongst Women Prisoners', *Howard Journal*, 33(1): 1–9.

Liebling, A., Muir, G., Rose, G. and Bottoms, A. (1997) *An Evaluation of Incentives and Earned Privileges: Final Report*, Institute of Criminology: University of Cambridge.

Linstead, S. (1994) 'Objectivity, Reflexivity, and Fiction: Humanity, Inhumanity and the Science of the Social', *Human Relations*, 47(11): 1321–46.

Lloyd, E. (1992) *Children Visiting Holloway Prison: Inside and Outside Perspectives on the All Day Visits Scheme at HMP Holloway*, London: Save the Children Fund.

Lloyd, G. (1984) *The Man of Reason: 'Male' and 'Female' in Western Philosophy*, London: Methuen and Co. Ltd.

Locke, J. (1967) *Two Treatises of Government*, Cambridge: Cambridge University Press.

Lombroso, C. and Ferrero, G. (1895). *The Female Offender*, New York: Fisher Unwin.

Loucks, N. (ed.) (1993) *Prison Rules: A Working Guide*, London: Prison Reform Trust.

Lucas, J. R. (1980) *On Justice*, Oxford: Oxford University Press.

Lygo, R. Sir. (1991) *Management of the Prison Service*, London: HMSO.

Lyon, J. and Coleman, J. (1996) *Understanding and Working with Young Women in Custody: Training Pack*, London: HMSO.

MacDonald, B. (1993) 'A Political Classification of Evaluation Studies', in Hammersley, M. (ed.) *Social Research: Philosophy, Politics and Practice*, London: SAGE.

MacKenzie, D. L. and Herbert, E. E. (1996) *Correctional Bootcamps: A Tough Intermediate Sanction*, Washington DC: National Institute of Justice.

Maden, T. (1996) *Women, Prisons and Psychiatry: Mental Disorder Behind Bars*, Oxford: Butterworth-Heinemann Ltd.

Maguire, A. (1994) *Why Me?* London: Routledge.

Maguire, M., Morgan, R. and Reiner, R. (eds) (1994) *The Oxford Handbook of Criminology*, Oxford: Oxford University Press.

Maher, L. (1992) 'Reconstructing the Female Criminal: Women and Crack Cocaine', *Southern Californian Review of Law and Women's Studies*, 2(1): 131–54.

Maher, L. (1997) *Sexed Work: Gender and the Politics of Resistance in a Brooklyn Drug Market*, Oxford: Clarendon.

Maher, L. and Daly, K. (1995) 'Women on the Street-Level Drug Economy: Continuity or Change?', *Criminology*, 34(4): 465–91.

Mahoney, M. and Yngvesson, B. (1992) 'The Construction of Subjectivity and the Paradox of Resistance: Integrating Feminist Anthropology and Psychology', *Signs: Journal of Women in Culture and Society*, 18(1): 44–73.

Mama, A. (1995) *Beyond the Masks: Race, Gender and Subjectivity*, London: Routledge.

Mandaraka-Sheppard, A. (1986) *The Dynamics of Women's Aggression in Women's Prisons in England*, Aldershot: Gower.

Marks, E. and de Courtivron, I. (1981) *New French Feminisms: An Anthology*, Brighton: The Harvester Press.

Martinson, R. (1974) 'What Works? – Questions and Answers about Prison Reform', *The Public Interest*, 35: 22-54.

Massey, D. (1994) *Space, Place and Gender*, Cambridge: Polity Press.

Mathiesen, T. (1965) *The Defences of the Weak: A Sociological Study of a Norwegian Correctional Institution*, London: Tavistock Publications.

184 Engendering Resistance

Mathiesen, T. (1974) *The Politics of Abolition*, Oslo: Scandinavian Studies in Criminology, Law in Society Series.

Mathiesen, T. (1990) *Prison on Trial: A Critical Assessment*, London: SAGE Publications.

Matza, D. (1969) *Becoming Deviant*, Englewood Cliffs, NJ: Prentice-Hall, Inc.

May, J. (1979) *Report of the Committee of Inquiry into the United Kingdom Prison Services*, Cmnd. 7673, London: HMSO.

McConville, S. (1981) *A History of British Penal Administration, Vol. 1: 1750–1877*, London: Routledge.

McConville, S. (1995) *English Local Prisons 1860–1900: Next Only to Death*, London: Routledge.

McGurk, B., Thornton, D. and Williams, M. (1987) *Applying Psychology to Imprisonment*, London: HMSO.

McNay, L. (1993) *Foucault and Feminism: Power, Gender and the Self*, Boston: Northeastern University Press.

Mead, G. H. (1934) *Mind, Self and Society: From the Standpoint of a Social Behaviourist*, Chicago: Chicago University Press.

Melossi, D. (1989) 'An Introduction: Fifty Years Later, *Punishment and Social Structure* in Comparative Analysis', *Contemporary Crises*, 13: 311–26.

Melossi, D. (1990) *The State of Social Control: A Sociological Study of Concepts of State and Social Control in the Making of Democracy*, Cambridge: Polity Press.

Melossi, D. and Pavarini, M. (1981) *The Prison and the Factory: Origins of the Penitentiary System*, London: Macmillan Press Ltd.

Merry, S. E. (1990) *Getting Justice and Getting Even: Legal Consciousness among Working-Class Americans*, Chicago: The University of Chicago Press.

Messerschmidt, J. (1986) *Capitalism, Patriarchy and Crime*, Totowa, NJ: Rowman, Littlefield.

Messerschmidt, J. (1993) *Masculinities and Crime*, Totowa, NJ: Rowman, Littlefield.

Morgan, R. (1991) 'Woolf: In Retrospect and Prospect', *The Modern Law Review*, 54(5): 713–25.

Morgan, R. (1992) 'Following Woolf: The Prospects for Prison Policy', *Journal of Law and Society*, 19(2): 231–50.

Morgan, R. (1994) 'Imprisonment', in Maguire, M., Morgan, R. and Reiner, R. (eds) *The Oxford Handbook of Criminology*, Oxford: Clarendon Press.

Morgan, R. (1996) 'Learmont: Dangerously Unbalanced', *The Howard Journal of Criminal Justice*, 35(4): 346–53.

Morris, A. (1987) *Women, Crime and Criminal Justice*, Oxford: Basil Blackwell.

Morris, A. and Wilkinson, C. (eds) (1988) *Women and the Penal System: Papers Presented to 19th Cropwood Round-Table Conference*, Cambridge: Institute of Criminology.

Morris, A. and Wilkinson, C. (1995) 'Responding to Female Prisoners' Needs', *The Prison Journal*, 75(3): 295–305.

Morris, A., Wilkinson, C., Tisi, A., Woodrow, J. and Rockley, A. (1995) *Managing the Needs of Female Prisoners*, London: HMSO.

Morris, N. (1994) 'Foreword', in Roberts, J. W. (ed.) *Escaping Prison Myths: Selected Topics in the History of Federal Corrections*, Washington: The America University Press.

Morrison, T. (1988) *Beloved*, New York: Penguin Books.

NACRO (1991a) *Black People's Experience of Criminal Justice*, London: NACRO.

NACRO (1991b) *A Fresh Start for Women Prisoners: Implications of the Woolf Report for Women*, London: NACRO.

NACRO (1996) *Women Prisoners: Towards a New Millennium*, London: NACRO.

Naffine, N. (1996) *Feminism and Criminology*, Philadelphia: Temple University Press.

Nagel, T. (1973) 'Rawls on Justice', *Philosophical Review*, 82: 220–34.

Nelken, D. (ed.) (1994) *The Futures of Criminology*, London: SAGE Publications.

Newburn, T. and Stanko, E. (eds) (1994) *Just Boys Doing Business? Men, Masculinities and Crime*, London: Routledge.

Newton, C. (1994) 'Gender Theory and Prison Sociology: Using Theories of Masculinities to Interpret the Sociology of Prison for Men', *The Howard Journal*, 33(3): 193–202.

Nicholson, L. (ed.) (1990) *Feminism/Postmodernism*, New York: Routledge.

Oakley, A. (1981) 'Interviewing Women: A Contradiction in Terms?', in Roberts, H. (ed.) *Doing Feminist Research*, London: Routledge and Kegan Paul.

Okin, S. M. (1989) *Justice, Gender and the Family*, New York: Basic Books.

Owen, B. (1998) *'In the Mix': Struggle and Survival in a Women's Prison*, Albany, NY: SUNY Press.

PAC (1996) *The Imprisonment of Women: Some Facts and Figures*, London: Penal Affairs Consortium.

Padel, U. and Stevenson, P. (1988) *Insiders: Women's Experience of Prison*, London: Virago Press.

Painter, K. (1992) 'Different Worlds: The Spatial, Temporal and Social

Dimensions of Female Victimisation', in Evans, D. T., Fyfe N. R. and Herbert D. T. (eds) *Crime, Policing and Place*, London: Routledge.

Park, R. and Burgess, E. (1925) *The City*, Chicago: University of Chigao Press.

Parker, T. (1965) *Women in Crime: Five Revealing Cases*, New York: Delacorte Press.

Parker, T. (1990) *Life After Life: Interviews with Twelve Murderers*, London: Secker and Warburg.

Pasquino, P. (1991) 'Criminology: The Birth of a Special Knowledge', in Burchell, G., Gordon, C. and Miller, P. (eds) *The Foucault Effect: Studies in Governmentality*, Chicago: The University of Chicago Press.

Pateman, C. (1988) *The Sexual Contract*, Cambridge: Polity Press.

Pilling, J. (1992) *Back to Basics: Relationships in the Prison Service*, Key Note Lecture presented to *ISTD*, 15 June 1992.

Platt, A. (1969) *The Child Savers: The Invention of Delinquency*, Chicago: University of Chicago Press.

Platt, T. and Takagi, P. (eds) (1980) *Punishment and Penal Discipline*, San Francisco: Crime and Social Justice Associations.

Player, E. (1994) 'Women's Prisons After Woolf', in Player, E. and Jenkins, M. (eds) *Prisons After Woolf: Reform Through Riot*, London: Routledge.

Player, E. and Jenkins, M. (eds) (1994) *Prisons After Woolf: Reform Through Riot*, London: Routledge.

PROP (1976) *Don't Mark His Face*, London: PROP.

PRT (1996) *Women in Prison: Recent Trends and Developments*, London: PRT.

PRT (1997) *Election Summary*, London: PRT.

Ramazanoglu, C. (1992) 'On Feminist Methodology: Male Reason Versus Female Empowerment', *Sociology*, 26(2): 207–12.

Ramazanoglu, C. (ed.) (1993) *Up Against Foucault*, London: Routledge.

Rawls, J. (1958) 'Justice as Fairness', *Philosophical Review*, 57.

Rawls, J. (1971) *A Theory of Justice*, Oxford: Oxford University Press.

Rawls, J. (1980) 'Kantian Constructivism in Moral Theory', *Journal of Philosophy*, 77: 515–72.

Rawls, J. (1992) 'Justice as Fairness: Political not Metaphysical', in Strong, T. B. (ed.) *The Self and the Political Order*, Oxford: Blackwell.

Rawls, J. (1996) *Political Liberalism*, New York: Columbia University Press.

Reinharz, S. (1992) *Feminist Methods in Social Research*, New York: Oxford University Press.

Rice, M. (1990) 'Challenging Orthodoxies in Feminist Theory: A Black Feminist Account', in Gelsthorpe, L. and Morris, A. (eds) *Feminist Perspectives in Criminology*, Milton Keynes: Open University Press.

Rich, A. (1980) 'Compulsory Heterosexuality and Lesbian Existence', *Signs: Journal of Women in Culture and Society*, 5(4): 631–90.

Richards, M., McWilliams, B., Batten, N., Cameron, C. and Cutler, J. (1995a) 'Foreign Nationals in English Prisons: I. Family Ties and their Maintenance', *The Howard Journal*, 34(2): 158–75.

Richards, M., McWilliams, B., Batten, N., Cameron, C. and Cutler, J. (1995b) 'Foreign Nationals in English Prisons: II. Some Policy Issues', *The Howard Journal*, 34(3): 195–208.

Richardson, G. (1994) 'From Rights to Expectations', in Player, E. and Jenkins, M. (eds) *Prisons After Woolf: Reform through Riot*, London: Routledge.

Richie, B. E. (1996) *Compelled to Crime: the Gender Entrapment of Battered Black Women*, New York: Routledge.

Ricoeur, P. (1981) *Hermeneutics and the Human Sciences*, Cambridge: Cambridge University Press.

Roberts, H. (ed.) (1981) *Doing Feminist Research*, London: Routledge and Kegan Paul.

Rock, P. (ed.) (1988) *A History of British Criminology*, Oxford: Clarendon Press.

Rock, P. (1994) 'The Social Organization of British Criminology', in Maguire, M., Morgan, R. and Reiner, R. (eds) *The Oxford Handbook of Criminology*, Oxford: Clarendon Press.

Rock, P. (1996) *Reconstructing a Women's Prison: The Holloway Redevelopment Project 1968–1988*, Oxford: Clarendon.

Rosaldo, M. Z. and Lamphere, L. (eds) (1974) *Women, Culture, Society*, Stanford: Stanford University Press.

Rose, N. (1989) *Governing the Soul: The Shaping of the Private Self*, London: Routledge.

Rosenblum, N. L. (ed.) (1989) *Liberalism and the Moral Life*, Cambridge, MA: Harvard University Press.

Rothman, D. (1971) *The Birth of the Asylum*, New York: Garland.

Rousseau, J.-J. (1993) *The Social Contract and Discourses*, London: Orion Publishing Group.

Rowbotham, S. (1979) 'The Women's Movement and Organizing for Socialism', in Rowbotham, S., Segal, L. and Wainwright, H. (eds) *Beyond the Fragments: Feminism and the Making of Socialism*, London: Merlin Press.

Rubin, H. J. and Rubin, I. S. (1995) *Qualitative Interviewing: The Art of Hearing Data*, Thousand Oaks, CA: SAGE Publications.

Ruggiero, V. (1991) 'The Disrespect of Prison', in *Respect in Prison*, Bishop Grosseteste College, Lincoln.

Rusche, G. and Kirchheimer, O. (1939, 1968) *Punishment and Social Structure*, New York: Russell and Russell.

Ryan, M. (1983) *The Politics of Penal Reform*, London: Longman.

Ryan, M. and Sim, J. (1995) 'The Penal System in England and Wales: Round Up the Usual Suspects', in Ruggiero, V., Ryan, M. and Sim, J. (eds) *Western European Penal Systems: A Critical Anatomy*, London: SAGE Publications.

Sampson, R. J. and Laub, J. H. (1993) *Crime in the Making: Pathways and Turning Points Through Life*, Cambridge, MA: Harvard University Press.

Sanchez, L. (forthcoming 1999) 'Sex/Law and the Paradox of Agency in the Everyday Practices of Women in the "Evergreen" Sex Trade', in Milovanovic, D. and Henry, S. (eds) *Constitutive Criminology at Work: Agency and Resistance in the Constitution of Crime and Punishment*, Albany, NY: SUNY Press.

Sandel, M. J. (1982) *Liberalism and the Limits of Justice*, Cambridge: Cambridge University Press.

Sargent, L. (ed.) (1981) *Women and Revolution: A Discussion of the Unhappy Marriage of Marxism and Feminism*, Boston: South End Press.

Schor, N. and Weed, E. (eds) (1994) *The Essential Difference*, Bloomington: Indiana University Press.

Schwartz, M. and Milovanovic, D. (eds) (1996) *Race, Gender, and Class in Criminology: The Intersection*, New York: Garland Publishing, Inc.

Scott, J. C. (1985) *Weapons of the Weak: Everyday Forms of Peasant Resistance*, New Haven CT: Yale University Press.

Scott, J. (1992) 'Experience', in Butler, J. and Scott, J. (eds) *Feminists Theorize the Political*, London: Routledge.

Scraton, P., Sim, J. and Skidmore, P. (1991) *Prisons Under Protest*, Milton Keynes: Open University Press.

Scull, A. (1977) *Decarceration: Community Treatment and the Deviant – A Radical View*, Englewood Cliffs, NJ: Prentice-Hall, Inc.

Sellin, T. (1944) *Pioneering in Penology: The Amsterdam Houses of Correction in the 16th and 17th Centuries*, London: Humphrey Milford.

Semple, J. (1993) *Bentham's Prison: A Study of the Panopticon Penitentiary*, Oxford: Clarendon Press.

Shaw, M. (1991) *Paying the Price: Federally Sentenced Women in Context*, Ottawa: Solicitor General of Canada.

Shaw, M. (1992) 'Issues of Power and Control: Women in Prison and Their Defenders', *British Journal of Criminology*, 32(4): 438–53.

Shaw, M. (1995) 'Conceptualizing Violence by Women', in Dobash, R. E., Dobash, R. P. and Noaks, L. (eds) *Gender and Crime*, Cardiff: University of Wales Press.

Shaw, M. (1996) 'Is There a Feminist Future for Women's Prisons?', in

Matthews, R. and Francis, P. (eds) *Prisons 2000: An International Perspective on the Current State and Future of Imprisonment*, London: Macmillan Press Ltd.

Sim, J. (1990) *Medical Power in Prisons: The Prison Medical Service in England 1774–1989*, Milton Keynes: Open University Press.

Sim, J. (1991) '"We Are Not Animals ..." Prisons, Protest, and Politics in England and Wales, 1969–1990', *Social Justice*, 18(3): 107–29.

Sim, J. (1992) '"When You Ain't Got Nothing You Got Nothing to Lose"; The Peterhead Rebellion, the State and the Case for Prison Abolition', in Bottomley, A. K., Fowles, A. J. and Reiner, R. (eds) *Criminal Justice: Theory and Practice*, London: British Society of Criminology.

Sim, J. (1994a) 'Tougher Than the Rest? Men in Prison', in Newburn, T. and Stanko, B. (eds) *Just Boys Doing Business? Men, Masculinities and Crime*, London: Routledge.

Sim, J. (1994b) 'Reforming the Penal Wasteland? A Critical Review of the Woolf Report', in Player, E. and Jenkins, M. (eds) *Prisons After Woolf: Reform through Riot*, London: Routledge.

Simon, J. (1974) 'Michel Foucault on Attica: An Interview', *Telos*, 19: 154–61.

Simon, J. (1993) *Poor Discipline: Parole and the Social Control of the Underclass, 1890–1990*, Chicago: The University of Chicago Press.

Skinner, Q. (1985) *The Return of Grand Theory in the Human Sciences*, Cambridge: Cambridge University Press.

Smart, C. (1976) *Women, Crime and Criminology: A Feminist Critique*, London: Routledge and Kegan Paul.

Smart, C. (1989) *Feminism and the Power of the Law*, London: Routledge.

Smart, C. (1995) *Law, Crime and Sexuality: Essays in Feminism*, London: SAGE Publications.

Smart, C. (1996) 'Deconstructing Motherhood', in Bortolaia Silva, E. (ed.) *Good Enough Mothering? Feminist Perspectives on Lone Motherhood*, London: Routledge.

Smith, C. (1996) 'The Imprisoned Body: Women, Health and Imprisonment', unpublished Ph.D., University of Wales.

Smith, D. (1994) 'Race, Crime and Criminal Justice', in Maguire, M., Morgan R. and Reiner R. (eds) *The Oxford Handbook of Criminology*, Oxford: Oxford University Press.

Smith, D. E. (1987) *The Everyday World as Problematic: A Feminist Sociology*, Milton Keynes: Open University Press.

Solomon, R. C. and Murphy, M. C. (eds) (1990) *What is Justice? Classic and Contemporary Readings*, Oxford: Oxford University Press.

Sommers, E. K. (1995) *Voices from Within: Women Who Have Broken the Law*, Toronto: University of Toronto Press.

190　*Engendering Resistance*

Sparks, R. (1994) 'Can Prisons be Legitimate? Penal Politics, Privatization, and the Timeliness of an Old Idea', *British Journal of Criminology*, 34 (special issue on prisons): 14–28.

Sparks, R. (1996) 'Penal "Austerity": The Doctrine of Less Eligibility Reborn?', in Matthews, R. and Francis, P. (eds) *Prisons 2000: An International Perspective on the Current State and Future of Imprisonment*, London: Macmillan Press Ltd.

Sparks, R. and Bottoms, A. (1995) 'Legitimacy and Order in Prisons', *The British Journal of Sociology*, 46(1): 45–62.

Sparks, R., Bottoms, A. and Hay, W. (1996) *Prisons and the Problem of Order*, Oxford: Clarendon Press.

Spierenburg, P. (1984) *The Spectacle of Suffering: Executions and the Evolution of Repression*, Cambridge: Cambridge University Press.

Spierenburg, P. (1991) *The Prison Experience: Disciplinary Institutions and Their Inmates in Early Modern Europe*, New Brunswick: Rutgers University Press.

Spivak, G. with Rooney, E. (1994) 'In a Word', in Schor, N. and Weed, E. (eds) *The Essential Difference*, Bloomington: Indiana University Press.

Stanko, E. (1985) *Intimate Intrusions: Women's Experience of Male Violence*, New York: Harper and Row.

Stanko, E. (1990) 'When Precaution is Normal: A Feminist Critique of Crime Prevention', in Gelsthorpe, L. and Morris, A. (eds) *Feminist Perspectives in Criminology*, Buckingham: Open University Press.

Stanley, L. and Wise, S. (1993) *Breaking Out Again: Feminist Ontology and Epistemology*, London: Routledge.

Straw, J. (1998) 'New Approaches to Crime and Punishment', *Prison Service Journal*, 116: 2–6.

Summers, A. (1981) *Damned Whores and God's Police: The Colonization of Women in Australia*, Ringwood, Victoria: Penguin.

Sumner, C. (1995) *The Sociology of Deviance: An Obituary*, Buckingham: Open University Press.

Sykes, G. (1958) *The Society of Captives: A Study of Maximum Security Prisons*, Princeton, NJ: Princeton University Press.

Sykes, G. and Matza, D. (1957) 'Techniques of Neutralization: A Theory of Delinquency', *American Sociological Review*, 22: 664–70.

Taylor, C. (1985a) *Human Agency and Language: Philosophical Papers 1*, Cambridge: Cambridge University Press.

Taylor, C. (1985b) *Philosophy and the Human Sciences: Philosophical Papers 2*, Cambridge: Cambridge University Press.

Taylor, C. (1989) *Sources of the Self: The Making of the Modern Identity*, Cambridge, MA: Harvard University Press.

Taylor, C. (1994) 'Politics of Recognition', in Gutman, A. (ed.) *Multi-*

culturalism: Examining the Politics of Recognition, Princeton, NJ: Princeton University Press.

Taylor, I., Walton, P. and Young, J. (1973) *The New Criminology*, London: Routledge and Kegan Paul.

Taylor, I., Walton, P. and Young, J. (1975) *Critical Criminology*, London: Routledge and Kegan Paul.

Thomas, D. A. (1995) 'Sentencing in England and Wales', in Clarkson, C. and Morgan, R. (eds) *The Politics of Sentencing Reform*, Oxford: Clarendon Press.

Thomas, C. and Petersen, D. (1977) *Prison Organization and Inmate Subcultures*, Indianapolis: The Bobbs-Merrill Company, Inc.

Thompson, E. P. (1975) *Whigs and Hunters: The Origin of the Black Act*, London: Penguin Books.

Thornton, D., Curran, L., Grayson, D. and Holloway, V. (1984) *Tougher Regimes in Detention Centres: Report of an Evaluation by the Young Offender Psychology Unit*, London: HMSO.

Toch, H. (1977) *The Ecology of Survival*, New York: The Free Press.

Toch, H. (1992) *Mosaic of Despair: Human Breakdowns in Prison*, Washington, DC: American Psychology Association.

Toch, H., Adams, K. and Grant, J. D. (1989) *Coping: Maladaptation in Prisons*, New Brunswick, NJ: Transaction Publishers.

Towl, G. and Bailey, J. (1993) 'Provisional Findings from a Survey of Groupwork in Prisons in England and Wales', *Division of Criminological and Legal Psychology Newsletter*, 35.

Tumim, S. (1997) 'Time to Cry Woolf and Cut Crime', *TLS*, March 21: 15.

Tyler, T. (1988) 'What is Procedural Justice? Criteria Used by Citizens to Assess the Fairness of Legal Procedures', *Law and Society Review*, 22(1): 103-35.

Tyler, T. R. (1990) *Why People Obey the Law*, New Haven, CT: Yale University Press.

Ussher, J. (1991) *Women's Madness: Misogyny or Mental Illness?* London: Harvester Wheatsheaf.

Vagg, J. (1994) *Prison Systems: A Comparative Study of Accountability in England, France, Germany, and the Netherlands*, Oxford: Clarendon Press.

von Hirsch, A. (1976) *Doing Justice*, New York: Hill and Wang.

Walker, A. (1982) *The Color Purple*, New York: Pocket Books.

Ward, D. and Kassebaum, G. (1964) 'Homosexuality: A Mode of Adaptation in a Prison for Women', *Social Problems*, 12(2): 159–77.

Ward, D. and Kassebaum, G. (1965) *Women's Prison: Sex and Social Structure*, Chicago: Aldine Publishing Company.

Ward, J. (1993) *Ambushed*, London: Vermillion.

Weber, M. (1958) *The Protestant Ethic and the Spirit of Capitalism*, New York: Charles Scribner's Sons.

Weber, M. (1968) *Economy and Society: An Outline of Interpretative Sociology Volumes One and Two*, Berkeley: University of California Press.

Weeks, J. (1987) 'Questions of Identity', in Caplan, P. (ed.) *The Cultural Construction of Sexuality*, London: Tavistock Publications.

Weir, A. (1995) 'Towards a Model of Self-Identity: Habermas and Kristeva', in Meehan, J. (ed.) *Feminists Read Habermas: Gendering the Subject of Discourse*, London: Routledge.

Weir, A. (1996) *Sacrificial Logics: Feminist Theory and the Critique of Identity*, New York: Routledge.

White, L. (1991) 'Subordination, Rhetorical Survival Skills, and Sunday Shoes: Notes on the Hearing of Mrs. G.', in Fineman, M. A. and Thomadsen, N. S. (eds) *At the Boundaries of Law: Feminism and Legal Theory*, New York: Routledge.

Whyte, W. (1965) *Street Corner Society*, Chicago: University of Chicago Press.

Williams, P. J. (1993) *The Alchemy of Race and Rights*, London: Virago Press.

Willis, P. (1977) *Learning to Labour: How Working Class Kids Get Working Class Jobs*, Farnborough, Hants: Gower.

Wilson, J. Q. and Herrnstein, R. J. (1985) *Crime and Human Nature*, New York: Simon and Schuster.

Wittig, M. (1992) *The Straight Mind and Other Essays*, London: Harvester Wheatsheaf.

Woodcock, S. J. (1994) *The Escape From Whitemoor Prison on Friday 9th September 1994*, Cmnd 2741, London: HMSO.

Wolf, M. (1992) *A Thrice Told Tale: Feminism, Postmodernism and Ethnographic Responsibility*, Stanford, CA: Stanford University Press.

Wollstonecraft, M. (1792) *A Vindication of the Rights of Woman*, 1995 edn, London: Everyman.

Woodrow, J. (1992) 'Mothers Inside, Children Outside', in Shaw, R. (ed.) *Prisoners' Children: What Are the Issues?* London: Routledge.

Woolf, L. J. (1991) *Prison Disturbances, April 1990*, Cmnd 1456, London: HMSO.

Woolf, V. (1938) *Three Guineas*, London: Harcourt Brace and Company.

Woolf, V. (1945) *A Room of One's Own*, London: Penguin.

Worrall, A. (1981) 'Out of Place: Female Offenders in Court', *Probation Journal*, 28: 90–93.

Worrall, A. (1990) *Offending Women: Female Lawbreakers and the Criminal Justice System*, London: Routledge.

Worrall, A. (1996) 'Gender, Criminal Justice and Probation', In McIvor, G. (ed.) *Working with Offenders*, London: Jessica Kingsley Publishers.

Wright, S. and Decker, S. (1994) *Burglars on the Job: Street Life and Residential Breakins*, Boston: Northeastern University Press.

Yngvesson, B. (1993) *Virtuous Citizens/Disruptive Subjects: Order and Complaint in a New England Court*, New York: Routledge.

Young, A. (1990) *Femininity in Dissent*, London: Routledge.

Young, A. (1993) 'Femininity on Trial', *Studies in Law, Politics and Society*, 13: 55–68.

Young, A. (1996) *Imagining Crime: Textual Outlaws and Criminal Conversations*, London: SAGE Publications.

Young, I. M. (1987) 'Impartiality and the Civic Public: Some Implications of Feminist Critiques of Moral Political Theory', in Benhabib, S. and Cornell, D. (eds) *Feminism as Critique: Essays on the Politics of Gender in Late-Capitalist Societies*, Cambridge: Polity Press.

Young, I. M. (1990) *Justice and the Politics of Difference*, Princeton, NJ: Princeton University Press.

Young, I. M. (1997) 'Unruly Categories: A Critique of Nancy Fraser's Dual Systems Theory', *New Left Review*, 222: 147–60.

Young, J. (1992) 'Ten Points of Realism', in Young, J. and Matthews, R. (eds) *Rethinking Criminology: the Realist Debate*, London: SAGE.

Young, J. (1994) 'Incessant Chatter: Recent Paradigms in Criminology', in Maguire, M., Morgan, R. and Reiner, R. (eds) *The Oxford Handbook of Criminology*, Oxford: Clarendon Press.

Young, J. and Matthews, R. (1992) *Rethinking Criminology: The Realist Debate*, London: SAGE Publications.

Young, P. (1992) 'The Importance of Utopias in Criminological Thinking', *British Journal of Criminology*, 32(4): 423–37.

Zamble, E. and Porporino, F. J. (1988) *Coping Behavior and Adaptation in Prison Inmates*, New York: Springer-Verlag.

Zedner, L. (1991) *Women, Crime and Custody in Victorian England*, Oxford: Clarendon Press.

Zimring, F. E. and Hawkins, G. (1991) *The Scale of Imprisonment*, Chicago: Chicago University Press.

Zimring, F. E. and Hawkins, G. (1995) *Incapacitation: Penal Confinement and the Restraint of Crime*, New York: Oxford University Press.

Index

Agency 125–53
    and its relationship to identity, 3, 26,
        62, 101, 117, 127, 137, 147,
        156, 160
    and resistance, 130, 143, 161
    and structure, 98, 130, 149
    in prison, 11, 131, 141, 143, 150–51,
        152
Autobiography, 5, 27

Beetham, D., 30
Benhabib, S., 99, 115
Bentham, J., 9, 16
Bottoms, T., 29–32, 61, 157
Braidotti, R., 101, 103, 157–8
Brown, W., 98, 129–30, 153n
Butler, J., 98, 101, 103, 107, 120, 122n,
    151

Cain, M., 83
Carlen, P., 24–5, 27, 28, 65n, 88
Children:
    maintaining relationships with, 140,
        148, 150
    of prisoners, 2, 84, 148–9
Choice:
    and autonomy, 51, 126, 132–3
    and evaluation, 61, 96, 120, 133
    in prison, 104, 130–31, 133–6, 145–
        6, 150, 152
Cixous, H., 100
Class, 117–20, 136, 137, 149, 150
Cohen, S., 33n, 83, 121n
Communitarian theory, 96, 99

Cornell, D., 99, 122n
Criminology:
    and theory, 67–70
    dualisms within, 20, 24, 33n, 69, 98
    feminist, 28, 90
    history of ideas, 69, 85, 92n
    transgressing, 8, 28, 69, 83, 157

Daly, K., 121n
Discipline, 15–16, 29
Domesticity, 23–5, 148
Drake Hall, 4, 76, 79, 82, 85, 104, 159

Eaton, M., 26–7, 73, 160
Education:
    in prison, 87, 103–4, 134
    women's level of, 2
Essentialism, 60, 98, 148, 151, 157
Ethnicity, 117–20, 135–6
Evaluation:
    by prisoners of power, 10, 126
    in relationship to identity, 40, 41,
        61, 62, 95–6, 99, 116, 136–7,
        160
    of the good, 47, 116
Experience:
    as truth, 27, 102, 139
    as basis for feminist research, 71–2

Fairness:
    in prison, 51
Family:
    as ideal, 25
    rights in, 54

195

and care, 5, 38, 56–9
and race, gender, class, 53
and rationality, 45, 99
as fairness, 39, 44, 45, 46, 51
gendered nature of, 5, 38, 52–6, 59–61
in prison, 1, 43, 44
practices of, 48, 53
procedural, 39, 63n
theories of, 45–7

Kristeva, J., 100

Lacey, N. 45, 53, 121–2n
Learmont Report, 38, 48–52, 53, 54, 55, 64n
Legitimacy, 4, 26, 29–32, 35n, 62, 162
challenges to, 97, 151
crisis of prisons, 41, 62
gendered nature of, 32, 96
Legitimate expectations, 44, 45, 46
gendered nature of, 38, 57
Lesbianism:
as resistance, 79
in early sociological literature, 22, 23
in prisons, 137–8, 152
Less Eligibility, theories of:
contemporary, 48
historical 12–13
Liebling, A., 27, 119, 142, 163n
Lloyd, G., 52

Maher, L., 128
Mama, A., 119
Mandaraka-Sheppard, A., 11, 25–6
Masculinity:
in criminology, 11, 157
in prison studies, 99, 121n
Mathiesen, T., 34n, 81–2, 111, 122n
Mead, G. H., 101–2
Morgan, R., 50, 63n
Morris, A., 92n, 135
Motherhood:
effect of imprisonment upon, 77, 105–6, 140, 150
ideals of, 25, 105–7, 144, 159

in relation to femininity, 106, 120, 148–9, 161

Oakley, A., 71

Padel, U., 27
Panopticon, panopticism, 16
Performativity, 101, 102, 103
Postmodern theory, 89–90, 97, 128, 129
Power:
and identity, 95–6, 115–6
and knowledge, 16, 18, 70, 71
as order, 10
as relational, 11, 16, 18, 96, 128, 161
negotiation of in prison, 3, 10, 126, 127, 155
of prison staff, 111, 116–7
of women in prison, 127, 152
to punish, 14–16
relations in research, 73, 78
theories of, 16–18, 30, 96, 126, 153n
Prisoners:
characteristics of, 2, 37, 57
numbers of, 1, 2, 8n
Prison:
Classes, 6, 104–5, 134–5
Community, 22, 111, 141
Compacts, 53–4
Conditions, 31
Culture, 20
gaining access to, 79–80
history of, 1, 9, 13, 19
literature about, 9–35, 157
labour, 12, 104, 134
management of, 30, 38, 43, 48, 57–9, 162
men's, 29, 30
Order, 26, 29, 31, 103, 117, 131, 139–40, 146
Origins of, 12, 32
privatizing, 1
Riots, 41, 42, 51, 63n, 140
Rules, 26, 38, 76
Security, 42, 48, 49, 50, 51
Staff, 43–4, 55, 78–9, 80, 116–17, 119